# HERO[barcode: D0958890]XIE

*The Wives, Mothers, Sisters,*
*Sweethearts and Nurses of their*
*"Dear, Dear Men in Gray,"*
*Telling a Proud*
*and Gallant History!*

MARY ANNA JACKSON—"After he had taken his departure for the army our home grew more lonely and painful to me from day to day . . ."

MARY CUSTIS LEE—"The prospects before us are sad indeed and as I think both parties are wrong in this fratricidal war there is nothing comforting even in the hope that God may prosper the right, for I see no right in the matter."

EMMA E. HOLMES—"Thursday (11th April 1861) . . . a day never to be forgotten in the annals of Charleston . . . Though every shot is distinctly heard and shakes our house, I feel calm and composed . . ."

LEORA SIMS—"The women are getting ready for any emergency. I am going to get me a bowie knife or look for some weapon of defense. We do not feel afraid of the Yankees but we must be ready for anything."

Also available from MOCKINGBIRD BOOKS:

**HEROINES OF DIXIE:**
**Winter of Desperation**

By Katharine M. Jones,                    $2.95

A MOCKINGBIRD BOOK

# HEROINES OF DIXIE:

*Spring of High Hopes*

Katharine M. Jones, Editor

MOCKINGBIRD BOOKS

To
The memory of my Grandmother
**Mary Turner Garrison**
Wife of
**Lieutenant William David Garrison**
16th South Carolina Regiment, C.S.A.

Library of Congress Catalog Card Number: 55-6825

SBN 89176-032-6

First Printing: December, 1974
Fifth Printing: June, 1988

Printed in the United States of America

Mockingbird Books, Inc.
P.O. Box 624
St. Simons Island, GA 31522

# INTRODUCTION

In some of the more recent studies of the subject it has been strongly suggested that the prime reason for the defeat of the Confederacy was a decline in, or loss of, the will to fight. There is a certain merit in the point though the more remarkable fact, considering the course of the conflict, is that the will to fight remained so strong so long.

For that, the women of the Confederacy were in large measure responsible. Not every woman could be classed as a "heroine of Dixie," as the title of the present work puts it, but it was commonly observed at the time by foe and friend alike, and has been repeatedly noted since, that it was among the women of the South that the spirit of resistance flamed highest.

The harder part of war is the woman's part. True of all wars, this was particularly true of the war of the Sixties in the South. For a few women, some of whom left memoirs which have become famous, there were the excitement and sustaining sense of accomplishment to be derived from contact with stirring events and association with notable personalities. For the great majority, however, there was more of strain and anxiety, of fear and loneliness, and of hardship and privation than there was of glamour and excitement. To all these were added, in large sections of the South, the aggravation and frustration of invasion and occupation by Federal troops—or, even worse the depredations of the lawless freebooters of either side, or neither, in those areas which were strongly held by neither army.

The story of the life of women in these years is scattered through diaries and lettters written without thought of publication, as well as through the comparatively small number of published memoirs. Of the latter, even, not many are well known and readily available. Searching out the facts about the lives of Confederate women, therefore, calls for diligence and patience, while presentation of the facts found requires judgment in selection and skill in organization. Miss Jones has brought to her work the qualities requisite for producing what is, in effect, a composite autobiography of Confederate women.

In doing so, she lets the actors tell the story in their own words, with a minimum of connective tissue to keep events in focus. There is no attempt to round up views from all sources on each phase of the story but the quotations given are each of sufficient length to preserve their flavor and effect.

The treatment is basically chronological, carrying the story forward from the first secession conventions to the last meeting of the Confederate Cabinet at Washington, Georgia, after which Miss Eliza Frances Andrews notes that "this, I suppose, is the end of the Confederacy."

The familiar passages from well-known diarists dealing with the Richmond scene are here but here also are bits of everyday life such as that on a remote farm in Texas where saving the meat at hog-killing time was a problem and where a hundred bales of cotton would "neither pay debts or buy groceries"—with touches of all the range of living in between.

To the author who has so patiently assembled and skillfully presented the story of the women of the Confederacy, the thanks of those interested in that story today are eminently due.

ROBERT S. HENRY

Alexandria, Virginia

# EDITOR'S FOREWORD

The military records and reports do not tell the story of the women of the Confederacy. They told it themselves—a few in magazine articles, pamphlets and books; many in letters and diaries. Only a part of it has been published; much survives in manuscripts cherished in family, historical society, public library and university collections. All manner of women told it—the rich and the poor, the educated and the ignorant.

A handful of these Confederate women saw active service as spies, hospital nurses, government clerks. The great majority were left back home, whether home was the big house or a cabin. They had vital work to do there. But almost from the outbreak of the struggle homes were broken up and women became exiles.

So their story is increasingly a story of refugees, of invaded and occupied cities, of burned and devastated dwellings, of hunger and want, of bitterness and human frailty. But it is also a story of love, of courage, of personal loyalty transcending heartbreak.

When the curtain rose, they expected the play to be over soon by a peaceful yielding of the North or a defeat of the Northern army. There were then some gleams of glamour about war—especially a war that might be over before it was well begun. With proud hearts these women watched the parade of their brave lads marching off to certain and easy victory, with the flags the women had been waving over them. Romances flowered quickly in those days. There was a gay, unquenchable humor in the ranks; anxiety and privation would leave little room for it behind the lines. There was the excitement of combat for the soldiers; there was a little waltzing on happy, rare occasions but much more waiting, watching, work for the women.

Though their Southern patriotism was intense, for the women devotion to the family came first—always—and none of them would knowingly and willingly have chosen a course of war that reversed this order of devotion. At the very start—just after the Act of Secession was passed—a woman of South Carolina said, "What do I care for patriotism? My husband is my country. What is my country to me if he be killed?" As they faced the grim reality of a long and bitter struggle, this became more and more the secret or avowed question of their deeply troubled hearts.

From Virginia to Texas I have searched out and read every piece of their writing I could lay hands on. I have selected what I humbly hope may bring their varied story into focus and continuity—their autobiography of the war years.

# ACKNOWLEDGMENTS

This anthology has been compiled with a constant sense of gratitude to all the people who have had a part in its making—the ladies of the Confederacy, whose diaries and letters I have shared, and the families of the ladies, the advisers, librarians and archivists who have helped me in my task. I owe a great debt to them for their contributions, their many kindnesses and valuable assistance.

I am grateful to Mr. Robert Selph Henry for completing the book with his introduction, for reading the galley proofs and for the usefulness of his book *The Story of the Confederacy*. I am indebted also to Dr. Bell I. Wiley of Emory University, who carefully read the proofs and offered suggestions. Of course, responsibility for any error is mine.

I wish to thank also those persons who have helped me find or given me permission to use the material reprinted in this book:

Mrs. Mary Verner Schlaefer, Mrs. T. B. Stackhouse, Mrs. Charles Blackburn, Mrs. Fitz Hugh McMaster, all of Columbia, South Carolina. Mr. Albert Neely Sanders of Furman University. Dr. James Rabun of Emory University. Dr. Robert H. Woody of Duke University. Dr. Harriet Holman of Erskine College. Mr. Zack Spratt of Washington, D.C. Dr. Mary Elizabeth Massey of Winthrop College. The library staff of Winthrop College. Mr. Frank Wardlaw, Director of the University of Texas Press. Dr. Llerena Friend, Librarian of the Barker Texas History Center, University of Texas Library. Miss Ruth Blair and Miss Bessie Duke Small of the Atlanta Historical Society. Miss Mary Verhoeff and Miss Mabel C. Weaks of the Filson Club, Louisville, Kentucky. Miss Margaret Jemison and

Mr. Richard B. Harwell of Emory University Library. Mr. and Mrs. E. R. Dobbins of Atlanta, Georgia. Mrs. Marie Bankhead Owen, Mrs. Hattie M. Allen, Miss Maud McLure Kelly, Sr. Peter Brannon, of the Alabama State Department of Archives and History. Mr. David C. Mearns, Chief, Manuscript Division of the Library of Congress. Miss Anna Loe Russell, Reference Librarian of the George Peabody College. Mr. Dan M. Robinson, State Librarian and Archivist. Mrs. Gertrude Morton Parsley, of the Tennessee State Library and Archives. Mr. V. L. Bedsole and Miss Marcelle F. Schertz of the Department of Archives, Louisiana State University. Miss Mattie Russell, Curator of Mss., Duke University Library. Dr. James Welsh Patton, Director, and Miss Anna Brooke Allen, Mrs. Carolyn Daniel, Mrs. Patterson Fisher and Mrs. John Watters, all of the Southern Historical Collection, University of North Carolina. Dr. William D. McCain, Director, Department of Archives and History, Jackson, Mississippi. Miss Georgia Clark, Reference Librarian, University of Arkansas. Mrs. Lilla M. Hawes, Director of the Georgia Historical Society. Miss Elizabeth Hodge, Reference Librarian, Public Library, Savannah, Georgia. The staff of the Georgia State Archives. Miss India Thomas, House Regent of the Confederate Museum, Richmond, Virginia. Dr. and Mrs. Robert Meriwether of the South Caroliniana Library, University of South Carolina. Mr. Henry R. Dwight of Pinopolis, South Carolina. Miss Georgia Faison, Reference Librarian, University of North Carolina Library. Mrs. Frank M. Ladd and Mr. Francis H. Inge of Mobile, Alabama. Mrs. Alfred S. Gaillard of Columbia, South Carolina. Mr. A. L. Alexander of Savannah, Georgia. Miss Susan Ware Eppes and Miss Alice B. Eppes of Tallahassee, Florida. Mr. Hunter McDonald and Mrs. Jesse E. Wills of Nashville, Tennessee. Mr. J. Lewis Scoggs of Berryville, Virginia. Mr. Warrington Dawson of Versailles, France. Mrs. M. D. Chase and Mr. Charles Stow of the Greenville Public Library. Miss Alice Adams of the Furman University Library. Miss Slann L. C. Simmons of the South Carolina Historical Society, Charleston, South Carolina.

Finally, I wish to express my appreciation to Mrs. Rosemary York and Mr. D. Laurance Chambers of The Bobbs-Merrill Company, whose understanding, wisdom and guidance made this book possible.

# TABLE OF CONTENTS

" . . . . it may truly be said of the Southern women of 1861–1865 that the simple narrative of their life and work unfolds a record of achievement, endurance, and self-sacrificing devotion that should be revealed and recognized as a splendid inspiration to men and women everywhere."

—MATTHEW PAGE ANDREWS

# I

# THE UNION IS DISSOLVED

*December 1860—May 1861*

*From the city of Charleston, South Carolina, on December 20, 1860, news was flashed to the outside world that the state of South Carolina had been proclaimed an independent Commonwealth. One hundred and sixty-nine delegates had unanimously passed an Ordinance of Secession from the Union.*

"We the People of the State of South Carolina in Convention Assembled, do declare and ordain, and it is hereby declared and ordained, That the Ordinance adopted by us in Convention, on the twenty-third day of May, in the year of our Lord one thousand seven hundred and eighty-eight under the name of the 'United States of America' is hereby dissolved."

*By February 1, 1861, Mississippi, Florida, Alabama, Georgia, Louisiana and Texas had passed Ordinances of Secession. Delegates from the seceded states met in Montgomery, Alabama, on February 4 to form a provisional government. On the ninth they sent a message to Mr. Jefferson Davis of Mississippi: "Sir: We are directed to inform you that you were this day unanimously elected President of the Provisional Government of the Confederate States of America, and to request you to come to Montgomery immediately."*

*The convention elected Alexander H. Stephens of Georgia Vice-President. The inaugural ceremonies were held on February 18. "The man and the hour have met," said Mr. William L. Yancey and the crowds cheered and a new song called "Dixie" was sung.*

*In early March, General Pierre Gustave Toutant Beauregard arrived in Charleston to command preparations for the*

1

*defense of the harbor from an expected attack by United States vessels. Repeated demands for the surrender of Fort Sumter met with refusal by Major Robert Anderson, its commander. On April 11 the Confederate Congress ordered the capture of the fort. On the fourteenth, after a bombardment of three days, Major Anderson departed from battered Sumter and a new flag was raised.*

*The Virginia state convention voted on April 17 to submit the Ordinance of Secession to the people, and three days later Robert E. Lee resigned his commission in the United States Army and was given chief command of the Virginia state forces. On May 6 an Arkansas convention voted for secession 69 to 1; on the seventh the Tennessee legislature submitted an ordinance to referendum vote; and on the twentieth North Carolina seceded.*

## 1. EMMA E. HOLMES—SOUTH CAROLINA
### SECEDES FROM THE UNION

*Emma E. Holmes, young lady of Charleston, South Carolina, was lame as a result of recent illness. This affliction prevented her active participation in the events associated with the secession of her state, and to relieve pent-up feelings she began a diary. Carefully and neatly penned, it became a record of life in her home city during 1861 and 1862.*

Charleston, South Carolina

On the 17th of December 1860 delegates elected by the people of South Carolina met in solemn convention in Columbia to withdraw our State from the Union. Smallpox was so prevalent there, that they as well as the Legislature adjourned to Charleston. On the 20th The Ordinance of Secession, declaring South Carolina a free and Independent Republic was passed unanimously at quarter past one, P.M. That evening the two Bodies met and marched in procession to Secession Hall, where it was signed amidst an immense throng. But few ladies were present, as it was so late before it was determined to sign it the same evening instead of the next day, as had been at first proposed.

The news flew upon the wings of the wind. . . .

## 2. SUSAN BRADFORD—FLORIDA PASSES
### THE ORDINANCE OF SECESSION

*Susan Bradford, daughter of Dr. Edward Bradford of Pine Hill plantation, Leon County, Florida, was born in 1846. Her forebears, who were descendants of Governor William Bradford of Plymouth Colony, had come to Florida in early territorial days and been leaders in the making of the new state. Susan's father had vast holdings of land. The plantation house was cared for by thirty servants, and more than three hundred slaves occupied the quarters and tilled the land. There was a French landscape gardener, and a New York governess for Susan. In the summer the family journeyed to the springs at Montvale or to resorts in the North. Susan was "just a little girl" when she began the diary which she kept through the years of conflict. It tells of the war as it touched her home and the surrounding Florida country.*

Pine Hill Plantation
Leon County, Florida

January 1, 1861.—A New Year has come to us now. As we sat around the long table today the conversation turned on the convention, so soon to meet in Tallahassee. Father said he considered this the most momentous year in the history of the South. He is for Secession and he does not think that war will necessarily follow. Brother Junius is a strong Union man and he thinks we will certainly have war; he says we will have war in any event. If the South secedes the North will fight to keep us, and if we do not secede all property rights will be taken from us and we will be obliged to fight to hold our own. He says he is for the fight but he wants to fight in the Union not out of it. Father thinks it is more honorable to take an open and decided stand and let all the world know what we are doing. Everyone at table who expressed an opinion was firmly set against the Republican party. Mother says she wants the negroes freed but she wants the United States Government to make laws which will free them gradually. All agree on one point, if the negroes are freed our lands will be worthless.

January 2, 1861.—Uncle Richard and Uncle Tom spent the morning with Father, the three brothers are going to Tallahassee tomorrow to the opening of the Secession Convention. They are so deeply interested.

January 3, 1861.—I would not write this morning because I wanted to put down in my diary the first news of the convention. Tonight Father has told me what they did; it was simply to organize and then they adjourned. Some of the delegates had not arrived and this will give them the opportunity to get to Tallahassee and present their credentials. Father says the Capitol was full of men from all over the State and they look very serious.

January 4, 1861.—I can hardly keep my mind on my books I am thinking so much of the probable action of the convention. I know Father must have been glad when the school bell rang this morning, it seems impossible for me to refrain from asking him questions, which, of course, must be troublesome.

January 5, 1861.—This is Saturday and Mother lets Lula make candy on Saturday and if she, my black mammy, will let us, we help with it. Cousin Rob is spending the day here and Lula has promised to teach us how to make the candy baskets. Cousin Rob does not care about the convention, he is going to school in town but comes home Friday after school and goes back Monday morning.

January 6, 1861.—This morning we went to Mount Zion to hear Mr. Blake preach. Today he spoke so earnestly of the representatives of the people of Florida, now in convention assembled in Tallahassee. He spoke of the heavy responsibility resting on them; of the high compliment paid them by the people of Florida, in trusting them with an issue of such paramount importance. He said we, none of us knew which way was best; we must trust in God and do good.

Mr. Blake took dinner with us and Eddie[1] came with him. He is just the shyest boy. When the company were all gone Father told me to ask Lula to get me ready to go with him to

---

[1] Mr. Blake was the Bradfords' neighbor as well as minister, and Eddie was his son.

town next morning. He said he was going to show me what a convention was like. I was so happy at the thought of going and my heart fell when Mother said: "Surely, Dr. Bradford, you are not going to take the child away from school?" but Father said, "Yes, I am going to take her with me in the morning, this is history in the making, she will learn more than she can get out of books, and what she hears in this way she will never forget." I am so glad. I am so excited I cannot hold my pencil steady but I must write this down.

January 7, 1861.—I am so glad it is not raining today. I am really going and, little diary, I will tell you all about the day when we get home.

8:30 P.M. We have just finished supper. Mother would not let me write until we had eaten, now she says I can only have one hour because I am going again tomorrow and must have a good sleep.

The convention was assembling in the hall of representatives when we entered the Capitol, and soon everybody was in place and Dr. DuBose made a very fine prayer.

After the preliminaries were disposed of a communication from the Governor was read and the first thing I knew Aunt Mary, who was sitting next caught me by the hand and said, "Look, there is the ambassador from South Carolina." A small man very erect and slender was being introduced by Mr. Villepique as Mr. Leonidas Spratt of South Carolina. Mr. Spratt bowed gravely and looking around upon the audience with a pair of brilliant, beautiful eyes, he began somewhat in this manner, though I probably will not get it quite right.

He said he felt some delicacy in appearing before this convention, coming as he did from a foreign power, but the heart of South Carolina was filled with love and sympathy for Florida, who now was standing where Carolina had so lately stood. Then he read aloud a communication from his state, recounting the grievances, which had led her to sever the ties which bound her to the Union. You never heard such cheers and shouts as rent the air, and it lasted so long. When quiet was restored Mr. Villepigue introduced Colonel Bulloch, of Alabama. He made a fine address but a short one. Said his own state was now deliberating as to what course she should pursue and had sent him to assure Florida of her cordial good-will. He sat down amid cheers for "Bulloch and Alabama."

Mr. Edmund Ruffin, of Virginia,[1] was introduced and said
he came to tell us that Virginia was with her Southern sisters
in feeling and, if the worse came to the worst, she would be
with them, heart and soul. He is a splendid looking man, quite
old and yet he is perfectly erect and only his snow-white hair
shows his age. He reminds me very much of dear Grandpa,
who is taking such a warm interest in these proceedings,
though he is so far away. I believe it will break his heart if
North Carolina does not secede.

When the speaking was over and a few resolutions had been
passed the convention adjourned and we came home. We left a
noisy crowd behind us. As far as we could hear there were
cheers for South Carolina; cheers for Mississippi; cheers for
Alabama and for Florida. Never before have I seen such excitement. It even throws the horse races in the shade. What
will tomorrow bring?

January 8, 1861.—We are at home again after a day filled
to over-flowing with excitement and interest. We were in such
a hurry to get to town that the convention had not assembled
when we reached the Capitol. There were groups of men talking earnestly and there were other men running hither and
thither with papers in their hands. Father has a great many
friends and I stood quietly beside him while he and they dis-
cussed the situation. The ambassador from South Carolina had
evidently made an impression on his audience of yesterday
and somebody had been busy last night, for in every direction
could be seen Palmetto cockades, fastened with a blue ribbon;
there were hundreds of them. When at last the hall of representatives was opened and Father and I took seats, Judge
Gwynn came in and pinned a cockade on Father and one on
me. Oh, I was so proud.

The members of the convention took their seats and Mr.
Blake, our dear Mr. Blake, whom we love so well, opened the
day's session with prayer. I had never seen a convention until
Father brought me here and it is strange to me. I wish I could
tell all I heard today but the language the members used is not

---

[1]He is generally accredited with firing the first shot on Fort
Sumter. In spite of the fact that he was sixty-seven years old, he
joined the Palmetto Guards and they gave him this honor. See
*Battles and Leaders of the Civil War*, I, 47.

familiar to me and some of the things they talk about are just as new. Then, too, I am just a little girl. A message was read on the floor of the convention, from Governor Brown of Georgia, to Governor Milton. As near as I can remember it was this way: "Georgia will certainly secede. Has Florida occupied the fort?"

Mr. Sanderson was very interesting. He recounted the rights which the states retained when they delegated other rights to the general government in the Constitution. He made it so perfectly clear that all and every state had the right to withdraw from the Union, if her rights and liberty were threatened. He said the Committee on Ordinances had carefully examined into the question and they could find no reason why Florida should not exercise her right to withdraw from a compact, which now threatened her with such dire disaster. I am going again tomorrow. My palmeto cockade lies on the table beside me.

January 9, 1861.—There has been a hot time in the convention today; the nearer they get to a final decision the hotter it gets. Colonel Ward made a most eloquent address to the convention. He told them that he was a Union man but it was in this way: in his opinion the South had done more to establish that Union than any other section; it was a Southern man who wrote the Declaration of Independence, it was a Southern man who led the American army, it was Southern men who framed the Constitution, a Southern man wrote our National Anthem and, in so doing, had immortalized the Star-spangled Banner and he proposed to hold on to that which we had done so much to bring about. He was willing to fight, if fight we must, but he wanted to fight in the Union and under that flag which was doubly ours. The heartiest applause greeted him as he sat down. It was plain to see that his audience was tremendously affected but the next speaker tore his fine argument to shreds. So it went on all day, some committee business would interrupt now and then but the most of the time was spent in debate for or against secession.

Our old friend, Mr. Burgess, says: "If Mrs. Harriet Beecher Stowe had died before she wrote 'Uncle Tom's Cabin,' this would never have happened." He says, "she has kindled a fire which all the waters of the earth cannot extinguish." Isn't it strange how much harm a pack of lies can do?

January 10, 1861.—It is night and I am very tired but there is much to tell. The Ordinance of Secession was voted on today. Bishop Rutledge made the opening prayer and it was very impressive. He pleaded so earnestly for God's guidance for these members, in whose hands lay the future of Florida. These men feel their responsibility I am sure, their faces are so serious and yet so alert. I heard something today about a flag which had been presented to Florida but I have not seen it yet.

After the committees were disposed of the Ordinance of Secession was voted on. The vote was 62 for and 7 against. The ordinance was declared adopted at 22 minutes after 12 o'clock. It was resolved that at one o'clock on the next day, January 11th, the Ordinance of Secession should be signed on the east portico of the Capitol. The convention then adjourned until the afternoon session.

Mississippi seceded last night and it seems we will have plenty of company. The Union men in the hall looked very sad. They have worked hard for their side, but they had only a few followers.

January 11, 1861.—We did not try to be early this morning, as the big event of the day did not take place until one o'clock. Capitol Square was so crowded you could see nothing but heads and the Capitol itself was full of people looking from the windows, which looked out on the east portico. Somehow Father and I had seats on the portico itself, close up to the wall where we were not in the way and yet we could both see and hear.

There was a table already there with a large inkstand and several pens, nothing more. A subdued murmur came from the assembled citizens but there was none of the noise and excitement which had prevailed on other days; all seemed impressed with the solemnity of the occasion for oh, it is solemn! I did not realize how solemn until Mr. Sanderson read the Constitution and I understood just why it was necessary for Florida to secede.

As the old town clock struck one, the Convention, headed by President McGehee, walked out on the portico. In a few moments they were grouped about the table on which some one had spread the parchment on which the Ordinance of Secession was written. It was impossible for me to tell in what order it was signed, the heads were clustered so closely around the table, but presently I heard Col. Ward's familiar voice. There was a little break in the crowd and I saw him quite plainly. He dipped his pen in the ink and, holding it aloft, he said, in the saddest of tones, "When I die I want it inscribed upon my tombstone that I was the last man to give up the ship." Then he wrote slowly across the sheet before him, "George T. Ward."

The stillness could almost be felt. One by one they came forward.

When at length the names were all affixed, cheer after cheer rent the air; it was deafening. Our world seemed to have gone wild.

General Call is an old man now; and he is a strong Union man. Chancing to look toward him I saw that the tears were streaming down his face. Everybody cannot be suited and we are fairly launched on these new waters; may the voyage be a prosperous one.

Nearly everybody seems to be happy and satisfied. The Supreme Court Judges, into whose hands the document just signed has been placed, have carried it to Miss Elizabeth Eppes to engross or adorn it with blue ribbon; the judges selected Miss Bettie because she is a granddaughter of Thomas Jefferson. I hope President Jefferson likes our Ordinance—I believe those who are gone know all we are doing here below.

Father says the rest of the proceedings of this convention will be confined to business matters and though he is planning to attend, he will leave me at home and let me go on with my studies. I wonder if I can collect my wits enough to learn my lessons. I will have Saturday to rest up in and Lula will make us some candy. . . .

## 3. AUGUSTA J. KOLLOCK—"WE ARE A FREE AND INDEPENDENT PEOPLE"

*Augusta J. Kollock was the young daughter of George J. Kollock of Savannah, Georgia. When the state seceded on January 19, her three brothers and various cousins were away at school. Augusta carried on an active correspondence with the absent members of her family despite the fact*

*that her father, who was a Yale man, repeatedly repri-*
*manded her for careless mistakes in spelling. Her brother*
*George was at Virginia Military Institute, a pupil of Profes-*
*sor Thomas Jonathan Jackson. To this brother, waiting im-*
*patiently for his father's permission to enlist, Augusta wrote*
*from their plantation home on the third day after the seces-*
*sion of Georgia.*

> The Retreat
> Chatham Co.
> *Republic of Georgia*
> Jan. 22nd [1861]

To George J. Kollock Jr.
V.M.I.
Lexington, Virginia

Dear Brother, I suppose you have seen by the papers that our
good State has seceded, and that now we are a *free & inde-*
*pendent people.* . . . The whole city has been wild with excitement ever since Sumter was taken, & has just begun to get
a little quiet, but I suppose we must prepare for hot times
now, that is if the Federal Government persists in the insane
policy of coercion. It is the most absurd thing I ever heard of,
& I rather think if they attempt it, they will find to their cost,
that it is not quite so easy to subdue us as they fancied. They
will be obliged to exterminate us. Of course you know that our
troops have possession of Pulaski. We cannot have any parties,
(though in truth no one has any heart for them) because all
the beaux are down at the Fort. Detachments of the Guards,
Blues, & Oglethorpe are down there all the time. Eddie Kollock either has joined or is about to join, a new company commanded by Col. Jones, the Pulaski Guards. If there is any war
Uncle George is pledged to join another new corps, under
Capt. Gallie, called the Savannah Artillery. In it are all the old
men in the city, I believe. Think of Uncle G! You must know
he is the only Unionist in the family, except Uncle William &
James W., but Coercion has turned even him out. George J.
has joined the Huzzars. The latter corps has adopted what they
call a "service uniform" which consists of a plain pair of dark
blue pants, with a duck-tail, tight fiitting sack coat of the same,
buttoned up the front with large silver buttons of the corps.
Both garments are made of *Georgia cassimere.* The pretty

dress uniform has been laid aside for a year, on account of the expense, which you know deterred many from joining the corps, & it is surprising how many recruits they have had, they now number 75 or more active members. Father says if there is war he will join again. There are three other new companies, the "Savannah Rifles," The "Blue Caps," Bob Grant commanding, (would you not like to join that corps) & the "Rattlesnakes." These three include all the rowdies in town, I believe. The Rattlesnakes was originally a secret society, a sort of vigilance committee I think, & the most extraordinary notices used to appear in the papers, for instance "Attention, Rattlesnakes Come out of your holes, and meet at the Canal bridge, at 9 o'clock this evening.

> By order of President Grand Rattle
> POISON FANG, Secretary"

Then the next day the notice would be to "crawl into your holes."

Fights & weddings are the order of the day. Notwithstanding the times there have been more weddings this winter than for several years. . . . My Christmas presents were not ready to send on in Mothers box, so they will have to go in the next. All are quite well here except Mother, she was complaining yesterday, but seems quite bright today. Goodnight, it is getting late. Love to you both. Yr. affectionate sister.

P.S. Fido is quite well, so is Pluto.

## 4. ELEANOR NOYES JACKSON—MONTGOMERY WELCOMES JEFFERSON DAVIS

*Eleanor Noyes Jackson, a native of Boston, Massachusetts, was the wife of Jefferson Franklin Jackson of Montgomery, Alabama. After her marriage she became an ardent Southerner and supported the Confederate cause with enthusiasm. When delegates from the seceding Southern states met in Montgomery to form their new provisional government, Mrs. Jackson witnessed the inauguration on the front steps of the Capitol. She saw President Davis ride up in a carriage drawn by six horses. She heard William L. Yancey say, "The man and the hour have met." The next day she wrote to her sister, Mary Noyes, of Boston, Massachusetts.*

Montgomery, Ala. Feb. 19, 1861

. . . I was one of the mass of people in front of the portico. The balconies and every front window were filled with ladies who went early.

My share of the interesting occasion was to furnish a most beautiful wreath of japonicas and hyacinths and small Spring magnolias—also a large bunch of flowers for the Vice-President.[1] I did not begin to collect the flowers until 9 o'clock in the morning, and went to the Garrett's place with a basket and brought it away full of those crimson and red variegated japonicas. The green of the wreath was arbor vitae and box. The front of the wreath was elevated and composed of a large crimson japonica, a small one and white hyacinths in the point against a back of arbor vitae. Below the japonicas were purple and white double hyacinths. On either side of the center were half-opened pink japonicas and the whole wreath was of dark and light flowers alternating. As the procession came through the capitol grounds I handed the flowers to Mr. Watts who was of the committee. After the inauguration Howell Cobb[2] handed him the wreath which he slipped on his arm, and gave Mr. Stephens his flowers. The ladies threw down small bunches of flowers which he gathered and held in his hand. . . .

A levee was held last night in Estelle and Concert Halls. The ladies trimmed Estelle Hall beautifully. Oh! the crowd, and such a one. The greatest variety of costumes you can imagine. People from town, people from country, young and old. Mrs. Watts Fitzpatrick just from Washington with black velvet dress—pointed lace bertha and sleeves trimmed with same— pearl ornaments. A lady next to her, perhaps with her head covered and shawl on. Men in fine clothes and men in homespun suit. Most of our ladies dressed prettily. Mrs. Thorington came with bonnet and cloak. I wore my brown silk with blue

---

[1] Alexander H. Stephens.

[2] Member of U.S. Congress from Georgia 1843-1851 and 1855-1857 (Speaker 1849-1851); Governor of Georgia 1851-1853; Secretary of the Treasury 1857-1860; President of the Confederate Congress 1861-1862.

brocaded flowers which had been entirely made over into a low-necked dress with skirt in puffs and ruffles. On my neck I wore my pretty colarett, and black lace shawl thrown around my shoulders. My head dress was of blue velvet with black and gold ornaments. My jewelry is blue you know. . . .

Every house, little and big, was illuminated from the capitol to the Exchange last night. The theater was illuminated, also Rocketts and bengal lights were thrown from opposite sides of the street constantly by the Estelle Hall. In short yesterday was a great day for Montgomery. . . .

## 5. VARINA HOWELL DAVIS—"I COULD NOT COMMAND MY VOICE TO SPEAK"

*Varina Howell Davis was thirty-five years old and the mother of three children when she became the First Lady of the Confederacy. She was described by William Howard Russell, the English war correspondent, as "a comely, sprightly woman, verging on matronhood, of good figure and manners, well dressed, ladylike and clever." She liked to wear a rose in her dark hair and she had a preference for gorgeous white silk dresses. She was above the average height, carried her head well and dressed her hair simply. One who saw her for the first time remarked, "She is brimming with zest for life."*

*Varina Howell was born in Natchez, Mississippi, on May 7, 1826, the daughter of William B. Howell and Margaret Louisa Kempe of Virginia. Her grandfather, Richard Howell, served as governor of New Jersey for eight successive terms. Varina, after a series of governesses, attended Madame Greenland's school in Philadelphia.*

*She met thirty-six-year-old Jefferson Davis in 1844. They were married the following year and lived at "Briarfield" near Natchez. That same year her husband was elected to Congress, and thereafter Varina found herself occupying various successive roles. She was a soldier's wife when Colonel Davis served in the Mexican campaigns, a senator's wife, a Cabinet member's wife when he was Secretary of War under President Pierce and a senator's wife again from 1857 until his resignation in 1861.*

*Mrs. Davis did not reach Montgomery in time to see her husband inaugurated Provisional President of the Confederate States of America. "Upon my weary heart," he wrote her, "was showered smiles, plaudits, and flowers; but, beyond them, I saw troubles and thorns innumerable. . . . I thought it would have gratified you to have witnessed it, and have been a memory to our children. . . ." She joined him on March 4.*

It was necessary to close up our home and abandon all we had watched over for years, before going to Montgomery; our library, which was very large and consisted of fine well-chosen English books, was the hardest to relinquish of all our possessions. After all was secured in the best manner practicable, I went to New Orleans en route to Montgomery, and remained a few days at my father's house. While there, Captain Dreux, at the head of his battalion, came to serenade me, but I could not command my voice to speak to him when he came on the balcony; his cheery words and the enthusiasm of his men depressed me dreadfully. Violets were in season, and the captain and his company brought several immense bouquets. The color seemed ominous. Perhaps Mr. Davis's depression had communicated itself to me, and I could not rally or be buoyed up by the cheerfulness of those who were to do battle for us. My journey up the Alabama River to join Mr. Davis in Montgomery was a very sad one, sharing his apprehensions, and knowing our needs to be so many, with so little hope of supplying them. . . .

When we reached the hotel where the President was temporarily lodged, the Provisional Congress had assembled, he had been inaugurated, and the day of my arrival the Confederate flag had been hoisted by the daughter of Colonel Robert Tyler, and the granddaughter of the ex-President. . . . [The flag had] a blue union containing the stars in white at equal distances; . . . one broad white and two red stripes the same width. Under it we won our victories, and the memory of its glory will never fade. It is enshrined in our hearts forever. . . .

The house chosen for us was a gentleman's residence, roomy enough for our purposes, on the corner of a street and looking toward the State Capitol. There were many charming people there, who were all intent on kind services to us; our memory of Montgomery was one of affectionate welcome, and if we should have judged from the hampers of blossoms poured out before us, it was a flowery kingdom. . . .

## 6. CAROLINE HOWARD GILMAN—CHARLESTON
### PREPARES FOR WAR

*Mrs. Gilman, daughter of a Boston shipwright, had lived in Charleston since 1819 where her husband Samuel Gilman, author of "Fair Harvard," served as pastor of the Unitarian church. Before the war she had published* The Rosebud, *one of the earliest periodicals for children; she had written* The Poetry of Travelling in the United States, Recollections of a New England Housekeeper, Recollections of a Southern Matron *and many stories and poems.*

*Mrs. Gilman had been a widow for a number of years when war came. The members of her family were divided in their loyalties. Two of her four daughters, her sister, and her niece Mrs. James Russell Lowell lived in Massachusetts and were ardent Northern sympathizers. With Mrs. Gilman in Charleston were the other daughters and their children, three of whom, Frank, Willie and Washington, had recently enlisted in the Confederate service.*

*To the daughters in Massachusetts, Mrs. Pickering Dodge of Salem and Mrs. Charles J. Bowen of Kingston, Mrs. Gilman wrote the letter that follows. She assumes, it seems, that they will share her attitude. The secessionist post office at Charleston was certainly exercising no censorship on mail going north that might give information to the enemy.*

Charleston, S.C., March 31, 1861

My dear Children:—

I was able to give the Wilkies great pleasure, by taking them with my permit to Sullivan's Island on Friday. The wharf presents a very animated appearance from the number of soldiers and the different uniforms—the Zouaves I think the most picturesque. Lieut. W. met us at the Cove, after we had passed the guard. In a short time Willie and Washington joined us. Lieut. W. borrowed the State wagon, and putting some of our

chairs for extra seats, the party were made very comfortable
for a drive to Fort Washington, the quarters of the Washington Light Infantry. Washington drove me in a buggy. The first
battery on the way, now finished and mounted, is the next lot
to mine, the terrible cannon pointing Sumter-wise. We stopped
to see the recruits (regulars) drill. The second battery is on
Mrs. McDowell's lot; the third is Fort Moultrie, where the
fearful machinery of war is so artistically arranged; the fourth
and fifth are near the Curlew grounds, and the Myrtles. After
our drive of three miles, so different from our Summer associations, we turned at East End, and saw the battery now
named Fort Washington, which our boys have been blistering
their hands in building. Lieut. Wilkie ordered the guns to be
fired that we might see the force of their action. The first regiment of rifles, including the Washington Light Infantry, are all
in tents, at the East End, and form quite a picturesque village.
We went first to the Officers' tent, where Lieut. Wilkie unrolled a new flag beautifully wrought with a Palmetto symbol
and recently presented by Mrs. Beauman of Charleston.
Knowing where to touch the heart of a W.L.I. man, I asked to
see the old Eutaw Standard. He unrolled it reverently. It is of
red damask and in tatters.

From the Officers' tent we went to Willie's. Willie was full
of fun as waiter, with his tin drinking cups, and Washington
was overrunning with sentiment about Carrie, who was absent,
and for whom he made a charming bouquet, with an appropriate kiss sentiment hidden in the centre. After about an hour of
chat and inspection we drove home, with Fort Sumter in view,
the calm waters and glittering beach in all their old beauty.
Fort Sumter looks like a noble stag at bay, with Morris Ft.
where the largest force is stationed, and James Fort bristling
with cannon in the rear, Sullivan's in front; and the floating
battery ready for the first note of reinforcement, for Beauregard says all is ready. When will it be surrendered? The men,
ours, have finished their work, and are growing impatient of
delay. It requires all the wisdom of their superiors to keep
them cool. Think of so many thousand men leaving plantations, mercantile life, shops, colleges, and every department of
labor, since December, and working like journeymen. The dragoons, who have been waited on all their lives, curry their own
horses.

Such is my faith in peace, that I carried down a gardener to arrange my flower beds.

MOTHER

## 7. EMMA E. HOLMES—FORT SUMTER SURRENDERS

*While two famous visitors to Charleston, Mrs. James Chesnut and William Howard Russell of the London* Times, *were writing their accounts of the bombardment and surrender of Fort Sumter, the lame girl, Emma E. Holmes, whose house shook from the thunder of the guns, sat at her desk and painstakingly set down the new scenes and new deeds in the once-quiet city of her birth.*

Charleston, South Carolina

Thursday 11th [April 1861] is a day never to be forgotten in the annals of Charleston. A despatch was received from Jeff. Davis with orders to demand the surrender of Fort Sumter immediately. At 2 P.M. two aide-de-camps went to Anderson with the summons, giving him until six to decide. The whole afternoon and night the Battery was thronged with spectators of every age and sex, anxiously watching and waiting with the momentary expectation of hearing the roar of cannon, opening on the fort, or on the fleet which was reported off the bar. Everybody was restless and all who could go, were out.

Friday April 12 1861

Carrie went up yesterday morning to Hattie's to help, in company with two or three others, to make a Confederate flag for the "Pride." When it was half finished, Mr. Hughes went home and told them Mr. Stevens had no flag to raise on his battery so they immediately got the material necessary and worked hard at night and early this morning they finished it and sent it down.

Beauregard went a second time last night at ten to urge the surrender but Anderson refused. The first time Anderson said if the fort was not battered he would have to surrender in three days for want of food. All last night the troops were under arms and at half past four this morning the heavy booming of cannon woke the city from its slumbers. The Battery was soon thronged with anxious hearts, and all day long they have continued—a dense, quiet, orderly mass—but not a sign of fear or anguish is seen. Everybody seems relieved that what has been so long dreaded has come at last, and so confident of victory that they seem not to think of the danger of their friends. Everybody seems calm and grave.

I am writing about half past four in the afternoon—just about twelve hours since the first shot was fired—and during the whole time shot and shell have been steadily pouring into Fort Sumter from Fort Stevens where our "Palmetto boys" have won the highest praise from Beauregard, from Fort Moultrie and the floating battery, placed at the cove. These are the principal batteries and just before dinner we received despatches saying *no one* has yet been hurt on either Morris or Sullivan's island and though the floating battery and Fort Stevens have both been hit several times, *no damage* has been done, while two or three breaches have been made in Fort Sumter. For more than two hours our batteries opened on Anderson, before he returned a single shot, as if husbanding his resources. At times the firing has been very rapid, then slow and irregular and at times altogether upon Fort Moultrie.

Though every shot is distinctly heard and shakes our house, I feel calm and composed. . . .

There are some few ladies who have been made perfectly miserable and nearly frantic by their fear of the safety of their loved ones, but the great body of the citizens seem to be so impressed with the justice of our Cause that they place entire confidence on the God of Battles.

Every day brings hundreds of men from the up-country and the city is besides filled with their anxious wives and sisters and mothers who have followed them.

Saturday April 13, 1861.

All yesterday evening and during the night our batteries continued to fire at regular intervals. About six in the afternoon the rain commenced and poured for some hours. The wind rose and it became quite stormy. But this morning was clear and brilliantly beautiful. Yesterday was so misty it was difficult to see what was going on at the forts. The wind was from the west today, which prevented us from hearing any firing and we were becoming anxious to know the meaning of stillness, when Uncle James sent to tell us Fort Sumter was on fire.

I could not wait for the Dr.'s permission but drove hurriedly to cousin Sallie's, whence I had a splendid view of the harbor —with the naked eye. We could distinctly see the flames amidst the smoke. All the barracks were on fire. Beyond lay the fleet of four or five vessels off the bar, their masts easily counted. They did not make the slightest effort to go to Anderson's relief. . . .

The scene at Fort Sumter must have been awful beyond description. They had soon been compelled to leave their barbette guns, from their exposed situation, many being disabled by our balls. Anderson fired his guns until he was compelled to retire to the case mates from the fury of the fire, on three sides at one time. . . . Both on Friday and Saturday, Anderson put his flag at half-mast as a signal of distress—the barracks being on fire three times on Friday—but "his friends" took no notice of it, and was not understood by our men though all sympathized deeply with him, and shouted applause every time he fired.

In the meantime the scene to the spectators in the city was intensely exciting. The Battery and every house, house top and spire was crowded. On White Point Garden were encamped about fifty cadets, having in charge, five, six, & twelve pounders placed on the eastern promenade. It was thought the vessels might attempt to come in and bombard the city, and workmen were busy all day in mounting four twenty-fours directly in front of Cousin S.'s.

With the telescope I saw the shots as they struck the fort, and the masonry crumbling, while on Morris Island we saw the men moving about on the sand hills. All were anxious to see, and most had opera glasses which they coolly used till they heard a report from Sumter, when they dodged behind the sand hills. . . .

During the morning a demand for cartridge bags for the Dahlgreen guns was made. The elder ladies cut and about twenty girls immediately went to work, all seated on the floor, while we set one to watch and report.

Soon the welcome cry was heard "the flag is down" but scarcely had the shout died away, when it was reported to be up again, but only visible with the glass. The staff being shot off, it was hastily fastened just above the parapets and very soon after at one o'clock the stars and stripes were struck and the white flag floated alone. We could scarcely believe it at first but the total cessation of hostilities soon proved it true.

After the staff was shot off Mr. Wigfall,[1] who was on Morris Island, not being able to see the flag when it was replaced, determined to demand the surrender in Beauregard's name. He sprang into a boat rowed by three Negroes, asked H. Gourdin Young of the P.G. to accompany him and went to the fort while shot and shell were falling all around from the batteries on Sullivan's Island. He crept into a port hole, asked to see Anderson and demanded the surrender. He was asked why the batteries continued firing as the White flag was up beside the U.S. flag. Wigfall answered that as long as the latter floated the firing would continue. It was immediately hauled down.

In the meantime a steamer had started from the City with several other aides, but they found Wigfall had anticipated them. The terms granted are worthy of South Carolina to a brave antagonist. Major Anderson and his garrison are to be allowed to march out with military honors—saluting their flag before taking it down. All facilities will be afforded for his removal together with company arms and property and all private property. He is allowed to determine the precise time of yielding up the Fort and may go by sea or land as he chooses. He requested that he might be sent on in the "Isabel" to New York.

What a change was wrought in a few moments in the appearance of the harbor. Steamers with fire engines were immediately despatched to the Fort. The garrison gathered on the wharf to breathe the fresh air and numbers of little sailing boats were seen darting like sea-gulls in every direction, conveying gentlemen to the islands to see their friends.

During the afternoon, a small boat came with a white flag from the fleet, bearing an officer who wished to make arrangements with Anderson about his removal.

As soon as the surrender was announced, the bells commenced to ring, and in the afternoon, salutes of the "magic seven" were fired from the cutter, "Lady Davis," school ship,

---

[1]Louis T. Wigfall was U. S. Senator from Texas when his state seceded. He immediately resigned and became a member of the Confederate Congress.

and "Cadet's Battery" in honor of one of the most brilliant
and bloodless victories in the records of the world. After thirty
three hours consecutive cannonading not one man hurt on either side—no damages of any consequence done to any of our
fortifications, though the officers quarters at Fort Moultrie and
many of the houses on Sullivan's Island were riddled, and
though the outer walls of Fort Sumter were much battered and
many of the guns disabled, besides the quarters burnt, still as a
military post it is uninjured. . . .

Sunday 14th. Major Anderson appointed 12 o'clock today
to give up the fort. The Governor, his wife & suite, General
Beauregard—suite—and many other military men besides
Mrs. Isaac Hayne and Hattie Barnwell who went down with
Lieut. Davis' sister, went down on board a steamer, whence
they witnessed the ceremony of raising the Confederate and
Palmetto flags. . . . Anderson and his men embarked on
board the "Isabel" but as the tide prevented them from leaving
immediately, they were obliged to be witnesses of the universal
rejoicing. . . .

Sunday afternoon I went on the Battery, which was more
crowded than ever. The cadets had a dress-parade at sunset
and the harbor was gay with steamers with flags flying from
every point. It did not seem at all like Sunday! . . .

## 8. MARY ANNA JACKSON—"OUR HOME GREW LONELY"

*Mary Anna Morrison, daughter of the Reverend R. H.
Morrison, Presbyterian minister of Charlotte, North Carolina,
was married on July 16, 1857, to Professor Thomas Jonathan
Jackson, of the Virginia Military Institute, Lexington, Virginia. He was thirty-three and she twenty-six. She had attended
the Moravian School in Salem, North Carolina, where she was
popular with both students and faculty. The groom's gift to his
lovely, black-haired bride was a gold watch and a dainty set of
seed pearls. After their wedding journey he brought her to
Lexington, where Professor Jackson purchased a small house
and a few acres of land. They planted a garden which was the*

*source of much pleasure to them. Many friends enjoyed the
hospitality of their home. In the following year, their first
child, a daughter, was born to live for only a few short weeks.*

*On April 21, 1861, Professor Jackson, a graduate of West
Point and a veteran of the Mexican campaign, was commissioned a colonel in the Virginia forces and ordered to Richmond. After his departure Mrs. Jackson went about the dreary
work of settling their business affairs, packing up, and dispos-
ing of no-longer-needed furniture. Acting on the wish and advice of her husband, she went back to her girlhood home in
North Carolina.*

Lexington, Virginia, April 21, 1861

About the dawn of that Sabbath morning, April 21, 1861,
our door-bell rang, and the order came that Major Jackson
should bring the cadets to Richmond immediately. Without
waiting for breakfast, he repaired at once to the Institute, to
make arrangements as speedily as possible for marching, but
finding that several hours of preparation would necessarily be
required, he appointed the hour for starting at one o'clock
P.M. He sent a message to his pastor, Dr. White, requesting
him to come to the barracks and offer a prayer with the command before its departure. All the morning he was engaged at
the Institute, allowing himself only a short time to return to
his home about eleven o'clock, when he took a hurried breakfast, and completed a few necessary preparations for his journey. Then, in the privacy of our chamber, he took his Bible
and read that beautiful chapter in Corinthians beginning with
the sublime hope of the resurrection—"For we know that if
our earthly house of this tabernacle be dissolved, we have a
building of God, a house not made with hands, eternal in the
heavens"; and then, kneeling down, he committed himself and
her whom he loved, to the protecting care of his Father in
heaven. Never was a prayer more fervent, tender, and touching. His voice was so choked with emotion that he could
scarcely utter the words, and one of his most earnest petitions
was that "if consistent with His will, God would still avert the
threatening danger and grant us peace!" . . .

When Dr. White went to the Institute to hold the short religious service which Major Jackson requested, the latter told
him the command would march precisely at one o'clock, and
the minister, knowing his punctuality, made it a point to close

the service at a quarter before one. Everything was then in readiness, and after waiting a few moments an officer approached Major Jackson and said: "Major, everything is now ready. May we not set out?" The only reply he made was to point to the dial-plate of the barracks clock, and not until the hand pointed to the hour of one was his voice to ring out the order, "Forward, march!"

After he had taken his departure for the army, our home grew more lonely and painful to me from day to day. . . .

## 9. MARY CUSTIS LEE—"THE PROSPECTS BEFORE US ARE SAD"

*Mary Custis Lee, wife of Robert E. Lee and mother of seven children, was in her fifty-fifth year when war came. The daughter of George Washington Custis and great-granddaughter of Martha Washington, she had spent almost her entire life at Arlington, across the Potomac from Washington. It was the scene of her courtship and marriage, the birthplace of her children—a beautiful and gracious home filled with heirlooms from Mount Vernon.*

*As the wife of an army officer she had lived for brief intervals in many places. After her father's death she edited a series of his articles which appeared in 1860 under the title of* Recollections and Private Memoirs of Washington, by his Adopted Son, George Washington Parke Custis, with a Memoir of the Author, by his daughter.

*On the day when her husband, after thirty years' distinguished service, resigned his commission in the United States Army, she wrote to their daughter Mildred at boarding school in Winchester, Virginia.*

> Arlington, Virginia
> April 20, 1861

With a sad heavy heart, my dear child, I write, for the prospects before us are sad indeed & as I think both parties are wrong in this fratricidal war, there is nothing comforting even in the hope that God may prosper the right, for I see no *right* in the matter. We can only pray that in his mercy he will spare us.

## 10. JUDITH BROCKENBROUGH McGUIRE—
### "I HEARD THE DRUMS BEATING IN WASHINGTON"

*Judith McGuire was the wife of the Reverend John P.
McGuire, principal of the Episcopal High School near Alexandria, Virginia. Born in Richmond in 1813, the daughter of
Judge William Brockenbrough of the Virginia Supreme
Court, she was widely connected throughout the state. Two
sons enlisted in the Confederate Army. Her daughters were in
school. Mrs. McGuire kept a diary from May 1861 till the
war's end "for the members of my family who are too young
to remember these days."*

Alexandria, Virginia

*At Home, May 4, 1861.*—I am too nervous, too wretched
to-day to write in my diary, but that the employment will
while away a few moments of this trying time. Our friends and
neighbors have left us. Every thing is broken up. The Theological Seminary is closed; the High School dismissed. Scarcely
any one is left of the many families which surrounded us. The
homes all look desolate; and yet this beautiful country is looking more peaceful, more lovely than ever, as if to rebuke the
tumult of passion and the fanaticism of man. We are left lonely indeed; our children are all gone—the girls to Clarke, where
they may be safer, and farther from the exciting scenes which
may too soon surround us; and the boys, the dear, dear boys,
to the camp, to be drilled and prepared to meet any emergency. Can it be that our country is to be carried on and on to the
horrors of civil war? I pray, oh how fervently do I pray, that
our Heavenly Father may yet avert it. I shut my eyes and hold
my breath when the thought of what may come upon us obtrudes itself; and yet I cannot believe it. It will, I know the
breach will be healed without the effusion of blood. The taking
of Sumter without bloodshed has somewhat soothed my fears,
though I am told by those who are wiser than I, that men must
fall on both sides by the score, by the hundred, and even by
the thousand. But it is not my habit to look on the dark side,
so I try to employ myself, and hope for the best. To-day our

house seems so deserted, that I feel more sad than usual, for on this morning we took leave of our whole household. Mr. McGuire and myself are now the sole occupants of the house, which usually teems with life. I go from room to room, looking at first one thing and then another, so full of sad associations. The closed piano, the locked bookcase, the nicely-arranged tables, the formally-placed chairs, ottomans and sofas in the parlor! Oh for some one to put them out of order! and then the dinner-table, which has always been so well surrounded, so social, so cheerful, looked so cheerless to-day, as we seated ourselves one at the head, the other at the foot, with one friend,—but one,—at the side. I could scarcely restrain my tears, and but for the presence of that one friend, I believe I should have cried outright. After dinner, I did not mean to do it, but I could not help going into the girls' room. . . . I heard my own foot-steps so plainly, that I was startled by the absence of all other sounds. There the furniture looked so quiet, the beds so fixed and smooth, the wardrobes and bureaux so tightly locked, and the whole so lifeless! But the writing-desks, work-boxes, and the numberless things so familiar to my eyes! Where were they? I paused, to ask myself what it all meant. Why did we think it necessary to send off all that was so dear to us from our own home? I threw open the shutters, and the answer came at once, so mournfully! I heard distinctly the drums beating in Washington. The evening was so still that I seemed to hear nothing else. As I looked at the Capitol in the distance, I could scarcely believe my senses. That Capitol of which I had always been so proud! Can it be possible that it is no longer *our* Capitol? And are our countrymen, under its very eaves, making mighty preparations to drain our hearts' blood? And must this Union, which I was taught to revere, be rent asunder? Once I thought such a suggestion sacrilege; but now that is dismembered, I trust it may never, never be reunited. We must be a separate people—our nationality must be different, to insure lasting peace and good-will. Why cannot we part in peace?

## 11. MARY CUSTIS LEE—I SET MY HOUSE IN ORDER

*Although the General wrote repeatedly from Richmond
urging his wife to leave Arlington, and although she had been
warned to leave by her young cousin, William Orton Williams,
who was attached to General Scott's office in Washington,
brave Mrs. Lee could not bring herself to go. She must first
place in best available security what they owned of intrinsic
value or historic interest. Now she had for a brief interval the
help of her son Custis who had been stationed at Fort Washington, a little way down the Potomac. The family plate and
the Washington letters and papers she sent to Richmond. The
family portraits and Washington's camp bed and equipment
were among the things she sent to Ravensworth, the country
home of her aunt, Maria Fitzhugh, near Alexandria. The Order of the Cincinnati china and the State china from Mount
Vernon with other cherished possessions she stored in the
closets and cellar of Arlington.*

*Finally, a few days after she wrote this letter to her hus-
band, she followed her three daughters to Ravensworth.*

Arlington, Virginia
May 9, 1861

I suppose ere this, dear Robert, you have heard of the arrival of our valuables in Richmond. We have sent many others to
Ravensworth & all our wine & stores, pictures, piano etc. I was
very unwilling to do this; but Orton was *so* urgent & even intimated that the day was fixed to take possession of these
heights, that I did not feel it was prudent to risk articles that
could never be replaced. Aunt Maria has been very kind in offering us an asylum there & in taking care of all our
things. . . . I sent the girls up last evening. . . . I thought
they could return if all was quiet. Custis was not ready to go;
so I determined to remain with him, being very uneasy lest he
should be arrested. I begin now to think, though it is all suspicion, that Orton was made the tool of some of the authorities
in Washington to alarm us, either to bring you out to defend
your home or get us out of the house. They are anxious at pres-

ent to keep up appearances & would gladly, I believe, have a
pretext to invade. . . . All day yesterday Gov. steamers were
going up to Georgetown—transports, steam tugs & all kinds of
crafts. Rumor Harpers Ferry is to be taken. Custis astonishes
me with his calmness; with a possibility of having his early &
beautiful home destroyed, the present necessity of abandoning
it, he never indulges in invectives or a word of reflection on
the cruel course of the Administration. He leaves that for his
Mamma & sisters.


## 12. VARINA HOWELL DAVIS—"THEY ARE THE FINEST SET OF MEN"

*Mrs. Davis and her children—Maggie, aged six, Jeff, Jr.,
aged three, and baby Joe—arrived in Montgomery in March
to occupy the lovely two-story dwelling which was now called
the White House of the Confederacy. She brought with her
some of their heirlooms from "Briarfield." Over the mantel of
her husband's new room she hung a sampler on which was
embroidered "Thy Will Be Done." "Queen Varina" entered
into her new duties with enthusiasm. The White House was the
center of much social activity. There were brilliant levees, dinners and luncheons. But social life was not the First Lady's
chief concern. She accompanied her husband on a hard, dangerous trip to examine the coast defenses of the Confederacy.
She found time to keep her absent friends informed of the
state of the nation. One such old friend was Clement Claiborne Clay, Jr., U.S. Senator from Alabama, 1853-1861, now
in ill health at his mountain home "Cosy Cot" near Huntsville,
but expecting to take his seat in the Confederate Senate in the
autumn. In this letter she pays her incidental respects left-
handedly to some Republican Senators in Washington.*

Executive Mansion [Montgomery, Alabama]
May 10th, 1861

My dear Mr. Clay,

Could I have supposed my letter could prove a tolerable
substitute to you for Mr. Davis I should long since have written to you. Mr. Davis seems just now only conscious of things

left undone, and to ignore the much which has been achieved, consequently his time seems all taken up with the cabinet planning (I presume) future operations. He comes home to eat his meals but always eats under a protest against the time occupied. "Oft in the stilly night," when he has seen his cabinet fall "like leaves in wintry weather" he is forced to come home for there is no one to help him to work. Sometimes the cabinet sans scotch cap depart surreptitiously, one at a time, and Mr. Davis while making things as plain as did the preacher "the virtues of the baptismal," finds his demonstrations made to one weak weary man, who has no vim to contend, to make the long short, he overworks himself & all the rest of mankind, but is so far quite well, though not fleshily inclined. There is a good deal of talk here of his going to Richmond as commander of the forces. I hope it may be done for to him military command is a perfect system of Hygiene and unless Mr. Spinola is around somewhere I don't suppose there is much danger. There have been some here who thought with a view to our sanitary condition that the government had better be moved to Richmond, and also that it would strengthen the weak fleshed, but willing spirited Border States.

For my part the only preference I have is be nearer Mr. Davis. I shall not attempt to stay here this summer. The children cannot stand warm weather.

This is a very pretty place and were not the climate as warm as is the enthusiasm of the people, it would be pleasant—but really all my patriotism oozes out, not unlike Bob Acres courage, at the pores, and I have deliberately come to the conclusion that Roman matrons did up their chores, patriotism, and such like public duties in the winter. I wish your health would suffice for you to come to see the Congress. They are the finest looking set of men I have ever seen collected together, grave, quiet, and thoughtful looking. Men, with an air of refinement which makes in my mind's picture gallery a gratifying pendant to Hamlen,[1] Durkee,[2] Dolittle[3] & Chandler.[4]

[1] Hannibal Hamlin, of Maine, seems intended—U. S. Senator 1848-1861, Vice-President 1861-1865.
[2] Charles Durkee, U. S. Senator from Wisconsin, 1855-1861,
[3] James R. Doolittle, U. S. Senator from Wisconsin, 1857-1869.
[4] Zachariah Chandler, U. S. Senator from Michigan, 1857-1875.

We are Presidents in embryo here. Shorn of much of our fair proportions, for instance Edward would carry prestige with him by insulting good friends, instead we have a negro door servant, who is disposed to believe all the people in the world bent on civility, and is happy to be rung up if he can testify his appreciation of their politeness.

The market is forlorn but this we give our best, and a warm welcome, and I hope are spared many of the critiques we have heard in Washington upon the indifferent fare of the entertainers, because our guests eat with l'entente cordiale, which I now find exists out of diplomatic papers, & is not a myth.

If you are able to come with your wife, and make us a visit we will have the concordances of Washington & Montgomery. I should sincerely rejoice to see you, and to show my little ones to you. Believe me time has not cooled the affectionate gratitude I feel for all your sympathy during Mr. Davis' illness, to me the darkest hour of my life, and it would be a happiness in your hour of prostration to say so to you. You are not able to bear hotel inconvenience, but if you will come to us, need only see people when you please. I think too Mrs. Clay would enjoy seeing the many friends and acquaintances she has here. Come immediately so as to see Mr. Davis before he leaves here for Virginia.

As to the children, I think you must like them, at best your God child—he is pretty as was Maggie in her babyhood, and so very gentle & loving, gets occasions of tenderness while playing, and runs up and puts his dirty little hands on either side of my face to kiss me. He talks sporadically—the words pronounced quite plainly, sometimes whole sentences, and then it is a month before another word is enunciated. Jeff is beaming, blustering, blooming, burly and blundering as ever. The repository of many hopes, promising of but little definite as yet. Little Maggie is gentle & loving, and considerate. She and I are good friends.

We all think of going out to Mrs. Fitzpatrick this evening with C. Brown & his wife, and Mr. and Mrs. Toombs to spend a night & day. We expect much pleasure. The Madam seems to be in fine spirits, as is also the Governor. Ben I have not seen—Mrs. Mallory is in town on a short visit. Mrs. Pope Walker is here, Mrs. Memminger, and Mrs. Toombs. The latter is the only person who has a house.[1] I could gossip on ad infinitum, but were my paper longer, my gossip might be stronger. Four pages are enough for a sick man one hopes to see soon.

Faithfully, your friend

VARINA DAVIS

[1] Mrs. Fitzpatrick was the handsome wife of Benjamin Fitzpatrick, former U. S. Senator. Ben was the Senator. C. Brown was "Constitution" Browne, i.e., R. M. Browne, *ad interim* Secretary of State and Assistant Secretary of State of the Confederacy, who had been editor of the Atlanta *Constitution*. The Governor of Alabama was Andrew B. Moore. In the Provisional Cabinet Robert Toombs, of Georgia, was Secretary of State; S. R. Mallory, of Florida, Secretary of the Navy; L. P. Walker, of Alabama, Secretary of War; C. G. Memminger, of South Carolina, Secretary of the Treasury.

# II

# THE CONFEDERACY IS INVADED

*May 1861—February 1862*

On May 23, 1861, the people of Virginia ratified the Ordinance of Secession, and the very next day Union troops carried out the threat of which Orton Williams had warned Mrs. Lee two weeks or so before. They crossed the Potomac from Washington and occupied Arlington and the little towns of Alexandria and Fairfax. Ben Butler—his name was to become a byword and a hissing to Southern women—started an advance from Fortress Monroe up the peninsula between the York and the James rivers toward Richmond. He did not get far, being turned back at Big Bethel.

On June 8 Tennessee ratified secession—the eleventh state to leave the Union. The roster of the Confederacy was now complete. Maryland wavered but stayed out. Kentucky strove vainly to be neutral. Some counties in western Virginia seceded into the Union. The Provisional Congress moved to Richmond.

In July Major-General Irvin McDowell with approximately 35,000 men invaded Virginia from the Washington camp. "On to Richmond!" they shouted. They would promptly quench this firey rebellion. At Manassas, twenty-five miles southwest of the Northern capital, they encountered Generals Beauregard and Joseph E. Johnston with about 31,000. On the twenty-first after some initial success the Union army was decisively defeated at what was later called in the South the First Battle of Manassas (Bull Run). Congressmen and others, men and women, who had come out in holiday spirit to view the spectacle of certain victory, skedaddled back to Washington in panic, adding to the confusion of the routed soldiers. During the battle Thomas Jonathan Jackson, commanding the Virginia brigade, won his first recognition and a new name.

31

*"There stands Jackson like a stone wall,"* cried *Brigadier-General Barnard E. Bee, soon to die. President Davis and the Southern commanders on the field did not feel they were strong enough to follow up the success with determined pursuit.*

*Elsewhere the South was not so fortunate in repelling invasion. The North was already intent on effecting a blockade of Southern ports. On August 29 Fort Hatteras and Hatteras Inlet on the North Carolina coast were captured by a Union fleet and army. Port Royal, Hilton Head, Beaufort and the surrounding sea islands off South Carolina fell to the enemy in November.*

*Further disasters came early in the New Year of 1862. The Conferedate fortification and garrison under General Henry A. Wise on Roanoke Island, scene of Sir Richard Grenville's abortive colony, were lost to an amphibious operation. In the West things went very badly indeed. Fort Henry on the Tennessee River was yielded to General Ulysses S. Grant on February 6, and on the sixteenth he took Fort Donelson on the Cumberland, and some 14,000 men, after a four days' seige. But the intrepid and resourceful Nathan Bedford Forrest, who was utterly opposed to the surrender, got his cavalry regiment out of Donelson in time. With the river forts gone, Nashville had to be evacuated by General Albert Sidney Johnston.*

*The day before that happened, Washington's Birthday, the Confederate permanent government had been inaugurated in Richmond.*

*Now the women speak as the tide of war flows toward them and some begin to withdraw before it.*

## 1. JUDITH BROCKENBROUGH McGUIRE—
### VIRGINIA IS INVADED

*During four days when Mrs. McGuire neglected her diary the sound of military activities over the river in Washington grew more ominous. Now she resumes—*

Alexandria, Virginia

*May 10 1861.* Since writing last, I have been busy, very busy, arranging and rearranging. We are now hoping that Alexandria will not be a landing-place for the enemy, but that the forts will be attacked. In that case, they would certainly be repulsed, and we could stay quietly at home. To view the progress of events from any point will be sad enough, but it would be more bearable at our own home, and surrounded by our family and friends. With the supposition that we may remain, and that the ladies of the family at least may return to us, I am having the grounds put in order, and they are now so beautiful! Lilacs, crocuses, the lily of the valley, and other spring flowers, are in luxuriant bloom, and the roses in full bud. The greenhouse plants have been removed and grouped on the lawn, verbenas in bright bloom have been transplanted from the pit to the borders, and the grass seems unusually green after the late rains; the trees are in full leaf; every thing is so fresh and lovely. "All, save the spirit of man, is divine."

War seems inevitable, and while I am trying to employ the passing hour, a cloud still hangs over us all and all that surrounds us. For a long time before our society was so completely broken up, the ladies of Alexandria and all the surrounding country were busily employed sewing for our soldiers. Shirts, pants, jackets, and beds, of the heaviest material, have been made by the most delicate fingers. All ages, all conditions, meet now on one common platform. We must all work for our country. Our soldiers must be equipped. Our parlor was the rendezvous for our neighborhood, and our sewing-machine was in requisition for weeks. Scissors and needles were plied by all. The daily scene was most animated. The fires of our enthusiasm and patriotism were burning all the while to a degree which might have been consuming, but that our tongues served as safety-valves. Oh, how we worked and talked, and excited each other! One common sentiment animated us all; no doubts, no fears were felt. We all have such entire reliance in the justice of our cause and the valor of our men, and, above all, on the blessing of Heaven! These meetings have necessarily ceased with us, as so few of any age or degree remain at home; but in Alexandria they are still kept up with great interest. We who are left here are trying to give the soldiers who are quartered in town comfort, by carrying them milk, pies, cakes, etc. I went in yesterday to the barracks, with the carriage well filled with such things, and found many young friends quartered there. All are taking up arms; the first young men in the country are the most zealous. Alexandria is doing her duty nobly; so is Fairfax; and so, I hope, is the whole South. We are very weak in resources, but strong in stout hearts, zeal for the cause, and enthusiastic devotion to our beloved South; and while men are making a free-will offering of their life's blood on the alter of their country, women must not be idle. We must do what we can for the comfort of our brave men. We must sew for them, knit for them, nurse the sick, keep up the faint-hearted, give them a word of encouragement in season and out of season. There is much for us to do, and we must do it. The embattled hosts of the North will have the whole world from which to draw their supplies; but if, as it seems but too probable, our ports are blockaded, we shall indeed be dependent on our own exertions, and great must those exertions be.

The Confederate flag waves from several points in Alexandria: from the Marshall House, the Market-house, and the several barracks. The peaceful, quiet old town looks quite warlike. I feel sometimes, when walking on King's street, meeting men in uniform, passing companies of cavalry, hearing martial music, etc., that I must be in a dream. Oh that it were a dream, and that the last ten years of our country's history were blotted out! Some of our old men are a little nervous, look doubtful, and talk of the impotency of the South. Oh, I feel utter scorn for such remarks. We must not admit weakness. Our soldiers do not think of weakness; they know that their hearts are strong, and their hands well skilled in the use of the rifle. Our country boys have been brought up on horseback, and hunting has ever been their holiday sport. Then why shall they feel weak? Their hearts feel strong when they think of the justice of their cause. In that is *our* hope.

Walked down this evening to see——.[1] The road looked lonely and deserted. Busy life has departed from our midst. We found Mrs. —— packing up valuables. I have been doing the same; but after they are packed, where are they to be sent? Silver may be buried, but what is to be done with books, pictures, etc.? We have determined, if we are obliged to go from home, to leave every thing in the care of the servants. They have promised to be faithful, and I believe they will be; but

---

[1] It was not uncommon for the diarists to omit names so as not to endanger their friends in case their journals should fall into enemy hands.

my hope becomes stronger and stronger that we may remain
here, or may soon return if we go away. Everything is so sad
around us! We went to the Chapel on Sunday as usual, but it
was grievous to see the change—the organ mute, the organist
gone; the seats of the students of both institutions empty; but
one or two members of each family to represent the absentees;
the prayer for the President omitted. When Dr. —— came to
it, there was a slight pause, and then he went on to the next
prayer—all seemed so strange! Tucker Conrad, one of the few
students who is still here, raised the tunes; his voice seemed
unusually sweet, because so sad. He was feebly supported by
all who were not in tears. There was night service, but it
rained, and I was not sorry that I could not go.

*May 15.*—Busy every moment of time packing up, that our
furniture may be safely put away in case of a sudden removal.
The parlor furniture has been rolled into the Laboratory, and
covered, to keep it from injury; the books are packed up; the
pictures put away with care; house linen locked up, and all
other things made as secure as possible. We do not hope to remove many things, but to prevent their ruin. We are constantly told that a large army would do great injury if quartered
near us; therefore we want to put things out of the reach of
the soldiers, for I have no idea that officers would allow them
to break locks, or that they would allow our furniture to be interfered with. We have a most unsettled feeling—with carpets
up, curtains down, and the rooms without furniture; but a constant excitement, and expectation of we know not what, sup-
plants all other feelings. Nothing but nature is pleasant, and
that is so beautiful! The first roses of the season are just appearing, and the peonies are splendid; but the horrors of war,
with which we are so seriously threatened, prevent the enjoyment of any thing.

I feel so much for the *Southerners* of Maryland; I am afraid
they are doomed to persecution, but it does seem so absurd in
Maryland and Kentucky to talk of armed neutrality in the present state of the country! Let States, like individuals, be independent—be something or nothing. I believe that the very best
people of both States are with us, but are held back by stern
necessity. Oh that they could burst the bonds that bind them,
and speak and act like freemen! The Lord reigneth; to Him
only can we turn, and humbly pray that He may see fit to say

to the troubled waves, "Peace, be still!" We sit at our windows, and see the bosom of our own Potomac covered with the sails of vessels employed by the enemies of our peace. I often wish myself far away, that I, at least, might not *see* these things. The newspapers are filled with the boastings of the North, and yet I cannot feel alarmed. My woman's heart does not quail, even though they come, as they so loudly threaten, as an avalanche to overwhelm us. Such is my abiding faith in the justice of our cause, that I have no shadow of doubt of our success.

*May 16.*—To-day I am alone. Mr. McGuire has gone to Richmond to the Convention, and so have Bishop Johns and Dr. Stuart. I have promised to spend my nights with Mrs. Johns. All is quiet around us. Federal troops quartered in Baltimore. Poor Maryland! The North has its heel upon her! I pray that we may have peaceful secession.

*May 17th.*—Still quiet. Mrs. Johns, Mrs. B., and myself, sat at the Malvern windows yesterday, *spying* the enemy as they sailed up and down the river. Those going up were heavily laden, carrying provisions, etc., to their troops. I think if all Virginia could see their preparations as we do, her vote would be unanimous for secession.

*May 21st.*—Mr. McGuire has returned. Yesterday evening we rode to the parade-ground in Alexandria; it was a beautiful but sad sight. How many of those young, brave boys may be cut off, or maimed for life. I shudder to think of what a single battle may bring forth. The Federal vessel *Pawnee* now lies before the old town, with its guns pointing towards it. It is aggravating enough to see it; but the inhabitants move on as calmly as though it were a messenger of peace. It is said that an undefended, indefensible town like Alexandria will hardly be attacked. It seems to me strange that they do not go immediately to the Rappahannock, the York, or the James, and land at once in the heart of the State. I tremble lest they should make a direct attack upon Richmond. Should they go at once to City Point, and march thence to the city, I am afraid it could hardly be defended. Our people are busy in their preparations for defense; but time is necessary—every day is precious to us. Our President and military chiefs are doing all that men can

do to forward preparations. My ear is constantly pained with
the sound of cannon from the Navy-Yard at Washington, and
to-day the drum has been beating furiously in our once loved
metropolis. Dr. S. says there was a grand dress parade—brothers gleefully preparing to draw their brothers' blood!

Day after to-morrow the vote of Virginia on secession will
be taken, and I, who so dearly loved this Union, who from my
cradle was taught to revere it, now must earnestly hope that
the voice of Virginia may give no uncertain sound; that she
may leave it with a shout. I am thankful that she did not take
so important a step hastily, but that she set an example of patience and long-suffering, and made an earnest effort to maintain peace; but as all her efforts have been rejected with scorn,
and she has been required to give her quota of men to fight
and destroy her brethren of the South, I trust that she may
now speak decidedly.

*Fairfax C. H., May 25.*—The day of suspense is at an end.
Alexandria and its environs, including, I greatly fear, our
home, are in the hands of the enemy. Yesterday morning, at
an early hour, as I was in my pantry, putting up refreshments
for the barracks preparatory to a ride to Alexandria, the door
was suddenly thrown open by a servant, looking wild with excitement, exclaiming, "Oh, madam, do you know?" "Know
what, Henry?" "Alexandria is filled with Yankees." "Are you
sure, Henry?" said I, trembling in every limb. "Sure, madam! I
saw them myself. Before I got up I heard soldiers rushing by
the door; went out, and saw our men going to the cars."

"Did they get off?" I asked, afraid to hear the answer. "Oh,
yes, the cars went off full of them, and some marched out, and
then I went to King Street, and saw such crowds of Yankees
coming in! They came down the turnpike, and some came
down the river; and presently I heard such noise and confusion, and they said they were fighting, so I came home as fast
as I could."

I lost no time in seeking Mr. ——, who hurried out to hear
the truth of the story. He soon met Dr. ——, who was bearing
off one of the editors in his buggy. He more than confirmed
Henry's report, and gave an account of the tragedy at the
Marshall House. Poor Jackson (the proprietor) had always
said that the Confederate flag which floated from the top of
his house should never be taken down but over his dead body.

It was known that he was a devoted patriot, but his friends had amused themselves at this rash speech. He was suddenly aroused by the noise of men rushing by his room-door, ran to the window, and seeing at once what was going on, he seized his gun, his wife trying in vain to stop him; as he reached the passage he saw Colonel Ellsworth[1] coming from the third story, waving the flag. As he passed Jackson he said, "I have a trophy." Jackson immediately raised his gun, and in an insant Ellsworth fell dead. One of the party immediately killed poor Jackson. The Federals then proceeded down the street, taking possession of public houses, etc. I am mortified to write that a party of our cavalry, thirty-five in number, was captured. It can scarcely be accounted for. It is said that the Federals notified the authorities in Alexandria that they would enter the city at eight, and the captain was so credulous as to believe them. Poor fellow, he is now a prisoner, but it will be a lesson to him and to our troops generally. Jackson leaves a wife and children. I know the country will take care of them. He is the first martyr. I shudder to think how many more there may be.

The question with us was, what was next to be done? Mr. McGuire had voted for secession, and there were Union people enough around us to communicate every thing of the sort to the Federals; the few neighbors who were left were preparing to be off, and we thought it most prudent to come off too. Pickets were already thrown out beyond Shuter's Hill, and they were threatening to arrest all secessionists.

With a heavy heart I packed trunks and boxes, as many as our little carriage would hold; had packing-boxes fixed in my room for the purpose of bringing off valuables of various sorts, when I go down on Monday; locked up every thing; gave the keys to the cook, enjoining upon the servants to take care of the cows, "Old Rock," the garden, the flowers, and last but not least, J——'s splendid Newfoundland. Poor dog, as we got into the carriage how I did long to take him! When we took leave of the servants they looked sorrowful, and we felt so. I promised them to return to-day, but Mr. —— was so sick this morning that I could not leave him, and have deferred it until day after to-morrow. Mr. —— said, as he looked out upon the

[1]E. Elmer Ellsworth, of the 11th New York or "First Fire Zouaves."

green lawn just before we set off, that he thought he had never seen the place so attractive; and as we drove off the bright flowers we had planted seemed in full glory; every flower-bed seemed to glow with the "Giant of Battles" and other brilliant roses. In bitterness of heart I exclaimed "Why must we leave thee, Paradise!" and for the first time my tears streamed. As we drove by "The Seminary," the few students who remained came out to say "Good-by." One of them had just returned from Alexandria, where he had seen the bodies of Ellsworth and Jackson, and another, of which we had heard through one of our servants who went to town in the morning. When the Federal troops arrived, a man being ordered to take down the secession flag above the market-house, and run up the "stars and stripes," got nearly to the flag, missed his foothold, fell, and broke his neck. This remarkable circumstance was told me by two persons who saw the body. Is it ominous? I trust and pray that it may be.

When we got to Bailey's Cross Roads, Mr. McGuire said to me that we were obliged to leave our home, and as far as we have a *right* to any other, it makes not the slightest difference which road we take—we might as well drive to the right hand as to the left—nothing remains to us but the barren, beaten track. It was a sorrowful thought; but we have kind relations and friends whose doors are open to us, and we hope to get home again before very long. The South did not bring on the war, and I believe that God will provide for the homeless.

About sunset we drove up to the door of this, the house of our relative, the Rev. Mr. Brown and were received with the warmest welcome. As we drove through the village we saw the carriage of Commodore Forrest[1] standing at the hotel door, and were soon followed by the C.'s of our neighborhood and many others. They told us that the Union men of the town were pointing out the houses of the Secessionists, and that some of them had already been taken by Federal officers. When I think of all this my heart quails me. Our future is so dark and shadowy, so much may, nay must, happen before we again become quiet, and get back, that I feel sad and dreary. I have no fear for the country—that must and will succeed; but

[1]Commodore French Forrest, whose home was "Claremont." He was later to command the Confederate navy yard at Norfolk.

our dear ones! the representatives of every State, almost every
family, from the Potomac to the Gulf of Mexico—how must
they suffer, and how must we at home suffer in their behalf!

This little village has two or three companies quartered in it.
It seems thoroughly aroused from the quiescent state which it
was wont to indulge. Drums are beating, colors flying, and
ever and anon we are startled by the sound of a gun. At Fairfax Station there are a good many troops, a South Carolina
regiment at Centreville, and quite an army is collecting at
Manassas Station. We shall be greatly outnumbered, I know,
but numbers cannot make up for the zeal and patriotism of
our Southern men fighting for home and liberty.

*May 29.*—I cannot get over my disappointment—I am not
to return home! The wagon was engaged. E. W. had promised
to accompany me; all things seemed ready; but yesterday a
gentleman came up from the Seminary, reporting that the public roads are picketed far beyond our house, and that he had
to cross fields, etc., to avoid an arrest, as he had no pass. I
know that there are private roads which we could take, of
which the enemy knows nothing; and even if they saw me,
they surely would not forbid ingress and egress to a quiet eld-
erly lady like myself. But Mr. —— thinks that I ought not to
risk it. The fiat has gone forth, and I am obliged to submit.

I hear that the house has been searched for arms, and that
J's old rifle has been filched from its corner. It was a wonderfully harmless rifle, having been innocent even of the blood of
squirrels and hares for some time past. I wonder if they do
suppose that we would leave good fire-arms in their reach
when they are so much wanted in the Confederacy, or if it is a
mere pretext for satisfying a little innocent curiosity for seeing
the interior of Southern homes? Ah, how many Northerners
—perhaps the very men who have come to despoil these
homes, to kill our husbands, sons and brothers, to destroy our
peace—have been partakers of the warm-hearted hospitality so
freely offered by our people! The parlours and dining-rooms
now so ignominiously searched, how often have they been
opened, and the best cheer which the houses could afford set
forth for them! I do most earnestly hope that no Northern
gentleman, above all, no Christian gentleman, will engage in
this wicked war of invasion. It makes my blood boil when I re-

member that our private rooms, our chambers, our very sanctums, are thrown open to a ruthless soldiery. But let me not do them injustice. I believe that they took nothing but the rifle, and injured nothing but the sewing-machine. Perhaps they knew of the patriotic work of that same machine—how it had stitched up many a shirt and many a jacket for our brave boys, and therefore did it wrong. But this silent agent for our country's weal shall not lie in ruins. When I get it again, it shall be repaired, and shall

> "Stitch, stitch, stitch,
>    Band, and gusset, and sea,"

for the comfort of our men, and it shall work all the more vigorously for the wrongs it has suffered. . . .

*29th, Night.*—Several of our friends from Alexandria have passed to-day. Many families who attempted to stay at home are escaping as best they may, finding that the liberty of the hoary-headed fathers of patriotic sons is at stake, and others are in peril for opinion's sake. It is too provoking to think of such men as Dr. —— and Dr. —— being obliged to hide themselves in their houses, until their wives, by address and strategy, obtain passes to get them out of town! Now they go with large and helpless families, they know not whither. Many have passed whom I did not know. What is to become of us all?

*Chantilly, June 1.*—We came here (the house of our friend Mrs. Stuart) this morning, after some hours of feverish excitement. About three o'clock in the night we were aroused by a volley of musketry not far from our windows. Every human being in the house sprang up at once. We soon saw by the moonlight a body of cavalry moving up the street, and as they passed below our window we distinctly heard the commander's order, "Halt." They again proceeded a few paces, turned and approached slowly, and as softly as though every horse were shod with velvet. In a few moments there was another volley, the firing rapid, and to my unpractised ear there seemed a discharge of a thousand muskets. Then came the same body of cavalry rushing by in wild disorder. Oaths loud and deep were heard from the commander. They again formed, and rode quite rapidly into the village. Another volley, and another, then such a rushing as I never witnessed. The cavalry strained by, the commander calling out "Halt, halt," with curses and imprecations. On, on they went, nor did they stop.

While the balls were flying, I stood riveted to the window, unconscious of danger. When I was forced away, I took refuge in the front yard. Mrs. B. was there before me, and we witnessed the disorderly retreat of eighty-five of the Second United States Cavalry (regulars) before a much smaller body of our raw recruits. They had been sent from Arlington, we suppose, to reconnoitre. They advanced on the village at full speed, into the cross-street by the hotel and courthouse, then wheeled to the right, down by the Episcopal church. We could only oppose them with the Warrenton Rifles, as for some reason the cavalry could not be rendered effective. Colonel Ewell,[1] who happened to be there, arranged the Rifles, and I think a few dismounted cavalry, on either side of the street, behind the fence, so as to make it a kind of breastwork, whence they returned the enemy's fire most effectively. Then came the terrible suspense; all was confusion on the street, and it was not yet quite light. One of our gentlemen soon came in with the sad report that Captain Marr of the Warrenton Rifles, a young officer of great promise, was found dead. The gallant Rifles were exulting in their success, until it was whispered that their captain was missing. Had he been captured? Too soon the uncertainty was ended, and their exultant shouts hushed. His body was found in the high grass—dead, quite dead. Two of our men received slight flesh-wounds. The enemy carried off their dead and wounded. We captured four men and three horses. Seven of their horses were left dead on the roadside. They also dropped a number of arms, which were picked up by our men.

After having talked the matter over, we were getting quite composed, and thought we had nothing more to fear, when we observed them placing sentinels in Mr. B's porch, saying that it was a high point, and another raid was expected. The gentlemen immediately ordered the carriages, and in half an hour

---

[1] Richard S. Ewell was to become a lieutenant-general and one of the Confederacy's great corps commanders. He was commissioned brigadier-general on June 17, 1861.

Mr. B's family and ourselves were on the way to this place. . . .

This evening we have been enjoying a walk about these lovely grounds. Nature and art have combined to make it one of the most beautiful spots I ever saw—"So clean, so green, so flowery, so bowery," as Hannah More wrote of Hampstead; and we look on it sadly, fearing that the "trail of the serpent may pass over it all." Can it be that other beautiful homes are to be deserted? The ladies of the family are here alone, the sons are where they should be, in the camp; and should the Northern army sweep over it, they cannot remain here. Colonel Gregg and others of a South Carolina regiment dined here yesterday. They are in fine spirits, and very sanguine.

*June 5.*—Still at Chantilly. Every thing quiet; nothing particularly exciting; yet we are so restless. Mrs. Casenove and myself rode to the camp at Fairfax Court-House a day or two ago to see many friends; but my particular object was to see my nephew, W. B. Newton, first lieutenant in the Hanover troop. He looks so cheerful, full of enthusiasm and zeal; but he feels that we have a great work before us, and that we have entered a more important revolution than our ancestors did in 1775. His bright political prospects, his successful career at the bar, his future in every respect so full of hope and promise—all, all laid aside. But it is all right, and when he returns to enjoy his unfettered country, his hardships will be all forgotten, in joy for his country's triumphs. . . .

Mrs. General Lee has been with us for several days. She is on her way to the lower country, and feels that she has left Arlington for an indefinite period. They removed their valuables, silver, etc., but the furniture is left behind. I never saw her more cheerful, and she seems to have no doubt of our success. We are looking to her husband as our leader with implicit confidence; for besides his great military abilities, he is a God-fearing man, and looks for help where alone it is to be found. Letters from Richmond are very cheering. It is one great barracks. Troops are assembling there from every part of the Confederacy, all determined to do their duty. Ladies assemble daily, by hundreds, at the various churches, for the purpose of sewing for the soldiers. They are fitting out company after company. The large stuccoed house at the corner of

Clay and Twelfth streets, so long occupied by Dr. John Brockenbrough,[1] has been purchased as a residence for the President. I am glad that it has been thus appropriated. . . .

## 2. BETTY HERNDON MAURY—"WE LEFT WASHINGTON"

*Betty was the eldest of the eight children of famous Matthew Fontaine Maury, whom Robert S. Henry characterizes as "father of the science of oceanography, discoverer of the Gulf Stream, once the great scientific light of the United States," and later on to be "one of the three naval commissioners through whose zeal and efforts the Confederacy was able to secure the ships that became her cruisers, and her only mobile Navy."*

*Betty was born in Fredericksburg, Virginia, in 1835. She was a child when the family moved to Washington, D. C., and her father began his distinguished career with the United States Naval Observatory. She often accompanied him on his lecture tours and in 1852 went with him to the Brussels Conference. Before they sailed home they were lavishly entertained in many foreign cities.*

*When she was twenty-one Betty married her cousin, Will A. Maury, a lawyer, whose father had been mayor of Washington. A daughter, Nannie Belle, was born to them in 1859.*

*When war came the Will Maurys withdrew to Fredericksburg and lived with John Minor, one of their numerous Virginia cousins and brother of Mary Berkeley Minor Blackford. Betty's father resigned his position in Washington and reported in Richmond. The Governor of Virginia appointed him to his council. Then, with the rank of commander in the Confederate Navy, he was put in charge of the Torpedo Bureau where he carried out dangerous experiments with electric mines. The two brothers nearest to Betty in age, John and Dick, enlisted in the army. Brother-in-law Tom was a surgeon who helped take care of the wounded. Cousin Dabney Herndon Maury*

[1] Mrs. McGuire's cousin.

*rose from captain of cavalry to commander of the District of the Gulf with headquarters at Mobile.*

Fredericksburg, Va.
At Cousin John Minor's
June 3d, 1861

A diary, faithfully kept, in such eventful times as these, must be interesting to our children even though it be indifferently written.

I commenced one about three weeks ago at our home in Washington, but in the hurry and confusion of getting off it was forgotten. I shall commence where I left off there, hoping to get that, one of these days, though God knows when or where we shall ever see our possessions there again. Will left his business, furniture and everything to come here and be with his people on the right side.

Last Thursday and Friday we got letters from Papa by private hand (there are no mails now between the North and the South) commanding us to come out of Washington at once.

On Friday Will went down to Alexandria to see if he could get a wagon, or conveyance of any kind to carry us to Manassas Junction. While he was gone it occurred to me that I had better go to the War Department and try to get a pass for us to leave the next day. So I got a hack and drove to the Department, intending to get Major John Lee[1] to go with me to see General Mansfield[2] and ask for the pass. Major Lee was out. After waiting half an hour for him I went over to General Mansfield's office. He refused to give us a pass. Refused even to give one to Nannie Belle and myself without Will. Said no one was allowed to cross the lines now. My heart died within me, and my eyes filled with tears. I began to despair. Just then Major Lee came in. He heard I had been waiting for him and had followed me over. He took me back to the Department and said we would go and ask the Secretary of War (Mr. Cameron). So we went up to Mr. Cameron's office, but he was home sick. Then we applied to General Scott. He gave one for Nannie Belle and myself but refused to allow Will to go. But when Major Lee learned that we were going in a hack across

[1]Major John F. Lee, in charge of the Bureau of Military Justice.
[2]Major-General J. K. F. Mansfield commanded the Department of Washington.

the country and through the "rebel camp" alone, he said it would never do for us to go without Mr. Maury.

Upon second application General Scott gave a pass to Will, first inquiring whether he was any relation to Captain Maury of the Observatory now in Richmond. The clerk who carried a note making the second application did not know, and said he was not. The old General little knew that I was his daughter.

Will was delighted when he saw the pass. Said that he could never have gotten it. I felt like all the strong minded women I knew.

Mr. Hasbrouck of Newburg, N.Y. came to see us that night. He came down hoping to get to Richmond to see Papa but was told there was danger of his being arrested so he gave it up. He could have come with perfect safety. Papa could get him back.

He speaks with the greatest regret and grief of Papa's resignation—talks as if he were dead. I told him that I was a hundred times prouder of my father now. That if he had considered his own personal welfare he would have remained with the North. The people of the North have always honored and appreciated him far more than those of the South. But he could not take sides against his own people, against his native state and against the RIGHT.

Mr. Hasbrouck wanted Will and myself to come up to Newburg and stay until the troubles were over. Saturday morning we left Washington. We gave up our house and stowed our furniture at cousin Charles's. Left a great many things undone but I reckon Mother will attend to them. There was a good deal of furniture in the house still to be moved. We missed the boat and came all the way to Alexandria in a hack. Will paid $25. for a carriage to take us to Manassas Junction. It could only take two small trunks, so I had to leave mine with the greater part of my clothes.

We were stopped by a sentinel every fifteen minutes of our ride for eight miles out of Alexandria. Nannie Belle was so delighted at the prospect of seeing her Grand Ma and Aunt Lucy that she would sing "Dixie" all the way. I was afraid it would make the soldiers suspect us. So in order to stop her I had to give her a sugar cracker whenever we came to a sentinel. She soon understood it and would call out "Mama here is another soldier. Give me a sugar tacker."

We were told that we would find a company of Federal cav-

alry close to the "rebel lines." So when it was nearly dark and
we were near Fairfax court house, we were stopped by two
dragoons. I was struck by their gentlemanly appearance. They
looked very different from the pickets we had passed. Will
handed them General Heintzleman's[1] pass that he had gotten
in Alexandria. They said that was signed by none of their
officers and would not do. Will then gave them General Scott's
pass. They laughed and said, they belonged to the Southern
troops. I exclaimed "Thank God, we are among our own people at last."

They told us we might go on to Fairfax courthouse but must
get a pass there. The night before (Friday) a company of
eighty horse had ridden into the village and attacked our
troops, fifty in number. They were repulsed with the loss of
three killed and three prisoners. They were expected again that
night. We lay down in our clothes, but were not disturbed.

Rose at four oclock and started at five for Manassas. We
stopped at the court-house and jail to get our pass. There
among a crowd of soldiers and horses I discovered our brother
Tom. He had arrived in the night with a company from Manassas. Were only stopped three or four times between Fairfax
and Manassas Junction. About three miles below Manassas a
South Carolina regiment is stationed. They are fortifying
themselves and throwing up breastworks. We reached Manassas too late for the eight oclock train and had to stay there till
Monday morning. There were no accommodations for us. The
tavern was filled with soldiers. I spent the day in the carriage
under the trees, with men, horses and tents all around us.

We had services during the day, the first time Nannie Belle
had ever been to "church." It was an imposing and affecting
sight to see so many soldiers worshiping God under the broad
canopy of Heaven. I was the only woman present. I saw a
great many acquaintances and friends there. We got a room at
night, but did not take off our clothes. The place was too public.

Our troops are fewer and more indifferently armed than I
expected to see. But with such indomitable spirits, and such
mothers and wives they can never be beaten. I saw some plain
country people there telling their sons and husbands good bye.
I did not hear the first word of repining or grief; only encour-

[1]Major-General Samuel P. Heintzelman.

agement to do their best and be of good service. One woman after taking leave of her husband said to two youths when telling them goodbye, "Don't mind my tears, boys, they don't mean a thing."

After they left, their mother shamed her and said: "How could you let them see you crying? It will unman them." These were plain people who talked about "Farfax" and said "farwell."

Will went to Richmond. I arrived here Monday evening in time for tea. Mama did not expect us, so there was no one at the cars to meet us.

Tuesday June 4th 1861

I went up to the sewing society with Aunt Mary and Molly.[1] The ladies are busy making tents for the soldiers and sheets and pillow cases for the hospitals.

Wednesday June 5th

Fanny (our cook) was not to be found this morning. She has gone off with all her possessions. It seems that she and Nanny[2] had some difficulty about ten days ago and Papa told her if she did not apologize to Nanny, he would send her to Farley Vale to Mr. Corbin.

Monday, June 10th 1861

My mother returned from Farley Vale on Saturday and Father came up from Richmond. He is rather blue—doesn't know how Jeff Davis and his "clique" will work. He has made it understood that now Virginia is given up to him and is one of the Confederate States, all the commissions and appointments given by her are null and void, and that if any retain their places it is a gift from him. Governor Wise is forming a legion for the protection of *Western* Virginia. It is likely to be very popular. Charley Blackford[3] is Captain in it.

Nanny and Mr. Corbin came up Sunday. The latter was dressed in a uniform Nanny had made for him. He had Papa's old navy buttons on his blue flannel shirt. Nanny says the U.S.

[1] Molly Maury, Betty's sister.
[2] Nanny Maury, another sister, wife of S. W. Corbin of Farley Vale plantation.
[3] Son of Mary Berkeley Minor Blackford.

stands for "United South." Mr. Corbin wears a sword taken from a French officer at Waterloo. Papa returned to Richmond this morning.

Fri. June 14, 1861

Went to church yesterday. Heard a sermon on patriotism. I fall far short of the mark of a true patriot. I am selfish and narrow minded. Nanny puts me to the blush continually. She is so patriotic and unselfish.

Sunday, June 16, 1861

Mr. Corbin came up this morning. He has been with his company to Mathias' Point. Says there is no battery there.

There is great jealousy between the Virginia and the Confederate forces. Papa thinks that the Confederate officers and politicians want to usurp too much power and are unjust towards many of the Virginia soldiers. I hope Tom will be able to keep his place.

Papa's post as one of the Governor's council is to be abolished tomorrow. We do not know what will become of him then.

Wed. June 19th

Papa returned to Richmond Monday morning. He has a scheme to blow up the enemy's vessels in the different rivers by submarine works of some kind.

I do not know whether he will be able to carry it out. It is a great secret now.

Will received a very cordial letter from Judge Badger a few days ago welcoming him to the South and inviting him to his house in Raleigh. Will would like very much to go and only hesitates because of the expense. But I suspect the temptation will prove too strong for him.

I have been busy for the last two days making a shirt for one of the soldiers.

Molly has a very devoted beau, who comes very often and stays very late.—But Johnny Scott will never do. He has a grandfather, two uncles and an aunt that are crazy!!!

Thur. June 20, 1861

The Convention in Richmond were surprised and delighted to see how much good the Governor's Council had done.

Thought the state could not do without it. But the Council thought they were unnecessary now that everything has been handed over to the Confederate States. So it has been abolished.

Papa is going up Saturday to see cousin Frank Minor. What a warm and true friend he is. He is very anxious that Papa shall be sent as Minister to England. Thinks it would be an appointment that would please the people and he would have more influence abroad than any other man. Cousin Frank need not take to himself the credit of having first thought of it. I have been wishing for it for more than a month. It is the only office in the gift of the Government that I covet for Papa. They surely would not send him into active service. He is too valuable and great a man for that.

Dick is chafing at being kept so long in Lexington. He wants to be in active service somewhere. Says he thirst for Yankee blood and cannot bear to be up there in Lexington behind those mountains when so many others are in the fields.

I have found an old satin cloak that I have been looking for to make a puffing round the bottom of my *three year old* brown silk to make it long enough. It is the only thick dress I have with me. All of my handsomest clothes were left in the trunk in Alexandria.

It is strange how one can become accustomed to almost any mode of life. Here we are now *almost* as happy as in our best days and we cannot look into the future of this world at all. We cannot form an idea as to where or in what condition we may be one month hence.

Fri. June 21—1861

Was interrupted yesterday to go down and see a soldier. It turned out to be my friend Nick Hill, one of *our* old law students. He came South to join the army more than a month ago and was sent back to Maryland on recruiting service. He came back yesterday morning and swam his horse across the Potomac. He brought a good many Marylanders with him and more will follow today. They went to Mr. Corbin's and he sent them up in a wagon. This is their place of rendezvous. Mr. Hill asked me to make some shirts for them. He is to bring the material today from Richmond.

Sat. June 22/61

Mr. Hill has not made his appearance yet with the shirts. No tidings of Fanny. I think she is too smart to be caught.

Wed. June 26th 1861

Have been hard at work this week on the clothes for Mr. Hill.

Six pairs of pantaloons, six jackets and eight shirts and have-locks—and all to be done in three days. I was in despair at first—but the ladies are so kind and ready to help. Every one that I asked took a part and the work now is comparatively easy. It will be done by tomorrow.

There are upwards of one hundred and fifty soldiers in the hospitals here. The sick suffer a great deal for want of proper medical attendance and good nursing. Many of the soldiers are laid on the floor when brought there and are not touched or their cases looked into for 24 hours.

Thurs. June 27/61

I never saw anything like the spirit here. The women give up the greater part of their time either to nursing the sick or sewing for the soldiers. It is the same case throughout the South.

Some of Papa's secret schemes are to be carried out now I am sure.

This is the time that Mr. Hill's clothes were to be done, and he has not brought me a single button or come to see anything about them. These suits are presents to the gentlemen that are with him.

Monday July 1st. 1861

Well! our secret expedition has returned.

Yesterday afternoon we heard a steam whistle and knew that no boat was expected here for a week. In a few minutes all Fredericksburg was at the wharf. It was the *St. Nicholas!* a prize! a Yankee Steamer that runs between Baltimore and Washington.

About two weeks ago Captain Hollins and Col. Thomas (a man that dresses like a Japanese)[1] went over to Maryland

---

[1]Richard Thomas was a wealthy Marylander. After he captured the *St. Nicholas* he was commissioned a colonel of Virginia Volunteers. He was himself captured and jailed in Baltimore.

and arranged with friends there to take the *St. Nicholas* by strategy. Col. Thomas went to Baltimore and with six or eight friends got on board the steamer as passengers. When they reached Point Lookout, Captain Hollins with a few friends came on board as passengers also, and when the boat was fairly out in the stream they walked up to the Captain and told him that he was their prisoner and that the boat was in the hands of Confederate officers. He made some show of resistance at first, but soon saw that it was of no use and surrendered. The boat was then run into Coan Creek on the Virginia shore opposite to Point Lookout, where Captain Lewis's party, including the four hundred Tennesseans were awaiting them. They had left the *Virginia* near the mouth of the Rappahannock and marched across country to Coan Creek the night before.

The plan was for the whole party to embark and under the Federal flag go up the Potomac, take the *Pawnee* and *Freeborn* at Aquia Creek. (They would never have suspected that the *St. Nicholas* was in the hands of Confederate officers until they were boarded) and then come around the mouth of the Rappahannock, take the blockading force there and come up with flying colors. But the Secretary of War would not allow the Tennesseans to embark. Said they might do any fighting that was necessary on shore, but not on board ship.

As it was, all embarked except Captain Lewis and a few others and went out into the Bay to see what they could find. The first vessel they met was a brig laden with coffee. It made no resistance. Some of the men were dreadfully frightened and begged on their knees for their lives. The Captain and crew were ordered aboard the steamer and two officers and five men were detailed to man the brig.

They then met a schooner filled with ice and another with coal both of which were taken in the same way. Mr. Thorburn and Dick were detailed for the coal schooner. Two of the Captains had their wives with them. One of them begged most piteously that her husband's life might be spared. There were thirty-nine prisoners in all. I saw them as they came by. They thought they were to be hung.

The Mayor went down last night to relieve their minds and say that no harm would be done them.

The passengers that were on the *St. Nicholas* were put off at Coan Creek. Clarence H. of Washington—Alice's old beau—

was among the number. He was returning from a fishing excursion. Expressed much surprise at seeing Dick. The two Captains' wives were at work yesterday cutting up their flags and making them into Confederate flags. The bunting of the South has given out. Col. Thomas went on board the *St. Nicholas*, dressed as a woman. The party on board did not know each other *very well*. Each one suspected the other and all suspected the "woman."

It was Captain Lewis's scheme. Papa only helped to carry it out. . . .[1]

There was no blockading vessel at the mouth of the Rappahannock when the prizes came in. Suppose she had gone for provisions.

Tuesday July 2nd 1861

The clothes for Mr. Hill's party are finished and packed in a clothes basket ready to be sent up to Citizen's Hall. They look very neat and substantial and comfortable.

Wed. July 3rd 1861

Will went to Richmond this Morning. Papa wrote word last night that he was suggesting him for Prize Commissioner. Some legal proceedings have to be gone through with whenever a prize is brought in, I believe. Do not know whether Will would like to have the place.

There are not more then thirty soldiers in the Hospital. The rest have been taken to private houses.

Fourth of July—1861

Not a gun was heard this morning. I hope our old National holidays will not be dropped by the Southern Confederacy.

Will returned from Richmond yesterday. Whether he got the appointment as Prize agent, or whether he would accept it if it was offered to him, or what he did in Richmond, I have not the most remote idea. I asked him to tell me where he went and what he did? He answered: "Oh! I went everywhere" and then told me he had tomatoes for dinner and that Jordan had a puppie for Nannie Belle. The rest he thought above my comprehension and reserved for some more fortunate male

[1] Prof. J. Russell Soley, U. S. N., gives an account of this exploit of June 29 in *Battles and Leaders*, II, 143.

friend. Everybody gives me credit for more sense than my husband does.

Papa has gone to Norfolk. Do not know what for. . . .

Wed. July 10th 1861

Papa came yesterday evening. His secret mission failed, but I am so thankful that he has gotten back safe that I care very little about the failure. He went down to Sewells Point to blow up some of the ships that are at the mouth of the James river. Five noble vessels he says are there. He aimed for the two flag ships—the *Minnesota* and the *Roanoke*—Commodores Stringham[1] and Pendergrast.[2]

Friday night and Saturday night he sent an officer in a boat to reconnoiter. But there was a little steamer flying round and round the vessels keeping watch. Sunday as he was spying them through a glass and noting their relative positions he saw the church flag up on two of them. It is a white flag with a cross on it. The stars and stripes are lowered a little and that put above it. When he thought that those men were worshiping God in sincerity and in truth and no doubt think their cause as righteous as we we feel ours to be, his heart softened towards them, for he remembered how soon he would be the means of sending many of them to eternity.

That night the party consisting of five skiffs, set off about ten o'clock. Papa was in the first boat with the Pilot and four oarsmen. Each of the other boats manned by an officer and four men, carried a magazine with thirty fathoms of rope attached to it.

The magazines were thick oak casks filled with powder in each of which there is a fuse. Two of these barrels, joined by the rope, were stretched across at the ebb tide and when directly ahead of the ship, let go. The rope then catching across the cable, the magazines would drift down under the ship—when the strain upon the rope would pull a trigger that would ignite the fuse. . . .

After putting the magazines under one ship, the boats that carried them were ordered back, and Papa went with the other two to plant the magazines under the other vessel.

[1]Silas H. Stringham, afterward rear-admiral.
[2]Lieutenant-Commander Austin Pendergrast.

They then rowed to some distance, and waited for the explosion, but it never came, thank God, for if it had Pa would have been hung long before now. At the first explosion the calcium light at Fortress Monroe would have been lit and the little steamer—whose steam was up—they could hear her—would have caught them within a few minutes. It took them an hour to get back.

If Papa's going again would ensure the destruction of every ship in the Yankee Navy, I would not have him go. If he had been lost then it would have been an everlasting stain upon the Southern Government that allowed so celebrated, valuable and clever a man as my father to risk his life in such an expedition. Europe would cry shame upon them.

Are not his brains worth more than two ships? He might have gone to the boats to see that all was right, but not in them to plant the magazines.

The Yankees would never have let him go. They appreciate his services better than that. Papa says, he was very much struck with the culpable negligence of the enemy. That he could have gone up and put his hand on those vessels with impunity.

Thur. July 11th

. . . Captain Thomas, the one who assisted in taking the *St. Nicholas*, has been captured in Washington.

Fri. July 12

William Blackford passed through here a few days ago with his cavalry company from Southwestern Virginia. He dined with us and gave us a very amusing account of their attempts at cooking. Said they bought half a bushel of rice one day. They nearly filled a pot with it and added a little water to boil. It soon commenced to swell, and they filled first one vessel and then another until every vessel that they had in camp was full, even their tin cups.

Monday 15—July 1861

Mamma has gone to Farley Vale with the children. I have undertaken the houskeeping. We have no cook since the old woman we had in Fanny's place, left us. Rebecca has been doing her best in that capacity, and we do the chamber work.

Thur. 16. July, 1861

The seceded counties in Western Virginia sent several members to the Congress at Washington. They elected a Governor some time ago—Governor Pierpont. There are between twenty and thirty disaffected counties, I believe.

Sat. July, 20—

Hurrah! we have beat the Yankees. The enemy was repulsed three times with considerable loss, 5 or 6 hundred, at Bull Run.[1] Our loss was not more than sixty.

Cousin Nanny and the children arrived last night. Cousin Dabney will be up tonight with Papa. They left Santa Fe the twenty sixth of May and did not stop one day on the way. They were forty days in crossing the plains in an *uncovered* wagon and camped out every night. They look like Indians they are so burned. Cousin Nanny tells us they had no wood on the plains, but used "buffalo-chips."

The Confederate Congress met today.

Sunday July 21

Distant firing has been heard all day.

Mon. July 22, 1861

There was an officer here last night who was in the fight at Bull Run. He says that the South Carolinians after firing threw down their muskets and charged with their bowie knives, seizing the Yankees by the collar and cutting them down.

Papa saw a gentleman yesterday, just from Washington. He said that many members of Congress and others went in carriages to see the fight last Thursday.

A company of five hundred cavalry are to pass through here, today, on their way to Manassas—The Hampton Brigade of South Carolina.

12 M

More news! More good news. Will has just come to tell me. The battle yesterday was more extensive than we thought. It extended along our whole line. The enemy is routed and we are in hot pursuit. Thank God, thank God. . . .

[1]There had been a small clash along the line of the Run on the eighteenth, which the Confederates called the Bull Run fight as distinguished from the big Battle of Manassas on the twenty-first.

Thursday, July 25

Uncle Charley and many gentlemen from here have been up to Manassas to see the battle field. He returned this evening, says that many of the soldiers (Yankees) are still lying upon the field: our men are burying them.

Sunday, July 28, 1861

The more we learn of the victory last Sunday the greater it seems to be. We took fifty odd cannon and four hundred wagons each one filled with stores and provisions of various kind and several stands of arms—new in their cases which were brought to arm the loyal citizens of Richmond. Their army was most completely equipped in every respect. They had blacksmiths shops and medicine wagons along. They never seemed to contemplate a defeat, and the arrogance and heartlessness of their preparations for victory are almost beyond conception. Many gentlemen and *ladies* came from Washington to witness the battle. Elegant dinners had been prepared at Fairfax C.H. and Centreville by French cooks, where they meant to regale themselves after their victory. Our soldiers found the tables set and many baskets of champagne and wine.

Abraham Lincoln professes to conduct this war on the most humane and merciful principles yet he has declared all medicines and surgical instruments contraband of war, a thing never before heard of among civilized people. And now having deprived us, as far as in his power, of all means of attending to our own sick and wounded, he leaves his poor soldiers to our care. They have never sent back for any of their wounded, or to bury their dead. Our soldiers buried them in trenches, fifty and sixty at a time.

Uncle Charley says that not one of the bodies he saw had shoes on. Our men took them. They were right. We have no leather. . . .

## 3. MARY BOYKIN CHESNUT—"A BATTLE HAS BEEN FOUGHT AT MANASSAS"

*The best-known of Confederate women diarists was born Mary Boykin Miller, March 31, 1823. Her father, Stephen Decatur Miller, was in turn congressman, Governor of South*

*Carolina, senator. At seventeen she married James Chesnut,
Jr., member of a prominent family and graduate of Princeton,
whose home was at Mulberry plantation near Camden, S.C.
He was active in politics and she in society. He was the first
Southerner to resign from the U.S. Senate and in July 1861
was a provisional member of the Confederate Senate. He became aide to General Beauregard at Fort Sumter, and then
served on the staff of President Davis, who greatly esteemed
his advice, took the Chesnuts into his intimate circle and made
him a sort of liaison officer between the Confederacy and
South Carolina. While he traveled back and forth, his wife,
when she did not accompany him, stayed at the Spotswood
Hotel, a favorite place for official families in Richmond. In
April 1864 he was appointed brigadier-general.*

*After the war the Chesnuts lived in a new house, Sarsfield.
Mary died there November 22, 1886, and was buried beside
her husband in the family cemetery at Knight's Hill. They had
no children.*

*On December 6, 1861, Mrs. Chesnut wrote on the first page
of a new diary—the one we have—"I have always kept a journal after a fashion of my own. . . . From today forward, I will
tell the story in my own way." It is a charming, vivacious way.
"The printed text," says Dr. Douglas S. Freeman, "is a remarkable human document. Of the complete devotion of Mrs.
Chesnut to the Southern cause, there could be no question, but
occasionally the reader hears champagne corks pop while boys
are dying in the mud. Then again there is all the poignancy of
woman's understanding of the sorrows of her sisters." To illus-
trate, he quotes the entries on the death of the gallant, impetu-
ous Francis S. Bartow. He adds: "Her qualities are oddly gal-
lic: One has to pinch oneself to realize that she is writing of
hungry Richmond and of the Anglo-Saxon South."[1]*

*By war's end the diary consisted of forty-eight slim volumes,
nearly 400,000 words with entries dated at Charleston, Montgomery, White Sulphur Springs, Columbia, Richmond, Camden. Mrs. Chesnut bequeathed it to her friend Isabella D.
Martin.*

*When writing his popular novel* House Divided, *Ben Ames
Williams based the character of Cinda Dewain largely on Mrs.*

---

[1]*The South to Posterity,* pp. 123-128. New York: Charles Scribner's Sons, 1951.

*Chesnut. Afterward he edited, under the title* A Diary from
Dixie, *the most complete edition of her journals in print.*

Richmond, Virginia

July 22d. [1861]—Mrs. Davis came in so softly that I did
not know she was here until she leaned over me and said: "A
great battle has been fought. Joe Johnston led the right wing,
and Beauregard the left wing of the army. Your husband is all
right. Wade Hampton is wounded. Colonel Johnston of the
Legion killed; so are Colonel Bee and Colonel Bartow. Kirby
Smith[1] is wounded or killed."

I had no breath to speak; she went on in that desperate,
calm way, to which people betake themselves under the greatest excitement: "Bartow, rallying his men, leading them into
the hottest of the fight, died gallantly at the head of his regiment. The President telegraphs me only that "it is a great victory." General Cooper[2] has all the other telegrams."

Still I said nothing; I was stunned; then I was so grateful.
Those nearest and dearest to me were safe still. She then began, in the same concentrated voice, to read from a paper she
held in her hand: "Dead and dying cover the field. Sherman's
battery taken. Lynchburg regiment cut to pieces. Three
hundred of the Legion[3] wounded."

That got me up. Times were too wild with excitement to
stay in bed. We went into Mrs. Preston's[4] room, and she made
me lie down on her bed. Men, women, and children streamed
in. Every living soul had a story to tell. "Complete victory,"
you heard everywhere. We had been such anxious wretches.
The revulsion of feeling was almost too much to bear. . . .

A woman from Mrs. Bartow's county was in a fury because
they had stopped her as she rushed to be the first to tell Mrs.
Bartow her husband was killed, it having been decided that

[1]For Edmund Kirby Smith, see page 177 *infra.*
[2]The senior Confederate officer, adjutant and inspector-general.
[3] General Wade Hampton's Legion had arrived from South Carolina in time for the infantry portion to participate in the most
severe fighting of the battle, in which he was wounded. He was for-
ty-three years old, six feet in height, broad-shouldered, deep-chest-
ed, a magnificent figure of a man.
[4]Wife of General John S. Preston and mother of Sally Buchanan ("Buck") Preston, the famous beauty whose ill-fated love affair
with General John B. Hood is mentioned on so many of Mrs.
Chesnut's pages.

Mrs. Davis should tell her. Poor thing! She was found lying on her bed when Mrs. Davis knocked. "Come in," she said. When she saw it was Mrs. Davis, she sat up, ready to spring to her feet, but then there was something in Mrs. Davis's pale face that took the life out of her. She stared at Mrs. Davis, then sank back, and covered her face as she asked: "Is it bad news for me?" Mrs. Davis did not speak. "Is he killed?" Afterwards Mrs. Bartow said to me: "As soon as I saw Mrs. Davis's face I could not say one word. I knew it all in an instant. I knew it before I wrapped the shawl about my head."

Maria, Mrs. Preston's maid, furiously patriotic, came into my room. "These colored people say it is printed in the papers here that the Virginia people done it all. Now Mars Wade Hampton had so many of his men killed and he wounded, it stands to reason that South Carolina was no ways backward. If there was ever anything plain, that's plain."

Tuesday.—Witnessed for the first time a military funeral. As that march came wailing up, they say Mrs. Bartow fainted. The empty saddle and the led war-horse—we saw and heard it all, and now it seems we are never out of the sound of the Dead March in Saul. It comes and it comes, until I feel inclined to close my ears and scream.

Yesterday, Mrs. Singleton[1] and ourselves sat on a bedside and mingled our tears for those noble spirits—John Darby,[2] Theodore Barker, and James Lowndes.[3] To-day we find we wasted our grief; they are not so much as wounded. I dare say all the rest is true about them—in the face of the enemy, with flags in their hands, leading their men. "But Dr. Darby is a surgeon." He is as likely to forget that as I am. He is grandson of Colonel Thomson of the Revolution, called, by the way of pet name, by his soldiers, "Old Danger." Thank Heaven they are all quite alive. And we will not cry next time until officially notified.

July 24th.—Here Mr. Chesnut opened my door and walked in. Out of the fulness of the heart the mouth speaketh. I had

[1] Mrs. Mat Singleton, mother of Mrs. Alexander Cheves Haskell.
[2] Surgeon of the Hampton Legion; he lived to go to Europe and get General Hood's wooden leg; married Mary Preston.
[3] "Toady" Barker and Captain James Lowndes, "the best of good company," old friends from South Carolina.

to ask no questions. He gave me an account of the battle as he saw it (walking up and down my room, occasionally seating himself on a window sill, but too restless to remain still many moments); and told what regiments he was sent to bring up. He took the orders to Colonel Jackson, whose regiment stood so stock still under fire that they were called "a stone wall." Also, they call Beauregard, Eugene, and Johnston, Marlboro. Mr. Chesnut rode with Lay's[1] cavalry after the retreating enemy in the pursuit, they following them until midnight. Then there came such a fall of rain—rain such as is only known in semitropical lands.

In the drawing-room, Colonel Chesnut was the "belle of the ball"; they crowded him so for news. He was the first arrival that they could get at from the field of battle. But the women had to give way to dignitaries of the land, who were as filled with curiosity as themselves—Mr. Barnwall,[2] Mr. Hunter,[3] Mr. Cobb, Captain Ingraham,[4] etc.

Wilmot DeSaussure[5] says Wilson[6] of Massachusetts, a Senator of the United States, came to Manassas, *en route* to Richmond, with his dancing shoes ready for a festive scene which was to celebrate a triumph. The New York Tribune said: "In a few days we shall have Richmond, Memphis, and New Orleans. They must be taken and at once." For "a few days" maybe now they will modestly substitute "in a few years."

They brought me a Yankee soldier's portfolio from the battlefield. The letters had been franked by Senator Harlan.[7] One might shed tears over some of the letters. Women, wives and mothers, are the same everywhere. What a comfort the spelling was! We had been willing to admit that their universal free-school education had put them, rank and file, ahead of us

[1] Captain John F. Lay.

[2] Robert W. Barnwell, of South Carolina, first Chairman of the Provisional Congress. Mr. Davis offered him the office of Secretary of State, but he declined it.

[3] R. M. T. Hunter, of Virginia, was named Secretary of State on this very day.

[4] Captain Duncan Nathaniel Ingraham.

[5] A friend from Charleston; Colonel Chesnut later gave him a position on the South Carolina Council.

[6] Henry Wilson, who was to be Vice-President of the United States in Grant's second administration (1872-1876).

[7] James Harlan, of Iowa.

*literarily,* but these letters do not attest that fact. The spelling is comically bad.

July 27th.—Mrs. Davis's drawing-room last night was brilliant, and she was in great force. Outside a mob called for the President. He did speak—an old war-horse, who scents the battle-fields from afar. His enthusiasm was contagious. They called for Colonel Chesnut, and he gave them a capital speech, too. As public speakers say sometimes, "It was the proudest moment of my life." I did not hear a great deal of it, for always, when anything happens of any moment, my heart beats up in my ears, but the distinguished Carolinians who crowded round told me how good a speech he made. I was dazed. There goes the Dead March for some poor soul.

Today, the President told us at dinner that Mr. Chesnut's eulogy of Bartow in the Congress was highly praised. Men liked it. Two eminently satisfactory speeches in twenty-four hours is doing pretty well. And now I could be happy, but this Cabinet of ours are in such bitter quarrels among themselves —everybody abusing everybody.

Last night, while those splendid descriptions of the battle were being given to the crowd below from our windows, I said: "Then, why do we not go to Washington?" "You mean why did they not; the opportunity is lost." Mr. Barnwell said to me: "Silence, we want to listen to the speaker," and Mr. Hunter smiled compassionately, "Don't ask awkward questions."

Kirby Smith came down on the turnpike in the very nick of time. Still, the heroes who fought all day and held the Yankees in check deserve credit beyond words, or it would all have been over before the Joe Johnston contingent came. It is another case of the eleventh-hour scrape; the eleventh-hour men claim all the credit, and they who bore the heat and brunt and burden of the day do not like that.

Everybody said at first, "Pshaw! There will be no war." Those who foresaw evil were called ravens, ill-foreboders. Now the same sanguine people all cry, "The war is over"—the very same who were packing to leave Richmond a few days ago. Many were ready to move on at a moment's warning, when the good news came. There are such owls everywhere.

But, to revert to the other kind, the sage and circumspect, those who say very little, but that little shows they think the war barely begun. Mr. Rives[1] and Mr. Seddon[2] have just called. Arnoldus Van der Horst[3] came to see me at the same time. He said there was no great show of victory on our side until two o'clock, but when we began to win, we did it in double-quick time.

Arnold Harris told Mr. Wigfall the news from Washington last Sunday. For hours the telegrams reported at rapid intervals, "Great victory," "Defeating them at all points." The couriers began to come in on horseback, and at last, after two or three o'clock, there was a sudden cessation of all news. About nine, messengers with bulletins came on foot or on horseback—wounded, weary, draggled, footsore, panic-stricken—spreading in their paths on every hand terror and dismay. That was our opportunity. Wigfall can see nothing that could have stopped us, and when they explain why we did not go to Washington I understand it all less than ever. Yet here we will dilly-dally, and Congress orate, and generals parade, until they in the North get up an army three times as large as McDowell's, which we have just defeated.

Trescot[4] says this victory will be our ruin. It lulls us into a fool's paradise of conceit at our superior valor, and the shameful farce of their flight will wake every inch of their manhood. It was the very fillip they needed. There are a quieter sort here who know their Yankees well. They say if the thing begins to pay—government contracts, and all that—we will never hear the end of it, at least, until they get their pay in some way out of us. They will not lose money on us. Of that we may be sure. . . .

There seems to be a battle raging at Bethel, but no mortal here can be got to think of anything but Manassas. Mrs. McLean[5] says she does not see that it was such a great victory, and if it be so great, how can one defeat hurt a nation like the North.

[1] William Cabell Rives, of Virginia, member of the Confederate Congress, formerly U. S. Minister to France and U. S. Senator.
[2] James A. Seddon, Member of Congress from Virginia; to become Secretary of War November 20, 1862.
[3] Descended from the Governor of South Carolina in 1792, who bore the same name.
[4] William Henry Trescot, from Columbia, S. C.
[5] *Née* Sumner, from the North, one of the clever women in Mrs. Davis' circle.

John Waties[1] fought the whole battle over for me. Now I
understand it. Before this nobody would take the time to tell
the thing consecutively, rationally, and in order. Mr. Venable[2]
said he did not see a braver thing done than the cool performance of a Columbia negro. He carried his master a bucket of
ham and rice, which he had cooked for him, and he cried:
"You must be so tired and hungry, marster; make haste and
eat." This was in the thickest of the fight, under the heaviest of
the enemy's guns.

The Federal Congressmen had been making a picnic of it;
their luggage was all ticketed to Richmond. Cameron[3] has issued a proclamation. They are making ready to come after us
on a magnificent scale. They acknowledge us at last foemen
worthy of their steel. The Lord help us, since England and
France won't, or don't. If we could only get a friend outside
and open a port.

One of these men told me he had seen a Yankee prisoner
who asked him "what sort of a diggins Richmond was for
trade." He was tired of the old concern, and would like to take
the oath and settle here. They brought us handcuffs found in
the debacle of the Yankee army. For whom were they? Jeff
Davis, no doubt, and the ring-leaders. "Tell that to the marines." We have outgrown the handcuff business on this side of
the water.

Dr. Gibbs[4] says he was at a country house near Manassas,
when a Federal soldier, who had lost his way, came in exhausted. He asked for brandy, which the lady of the house
gave him. Upon second thought, he declined it. She brought it
to him so promptly he thought it might be poisoned; his mind
was; she was enraged, and said: "Sir, I am a Virginia woman.
Do you think I could be so base as that? Here, Bill, Tom, dis-
arm this man. He is our prisoner." The negroes came running,
and the man surrendered without more ado.

Another Federal was drinking at the well. A negro girl said:
"You go in and see Missis." The man went in and she followed, crying triumphantly: "Look here, Missis, I got a pris-

---

[1] The Waties were a well-known South Carolina family; William
Waties signed the South Carolina Ordinance of Secession.

[2] Charles S. Venable, later on General Less's staff.

[3] Simon Cameron, of Pennsylvania, U. S. Secretary of War.

[4] Dr. Hampton Gibbes, of Columbia, S. C., active in the medical
service.

oner, too!" This lady sent in her two prisoners, and Beauregard complimented her on her pluck and patriotism, and her presence of mind. These negroes were rewarded by their owners. . . .

## 4. ROSE O'NEAL GREENHOW—"MY HOME WAS CONVERTED INTO A PRISON"

*Mrs. Greenhow, a native of Maryland, was the widow of Robert Greenhow, prominent Washingtonian and friend of President Buchanan, John C. Calhoun, Martin Van Buren and other political leaders of ante-bellum days. Shortly after the war began, she became a leading figure in the Confederate espionage system. The record book of "Old Capitol Prison" in Washington listed her as "a dangerous, skillful spy."*

*From Washington she sent two messages in code to General Beauregard, and on this information he based his defense at First Manassas. After the battle the Federal War Department instructed Allan Pinkerton, head of the Federal Secret Service, to keep Mrs. Greenhow under surveillance. Pinkerton reported that she had "alphabets, numbers, ciphers, and various other ways of holding communication with the Confederate officials." Mrs. Greenhow's home, when she was imprisoned, was at 398 16th Street. In 1861 she was forty-four years old and the mother of four daughters.*

On the morning of the 16th of July, 1861, the Government papers at Washington announced that the "grand army" was in motion and I learned from a reliable source (having received a copy of the order to McDowell) that the order for a forward movement had gone forth.

There was great commotion amongst the military men. Officers and orderlies on horse were seen flying from place to place; the tramp of armed men was heard on every side—martial music filled the air. "On to Richmond" was the war cry. So with drums beating and flying colours, and amidst the shower of posies thrown by the Yankee maidens, the grand army moved on into Virginia.

At twelve o'clock on the morning of the 16th of July, I dispatched a messenger to Manassas, who arrived there at eight o'clock that night.[1] The answer received by me at mid-day on the 17th will tell the purport of my communication—

"Yours was received at eight oclock at night. Let them come: we are ready for them. We rely upon you for precise information. Be particular as to description and destination of forces, quantity of artillery etc."

Signed, "THOMAS JORDAN, ADJT GEN."

On the 17th of July, I dispatched another message to Manassas, for I had learned of the intention of the enemy to cut the Winchester railroad, so as to intercept Johnston and prevent his reinforcing Beauregard who had comparatively but a small force under his command at Manassas.[2]

On the night of the 18th news of a great victory by the Federal troops at Bull Run reached Washington. Throughout the length and breadth of the city it was cried. The accounts were received with frantic rejoicings, and bets were freely taken in support of Mr. Seward's wise saws—that the rebellion would be crushed out in thirty days. My heart told me that the triumph was premature yet, O my God! how miserable I was for the fate of my beloved country which hung trembling in the balance.

[1]This messenger was Betty Duvall, a Maryland girl. Disguised as a farm woman, she rode across the Chain Bridge out of Washington in a farm cart. On the Virginia side of the Potomac, she secured riding clothes and a horse from friends, and galloped for Fairfax County Courthouse, where she ran into a Confederate picket commanded by General Milledge R. Bonham. From what he said was the longest, most beautiful roll of hair he had ever seen "she took a small packet, not larger than a silver dollar, sewed up in silk." He promised to convey it to General Beauregard.

[2]"About July 10th 1861, Miss Duvall of Washington brought to Fairfax Court House, Headquarters for General Bonham, the first message from Mrs. Rose Greenhow telling of the intended positive advance of the Union Army across the Potomac. On the night of July 16, 1861, I received by special messenger (a Mr. Donellan) the second dispatch (in cipher also) of Mrs. Greenhow telling of the Union Army, 55,000 strong, would positively commence that day to advance from Arlington and Alexandria on Manassas via Fairfax C. H.

"G. T. BEAUREGARD"
*(Official Records of the Union and Confederate Armies.)*

On Sunday (21st) the great battle of Manassas was fought ——which ended in the total defeat of the entire "Grand Army." In the world's history such a sight was never witnessed: statesmen, Senators, Congressmen, generals and officers of every grade, soldiers, teamsters—all rushing in frantic fright, as if pursued by countless demons. For miles the country was thick with ambulances, accoutrements of war etc. The actual scene beggars description so I must relinquish the effort to portray it. The news of the disastrous rout of the Yankee army was cried through the streets of New York on the 22nd. The whole city seemed paralysed by fear.

For days the wildest disorder reigned in the Capitol. The streets of Washington were filled with stragglers, each telling the doleful tale.

It would be idle to recount the gasconade of those who fled from imaginary foes, or to describe the forlorn condition of the returning "heroes" who had gone forth to battle flushed with anticipated triumph and crowned in advance with the laurel of victory. Alas! their plight was pitiable enough. Some were described as being minus hat or shoes. Amongst this latter class was Colonel Burnside,[1] who on the morning that he sallied forth for Virginia is said to have required two orderlies to carry the flowers showered upon him by the women of Northern proclivities. The Northern troops had been taught to believe that a bloodless victory awaited them, and so possessed were they with the idea of their philanthropic mission as liberators of an oppressed people that many officers took far more pains to prepare white gloves and embroidered vests for "the balls" to be given in their honor in Richmond than in securing cartridges for their muskets.

When consulted on the subject I said "No doubt they would receive a great many balls, but I did not think that a very recherché toilet would be expected."

The fanatical feeling was now at its height. Maddened by defeat, they sought a safe means of venting their pent up wrath. The streets were filled with armed and unarmed ruffians; women were afraid to go singly in the streets for fear of

[1] In April 1861 Ambrose E. Burnside had organized the 1st Rhode Island Regiment at the request of the governor, and become its colonel; it was among the first regiments to reach Washington.

insult; curses and blasphemy rent the air and no one would have been surprised at any hour at a general massacre of peaceful inhabitants. This apprehension was shared even by the better class of United States army officers.

On Friday Aug. 23, 1861, as I was entering my own door on returning from a promenade, I was arrested by two men, one in citizens clothes and the other in the dress of an officer of the United States Army. This latter was called Major Allen, and was the chief of the detective police of the city. They followed close upon my footsteps. As I ascended my steps the two men ascended also before I could open the door and asked "Is this Mrs. Greenhow?" I answered "Yes". "Who are you and what do you want?" "I come to arrest you"—"By what authority?" The man Allen, or Pinkerton (for he had several aliases) said: "By sufficient authority." I said: "Let me see your warrant." He mumbled something about verbal authority from the War and State Department and then they followed me into the house. By this time the house had become filled with men, and men also surrounded it outside like bees from a hive. An indiscriminate search now commenced throughout my house. Men rushed with frantic haste into my chamber. My beds, my wardrobes were all up-turned. My library was taken possession of and every scrap of paper was seized.

As the evening advanced I was ordered upstairs accompanied by my friend, Miss Mackall, a heavy guard of detectives being stationed in the room with us. I was never alone for a moment. Wherever I went a detective followed me. If I wished to lie down he was seated a few paces from my bed. If I desired to change my dress or anything else, it was obliged to be done with open doors, and a man peering in at me. But, alas! I had no alternative but to submit, for when I remonstrated with detective Captain Dennis, I was met by the answer that it was the order of the Provost Marshal.

The work of examining my papers had commenced. I had no reason to fear of the consequences from the papers which had as yet fallen into their hands. I had a right to my own political opinions. I am a Southern woman, born with Revolutionary blood in my veins, Freedom of speech and of thought were my birthright, guaranteed, signed and sealed by the blood of our fathers.

The search went on. I desired to go to my chamber, and

was told that a woman was sent for to accompany me. It did not, even then, flash upon my mind that my person was to be searched. I was, however, all the more anxious to be free from the sight of my captors for a few moments; so feigning the pretext of change of dress etc. as the day was intensely hot, after great difficulty and thanks to the slow movements of these agents of evil, I was allowed to go to my chamber and I then resolved to destroy some important papers which I had in my pocket, even at the expense of my life. (The papers were my cipher, with which I corresponded with my friends at Manassas.) Happily I succeeded without such a painful sacrifice.

The detective Dennis rapped at my door, calling Madam! Madam! and then opened it, but seeing me apparently legitimately employed he withdrew.

Shortly after the female detective arrived. Like all detectives, she had only a Christian name, Ellen. Well, I was ushered into my chamber, a detective standing guard outside to receive the important papers believed to be secreted on my person.

I was allowed the poor privilege of unfastening my own garments, which, one by one, were received by this pseudo-woman, and carefully examined until I stood in my linen. After this I was permitted to resume. I now began fully to realize the dark and gloomy perils which environed me.

The chief of detectives having gone out, several of the subordinates left in charge now possessed themselves of rum and brandy which aided in developing their brutal instincts: and they even boasted in my hearing of the "nice times" they expected to have with the female prisoners.

As every evil is said to be checkmated by some corresponding good, I was enabled by this means to destroy every paper of consequence. I had placed them where they could be found by me at any hour of the day or night, and was not slow to avail myself of the state of inebriation in which the guards were plunged. Stealing noiselessly to the library in the dark, I mounted up to the topmost shelf, took, from the leaves of a dusty folio, papers of immense value to me at the moment, concealing them in the folds of my dress, and returned to my position on the bed without my gaolers having missed me. The papers were more numerous than I imagined and the difficulty was how to dispose of them. I remembered, however, that in the search of my person in the morning my boots and stockings had not been removed; so Miss Mackall, who was held in durance but had been assured she would be released that night, concealed the papers in her stockings and boots. Between the hours of three and four on the 24th Miss Mackall was permitted to depart under escort of a detective guard who were then stationed around her house for the following day.

A very large sum had been offered for my cipher. This stimulated the zeal of the employees of the Government to a very remarkable degree. The tables were filled with fragments of old letters and scraps in cipher, in several languages, from early morning till late at night. For seven days they puzzled over them. I had no fear.—One by one they allowed the clue to escape them. Only once was I frightened. Miss Mackall, who like myself was always on the alert, abstracted from a heap of papers a sheet of blotting paper upon which was the whole of my dispatch to Manassas on July 16.

On Friday the 30th of August I was informed that my house was to be converted into a prison.

One morning as I opened my chamber door to pass to the library I saw the detective Allen taking an old lady up the stairs. It was the venerable mother of the martyr Jackson[1] killed in Alexandria, and I honored her gray hairs as being his mother. She was placed in an adjoining room to mine and kept until about twelve oclock at night when she was released. . . .

I received a visit from my sister, Mrs. James M. Cutts, and my niece, Mrs. Stephen A. Douglas, accompanied by Colonel Ingolls, U.S.A.,[2] the permit to see me making the presence of an officer obligatory and limiting the visit to fifteen minutes. . . .


## 5. VARINA HOWELL DAVIS—OUR NEW HOME

*When Mrs. Davis, with the children and her young sister Margaret Howell, came to Richmond the city gave her lavish welcome. The elegant, spacious house which it purchased for*

---

[1] See page 36 *supra*.

[2] General Rufus Ingalls, chief quartermaster of the Army of the Potomac.

*the President's family had been built, as Judith McGuire mentioned, By Dr. John Brockenbrough, onetime president of the Bank of Virginia. To go with it were a handsome carriage and four white horses.*

*The newspapers were eloquent. "Mrs. Davis," said the Dispatch, is "a tall, commanding figure, with dark hair, eyes and complexion, and strongly marked characteristics, which lie chiefly in the mouth. With firmly-set yet flexible lips there is indicated much energy of purpose and will, but beautifully softened by the usually sad expression of her dark, earnest eyes. Her manners are kind, graceful, easy, and affable, and her receptions are characterized by the dignity and suavity which should very properly distinguish the drawing-room entertainments of the Chief Magistrate of a republic."*

*An Englishman, the Reverend William Malet, who visited the Executive Mansion, summed up the general verdict. "Mrs. Davis," he wrote, "is the right lady in the right place."*

In July [1861] we moved to the "old Brockenbrough house," and began to feel somewhat more at home when walking through the old-fashioned terraced garden or the large airy rooms in the seclusion of family life.

The mansion stands on the brow of a steep and very high hill, that is sharply defined against the plain at its foot through which runs the Danville railway that leads to the heart of Virginia.

The house is very large, but the rooms are comparatively few, as some of them are over forty feet square. The ceilings are high, the windows wide, and the well-staircases turn in easy curves toward the airy rooms above. The Carrara marble mantels were the delight of our children. One was a special favorite with them, on which the whole pilaster was covered by two lovely figures of Hebe and Diana, one on either side in bold relief, which, with commendatory taste, were not caryatides. The little boys, Jefferson and Joe, climbed up to the lips of these "pretty ladies" and showered kisses on them. The entablature was Apollo in his chariot, in basso relievo. Another was a charming conception of Cupid and Psyche, with Guido's Aurora for the entablature. . . .

Every old Virginia gentleman of good social position who came to see us, looked pensively out on the grounds and said, with a tone of tender regret, something like this: "This house

was perfect when lovely Mary Brockenbrough used to walk
there, singing among the flowers;" and then came a description
of her light step, her dignified mien, sweet voice, and the other
graces which take hold of our hearts with a gentle touch, and
hold them with a grip of steel. At first it seemed odd, and we
regretted our visitor's disappointment, but after a while Mary
came to us, too, and remained the tutelar goddess of the garden. Her name became a household word. "Whether Mary
would approve," was a question my husband playfully asked,
when he liked the arrangement of the drawing rooms.

Mrs. James Grant lived in another fine old house next door
to us, and with her we formed a lasting friendship, which was
testified on her part by every neighborly attention that kind
consideration could suggest. If Mr. Davis came riding up the
street with General Lee, their staff officers clattering after
them, Mrs. Grant heard them and sent some dainty which her
housewifely care had prepared, or fruit from her farm on the
outskirts of Richmond. If our children were ill, she came full
of hope and kind offices to cheer us by her good sense and
womanly tenderness. The very sight of her handsome face
brought comfort to our hearts. She fed the hungry, visited the
sick, clothed the naked, showed mercy to the wicked, and her
goodness, like the city set upon the hill, "could not be
hid." . . .

On my first introduction to the ladies of Richmond, I was
impressed by the simplicity and sincerity of their manners,
their beauty, and the absence of the gloze acquired by association in the merely "fashionable society." They felt the dignity
attached to personally conducting their households in the best
and most economical manner, cared little for fashionable
small-talk, but were full of enthusiasm for their own people,
and considered wisely and answered clearly any practical question which would tend to promote the good of their families or
their country.

I was impressed by a certain offishness in their manner towards strangers; they seemed to feel that an inundation of people perhaps of doubtful standards, and, at best, of different
methods, had poured over the city, and they reserved their
judgment and confidence, while they proffered a large hospitality. It was the manner usually found in English society toward
strangers, no matter how well introduced, a wary welcome. In
the more southern and less thickly settled part of our country,

we had frontier hospitality because it was a necessity of the case. In Virginia, where the distances were not so great, and the candidates for entertainment were more numerous, it was of necessity more restricted.

We were fortunate in finding several old friends in Richmond. The Harrisons, of Brandon, and the handsome daughters of Mr. Ritchie, who had been for many years dear and valued friends. During our stay there we made other friends. . . .

## 6. LEORA SIMS—"OUR CAUSE WE KNOW IS JUST"

*When war came fire-eating, hospitable Leora Sims of Columbia, South Carolina, was nineteen, a recent graduate of the Barhamville School for young ladies. When the first cavalry company was raised in Columbia her mother gave it her carriage horses, and Leora gave her favorite saddle horse, which was later killed on a Virginia battlefield.*

*At Appomattox the morning of April 9, 1865, it was Leora's father, Captain Robert Moorman Sims, who carried General Lee's message from Longstreet to Gordon to cease fire as a truce would be asked. Longstreet spoke of him as "Captain Sims, of the Third Corps staff, serving at my headquarters since the fall of A.P. Hill."[1] According to family tradition, his white handkerchief was used as the flag of surrender. After the war Leora married Richard O'Neale of Columbia, who had spent five birthdays in the Confederate Army and was with General Lee at Appomattox.*

*Leora wrote frequently to her dear school friend, Mary Elizabeth Bellamy of Wilmington, North Carolina.*

Home
Columbia, South Carolina
November 14, 1861

My dear dear Mary

. . . Since we last interchanged communications what an increase in this mighty revolution. Virginia, the home of our loved Washington, the resting place of many great and noble,

---

[1]D. S. Freeman, *Lee's Lieutenants*, III, 733. New York: Charles Scribner's Sons, 1937.

has been laid waste, and in the midst of the true and gallant, we find, thickly woven, traitors and Yankees of the blackest dye, if that race will admit of comparison. I cannot realize that our loved Carolina is now the abiding place of our enemies. You have the invaders at Cape Hatteras and we at Port Royal. Our people have acted nobly; some cotton has fallen into the hands of the enemy; and for my part, and it is so with nearly every one in this state—we would rather have lost our men, than that the Yankees should have been gratified. . . . Some of our men did daring deeds on that battle field [Port Royal] but you have heard them, twice told, ere this. I do love the noble people of the Southern Confederacy. When we look over all the innumerable deeds of magnanimity & self denial, every true heart bounds with pleasure. Though our cause we know is just, and will eventually triumph, it may be sealed in blood or bathed in blood more properly. How many beloved ones have "fought their last battle, and now sleep their last sleep." . . . Pa was in the Battle of Manassas. We have a good many trophies from the battle field. . . .

Mary, if you all conclude to leave Wilmington, Ma & every one in the house and me especially, beg and insist that you come right to us. In these days of confusion, we never know one day what will be the circumstances of the next. I want our people to whip the Yankees badly & I do not care how they do to accomplish that end, for an invader so hateful cannot be dealt with as other enemies. Our people are not going to stop for the want of guns, they are being armed (or some) with spikes, knives, saws & anything that will do to kill and cut the Yankees to pieces. The women are getting ready for any emergency. I am going to get me a bowie knife or look for some weapon of defense. We do not feel afraid of the Yankees but we must be ready for anything. "Booty & Beauty" for their watch word, the women may expect no quarter, and if I ever fall into their hands, I earnestly pray I may be enabled to give them one "fire eater" to deal with. . . . We have but one motto—Determination. And with God as our guide we will eventually overcome all these heart rending trials. I do not think this war will last long but you know I am always looking on the bright side. Now my dear friend, do come and stay with us, your Mother and all the children, and anyone else of your family or friends. We would ever welcome citizens from our Sister state to a home in our midst, but now we feel especially

near to you all, and nothing would gratify us more than for
you all to seek a safe retreat in our Home. Come one and all.
Every body sends much love to you. Give my love to your
dear Mother. Write soon to your old classmate and your companion in these times of uncertainty & confusion.

I am as ever your devoted friend.

BABE

## 7. MRS. DORIAN HALL—"I HOPE THIS STATE OF AFFAIRS WILL NOT LAST LONG"

*Mrs. Hall was a member of an affluent Alabama family
and the mistress of a large plantation at Lowndesboro. When
her eldest son, Dr. William Hall, enlisted, she took over the
added responsibility of his near-by plantation. She wrote these
letters to him when he was stationed at Wilmington, North
Carolina. Lieutenant-General Braxton Bragg commanded the
Army of Pensacola.*

January 6th, 1862

My dear William.

Your letter from Wilmington was received on last Friday. It
was a long time getting here. You did not say anything about
your health. I felt anxious as I had understood you was complaining while at the plantation. I was very much astonished
when hearing you had remained down there that you did not
write a line to let me know what detained you, and particularly when I was told you was not well.

They are all well at the Valley but there are quite a number
of cases at big Swamp of sore throat. We have had the finest
weather for picking cotton I ever saw. I hope we will soon finish if this weather continues. Last week it was very warm.
Some persons have lost their meat, but today it is turning cold,
so much so we are expecting to kill some hogs this afternoon
altho I don't like to kill in the afternoon but its late in the season, and probably we should embrace it.

Such a December I dont recollect ever to have seen; so dry
& pleasant. During the Christmas it was equally pleasant.
There was quite a fine congregation at the Episcopal Church

—the sermon good. The church looked very pretty. By the way did you tell Mr. Powers to send a wagon load of corn to the minister for me. I dont wish to send one if he has already had one. My last cotton only brought me 6½ cts & one dollar and a quarter profit. I was glad after I found cotton had gone down that you did not send any up—letters come here for you that I could have sent to you had we but known where you were. . . .

I will get Capt. Clowndes to sell 20 bales of your cotton as soon as it will bring anything, but don't wish to sell it at 6½ cts. . . .

I am very anxious to hear from you　　goodby My dearest Son

YOUR MOTHER

January 9th 1862

My dear William:

Capt. Clowndes sold 20 bales of your cotton at 6¾ cts sent the proceeds to me　　he wrote me that good cotton was selling at 7⅛ cts but yours only brought 6¾ a quarter of a cent more than mine & it was good. We will wait now & see if the times will not change for the better. Judge Bragg thinks we will be able to sell by the first of May. I sincerely hope we will. It is a very destructive state of affairs now. Ruinous to us & our country. . . . I am engaged in setting out & transplanting tins of various lines of fruit and shade trees. Judge Bragg is suffering very much from dyspepsia worse than usual. I am anxious to hear from you very anxious. It is painful to hear of so much sickness & death among our Soldiers in various parts of the country but I hope the state of affairs will not last long & those who are away from their homes will soon return not be called out again on such a mission. There has been a petition sent on to Richmond by the Mobile people for Gen. Bragg to move his headquarters to Mobile. They feel pretty badly scared about their safety. Mrs. Bragg, Miss Mary Ellis,[1] are at Pensacola now I suppose.

With a Mothers love　　Good bye　　I hope to hear from you soon.

---

[1]Mrs. Bragg's sister, from Louisiana. She lived to be a hundred years old.

## 8. MARY BYSON—HARD TIMES IN TEXAS

*Mary lived with a young member of her family, Bettie Hooks, and her husband at Red River, Texas. Letters to her friend Margaret Butler, at her plantation home near St. Francisville in West Feliciana Parish, Louisiana, give a glimpse of economic conditions.*

Red River     January 16th 1862

My dear Margaret

You must excuse my not writing sooner as Bettie sent me up to Paris to get her some things for house-keeping, before they were all gone and I was absent nearly three weeks and only expected to be gone three days. . . .

I bought me one common calico in Paris, light purple. Bettie says too light for winter, gave twenty-five cents a yard, and not very thick. It was the darkest one I could find. I think the merchants must have packed away their goods and bring out a piece at a time. I would have got some last summer if I had thought they would have been so scarce. In hunting around for things for Bettie I chanced upon a pair of Congress gaiters, very soft and nice, just as good as I could find in the City, for three dollars so I shall not be barefooted for some time yet. There is an old Dutch shoemaker near here makes very nice shoes, but not very fashionable so they are comfortable. I do not mind the style. He told Mr. Hooks he had some very nice calfskin to make ladies shoes.

A regiment of infantry passed through Paris while I was there on their way to Kentucky. They had measles and typhoid fever, some died there. Poor fellows they say they are very much neglected when they are sick. They had orders from headquarters to get to Kentucky as soon as possible. . . .

Meat and bread are very plentiful here. Mr. Hooks will make enough meat this year for his own use. He was very much afraid of losing it at one time, but the weather turned cold in time to save it, and they will make one hundred & forty or fifty Bales of Cotton, but it will neither pay debts or buy groceries at this time. I thank you very much for thinking of me. I was in hopes I could go down this Spring, but no one can raise any money. Turkey gobblers were selling from thirty to fifty cents, eggs ten cents, sometimes five, can't get any paper money changed but can take it out in goods. Confederate bonds are not much thought of up here. Sugar & Tea are very scarce. Bettie let her Mother have some of her white sugar, and I am afraid it will give out before she can get it up from New Orleans. White Sugar is selling for twenty-five cents a pound. . . . Hard times is all the talk, besides the war. I expect I will have to give up tea as there is none in the country. I sent by Mr. Wright for some, but I am afraid we will not get any as they say everything is so scarce in New Orleans. I wish I was with you going to church. Sometimes I am afraid I shall become quite heathenish. I will try and write regularly as long as my paper lasts. . . .

My best love to your Mother and all the family and remember me to all inquiring friends. I was in hopes of going down but I think I might as well give it out as the stage has quit running.

God bless you all<br>
Yours truly M. BYSON

## 9. ROSE O'NEAL GREENHOW—OLD CAPITOL PRISON

*Mrs. Greenhow was a prisoner in her own house in Washington for six months. It became known as "Fort Greenhow." Despite the carefully guarded area, information sent by Mrs. Greenhow continued to reach Confederate lines. Allan Pinkerton reported: "She has not ceased to lay plans, to attempt the bribery of officers having her in charge, to make use of signs from the windows of her house to her friends on the streets. . . ."*

*A letter written in code by Mrs. Greenhow on December 26, 1862, was found in the archives of the Confederate War Department when Richmond was evacuated. It was deciphered and published in the* Official Records of the Union and Confederate Armies.

*The Miss Poole to whom Mrs. Greenhow refers in the following passage from her book was a fellow prisoner in the Greenhow house.*

On Saturday, January 18th [1862] at two o'clock, I learned incidentally, that I was to be removed from my house to another prison. I was sitting in my library reading. I immediately sent for the officer of the guard to know the facts. He told me he had orders not to communicate with me on the subject, but he would go to the Provost Marshal and obtain further instructions. He returned with orders fixing the hour for my removal. Detective Allen had the ordering and regulations of the arrangements. A covered wagon surrounded by a file of soldiers was ordered by Allen to be my conveyance to my prison. Believing that I should feel humiliated by this indignity, Lieutenant Sheldon however positively refused to obey this order.

Miss Poole, at this time, took the oath of allegiance, and fifty dollars in gold from the Yankee Government, and went on her way rejoicing. The woman Baxley also applied to be released upon similar terms which was refused and she was sent to the Old Capitol Prison upon which occasion I saw her for the first time. About four o'clock I turned my back upon what had been a happy home.

I reached the Old Capitol Prison[1] just at dark; the whole guard were under arms to receive me; a general commotion was visible in all directions and it was evident that a great deal of interest and curiosity was felt as to the destination of "so noted a rebel."

After the lapse of some half-hour I was taken up to the room which had been selected for me by General Porter.[2] It was situated in the back building of the prison on the northwest side, the only view being that of the prison yard and was chosen purposely so as to exclude the chance of my seeing a friendly face. It is about ten feet by twelve and furnished in the rudest manner—a straw bed with a pair of newly-made unbleached cotton sheets, a small feather pillow—a few wooden chairs, a wooden table and a glass six by eight inches com-

[1]The dingy brick building at the corner of First and A streets had been erected for the use of Congress in 1815, while the noble edifice across the parkway, burned by British soldiers, was being restored. Before it was turned into a military prison it had been a boardinghouse. Rose Greenhow's idol, John C. Calhoun, had lived there. See *Reveille in Washington, 1860–1865,* by Margaret Leech, p. 134. New York: Harper & Brothers, 1941.

[2]Andrew J. Porter, Provost-Marshal.

pleted my adornment; soldiers rations being only allowed me
by this magnanimous Pennsylvanian. . . .

I have been one week in my new prison. My letters now all
go through the detective police who subject them to a chemical
process to extract the treason.

My existence is now a positive blank. Day glides into day,
with nothing to mark the flight of time and hope paints no silver lining to the clouds which hang over me. . . .

## 10. MARY H. JOHNSTONE—PERSONAL OBSERVATIONS AT SOME OF THE CAMPS AND HOSPITALS

*Mrs. Johnstone, of Savannah, Georgia, at the request of
Vice-President Stephens, made a survey of medical conditions
at camps and hospitals in Virginia.*

Savannah    Feby 3rd, 1862

To Alexander H. Stephens
    Private
Sir

In compliance with a request made by Mr. Duncan in *your*
name to my adopted son, Cap Waring, I commit to paper the
result of my personal observation at some of the camps & hospitals in Va. No doubt to the emergency, & to a want of practical experience in the organization & management on a large
scale of this very necessary appendage to an army in war, may
be attributed much that is reprehensible, but no great improvement can be expected so long as surgeon appointments remain
a political preferment, and are consequently made with so little reference to the most important qualifications to the position.

The man's life in the Army is not sufficiently valued—
though it is there of so great moment, and most recklessly in
some cases have the scales of life been intrusted to inexperi-
enced, if not incompetent hands. Surely, where neither Patient
nor friend has a choice in the medical adviser, & the one freely
offers his life for his country, the other more than life! Common justice requires a judicious selection by those in authority;
above all, that power for good or for ill should not be confided

to the Intemperate; Without desiring to make a charge, I simply ask, in the name of those being thus sacrificed, that professional men of more experience be chosen, and that a more rigid examination into their habits be instituted. This one vice of Intemperance ought to be sufficient to condemn any applicant for the post, and be a reason for dismissal when already appointed. . . .

. . . There should be local hospitals. Camp fevers, it is said, are incurable under canvass, & the camp Hospitals, where even under roof, are devoid of comfort, even necessaries, & yet to remove an ill person any distance is death in most cases. Supposing it be not possible to procure a suitable building in the direct vicinity of the encampment to form a proper hospital, then it remains but to permit friends, or persons willing to receive a few patients, to do so. . . .

It is a fact which came under my own knowledge that the private medicine chest of a company, recently arrived at Manassas, was in request immediately for the whole regiment to which it was attached. . . .

The few observations I was enabled to make upon my recent sojourn at Manassas are such as would strike any kind of practised eye, but many valuable suggestions might occur to one habitually a visitor, whose business it might be to investigate matters, & to be responsible for the faithful discharge of duty in every department. An Inspector General whose character & experience in his profession should command respect from his fellow surgeons, and of kindliness of heart not to consider the smallest matter that might contribute to the poor soldiers comfort beneath his notice.

This supervision should extend, not only over nurses & the minutiae of their duties, but also over surgeons themselves, and he should be invested with authority in turn, should be cashiered in default of moral courage to exercise this discretion.

Wishing you success in the beautiful & important work to which you are so charitably devoting your attention, I am, Sir, one most earnestly interested in the same cause.

MARY H. JOHNSTONE

## 11. LOUISA FREDERIKA GILMER—"MY HUSBAND WAS A PRISONER AT FORT HENRY"

*In 1861 Mrs. Gilmer, a native of Georgia and the mother of two young children, was living in San Francisco where her husband, Jeremy F. Gilmer, was stationed with the United States Army. When war broke out he promptly resigned his commission and they returned to Georgia, to make their home in Savannah. Then Mr. Gilmer was appointed major of engineers in the Western army under General A. S. Johnstone and departed for Tennessee. He was at Fort Henry when it fell to General Grant. In a letter to her father, A. L. Alexander of Washington, Georgia, Mrs. Gilmer gives the news she had from Tennessee.*

Savannah Feb. 10th 1862
Monday night

My dear Father

I suppose you have seen in the papers the telegraphic account that Mr. Gilmer was a prisoner at Fort Henry & also from Maj. Rains' account that he afterwards escaped. Maj. Rains had the first intimation to that effect & was kind enough to telegraph me to that effect on Sat. morning—too late this to save me from a dreadful nervous headache from which I am but just coming out.

Sat. night I had a telegram from Mr. G. dated in Clarksville, Tenn. telling me he had reached there safely—but giving no further particulars—and today I had another dated at Fort Donelson, where he is now gone & expects to remain I presume until the fight is over there. I felt sure when I first heard Friday night that Fort Henry was taken that he was in all probability either a prisoner or killed. He was just starting there when his last letter to me was mailed and I was in such a state by the time I recd Maj. Rains telegraph that I could not hold my head up. I have been in bed ever since. It seems a dreadful state of affairs there. That the Tennessee country is in possession of the enemy & if they have as stated pushed all the way into Alabama, then it is simply disgraceful to our people.

I feel too sick to write but only thought you would feel anxious & wanted you to know all I know.

All seems quiet here yet.

Affectionately

L

## 12. MISS A. M. B.—THE UNION FLAG WAS RAISED IN NASHVILLE

*The sensitive observer who is known only by these initials lived near Nashville. After the occupation her home and the countryside about it were to remain in enemy hands throughout the war. Miss A. M. B. served in the hospitals of Nashville and Murfreesboro. Once she was arrested, charged with being a "Rebel letter carrier."*

*General John B. Floyd and General Gideon J. Pillow, the ranking officers, escaped across the Cumberland River with Floyd's Virginia brigade. This left the third officer, General Simon Bolivar Buckner, to yield Fort Donelson to his old West Point friend, General Grant.*

Saturday, the 15th of February, was a rainy, drizzling, sleeting, chilly day, when the bell tolled from our market house, ordering the citizens to assemble in solemn conclave. One old marketer on hearing its mournful echoes said, "I have done bin cummin' to this market for these twenty years and I never heard that bell make such a queer noise before!" We told him our forces at Donelson would have to retreat and we would be in the hands of the enemy. The following Sabbath was a day long to be remembered by those in and around Nashville. The Confederate forces were retreating South, and no citizen was allowed to cross the bridge until the army were over. Hurried words of parting were said by the young men who stopped at their homes, while many mothers pressed the manly forms of their sons to their hearts for the last time, and printed the good-bye kiss on their lips, while the tears choked their utterance. Everything was in a state of confusion, commissary stores were thrown open to the citizens, and stalwart women commenced rolling flour barrels, shouldering sides of bacon, and gathering up clothing until they had sufficient supplies to open a neighborhood store. Gens. Floyd and Pillow after the army had crossed ordered the suspension and railroad bridges over the Cumberland destroyed as a strategic move for a successful retreat of their forces.

Every day we expected to see the Federal army; but a week passed when, on Sabbath morning, the 23rd of February, Buell's[1] advance of a hundred cavalry entered the suburbs of Edgefield and camped. The ciizens were much excited, but our apprehensions for safety were quieted when a friend told us the Federals "were having their horses shod, paying for the work in gold, and behaving themselves very well."

No attempt was made by the enemy to cross the river for another week, when thirty transports under protection of ten gun-boats, commanded by Gen. Nelson,[2] came crawling up the Cumberland slowly as though each bluff was a masked battery, and every mile of water a net work of torpedoes. The skies, as if in sympathy, covered the whole face of the country with water. What remained to grace the triumph of a conqueror was only some old men, women and children, with a few Confederate soldiers, too sick to follow their commands. It was a silent surrender with no exclamations of triumph or display of pageant. The Union flag was raised on the capitol building. . . .

## 13. CONSTANCE CARY—THE INAUGURATION OF JEFFERSON DAVIS AS PERMANENT PRESIDENT

*Constance Cary spent her girlhood at "Vaucluse," a plantation near Alexandria, Virginia. When the Federals came that way they destroyed the house and turned the site into an army camp. Constance, her mother and her aunt fled to Richmond where they found lodgings in an overcrowded, dilapidated hotel. After some months they moved to a pleasant house on*

[1] Brigadier-General Don Carlos Buell, in command of the Federal Army of the Ohio at Louisville, had been ordered toward Nashville with 50,000 men.

[2] Brigadier-General William Nelson, in command of the 4th Division of Buell's Army of the Ohio, called "Bull" because of his stature and roaring manner.

*Franklin Street. It soon became the gathering place for a wide
circle of friends and acquaintances, who made talented, vivacious, sixteen-year-old Constance a great favorite. She took
leading roles in tableaux vivants and amateur theatricals; her
performance as Lydia in* The Rivals *captured all hearts, including that of Burton N. Harrison, the handsome private secretary of President Davis. Mrs. Chesnut spoke of her as "the
clever Conny," and said she had "a classically perfect profile."*

That 22d of February [1862] was a day of pouring rain,
and the concourse of umbrellas in the square beneath us had
the effect of an immense mushroom-bed. As the bishop and
the President-elect came upon the stand, there was an almost
painful hush in the crowd. All seemed to feel the gravity of
the trust our chosen leader was assuming. When he kissed the
Book a shout went up; but there was no elation visible as the
people slowly dispersed. And it was thought ominous afterwards, when the story was repeated, that, as Mrs. Davis, who
had a Virginia negro for coachman, was driven to the inauguration, she observed the carriage went at a snail's pace and
was escorted by four negro men in black clothes, wearing
white cotton gloves and walking solemnly, two on either side
of the equipage. She asked the coachman what such a spectacle could mean, and was answered, "Well, ma'am, you tole me
to arrange everything as it should be; and this is the way we
do in Richmond at funerals and sich-like." Mrs. Davis promptly ordered the out-walkers away, and with them departed all
the pomp and circumstance the occasion admitted of. In the
mind of a negro, everything of dignified ceremonial is always
associated with a funeral!

About March 1st martial law was proclaimed in Richmond,
and a fresh influx of refugees from Norfolk claimed shelter
there. When the spring opened, as the spring does open in
Richmond, with a sudden glory of green leaves, magnolia
blooms, and flowers among the grass, our spirits rose after the
depression of the latter months. If only to shake off the atmos-
phere of doubts and fears engendered by the long winter of
disaster and uncertainty, the coming activity of arms was welcome! Personally speaking, there was vast improvement in our
situation, since we had been fortunate enough to find a real
home in a pleasant brown-walled house on Franklin street, divided from the pavement by a garden full of bounteous green-

ery, where it was easy to forget the discomforts of our previous mode of life. The gathering of many troops around the
town filled the streets with a continually moving panorama of
war, and we spent our time in greeting, cheering, choking with
sudden emotion, and quivering in anticipation of what was yet
to follow. We had now finished other battle-flags begun by
way of patriotic handiwork, and one of them was bestowed
upon the "Washington Artillery" of New Orleans, a body of
admirable soldiers who had wakened to enthusiasm the daughters of Virginia in proportion, I dare say, to the woe they had
created among the daughters of Louisiana in bidding them
good-bye. One morning an orderly arrived to request that the
ladies would be out upon the veranda at a given hour; and,
punctual to the time fixed, the travel-stained battalion filed
past our house. These were no holiday soldiers. Their gold was
tarnished and their scarlet faded by sun and wind and gallant
service—they were veterans now on their way to the front,
where the call of duty never failed to find the flower of Louisiana. As they came in line with us, the officers saluted with
their swords, the band struck up "My Maryland," the tired soldiers sitting upon the caissons that dragged heavily through the
muddy street set up a rousing cheer. And there in the midst of
them, taking the April wind with daring color, was our flag,
dipping low until it passed us.

A few days later, on coming out of church—it is a curious
fact that most of our exciting news spread over Richmond on
Sunday, and just at that hour—we heard of the crushing blow
of the fall of New Orleans and the destruction of our ironclads.[1] As the news came directly from our kinsman, General
Randolph,[2] the Secretary of War, there was no doubting it;
and while the rest of us broke into lamentation, Mr. Jules de
St. Martin, the brother-in-law of Mr. Benjamin,[3] merely
shrugged his shoulders, with a thoroughly characteristic gesture, making no remark.

[1] The forts surrendered on April 28. The next day Farragut took
formal possession of the city.
[2] George W. Randolph, Secretary of War from March to November 1862.
[3] Judah P. Benjamin, having first been Attorney-General, and
then Secretary of War, became Secretary of State on March 17,
1862.

"This must affect your interests," some one said to him inquiringly.

"I am ruined, *voilà tout!*" was the rejoinder—a fact too soon confirmed.

# III

# A FRIGHTING SPRING

*March—May 1862*

On March 8, 1862, the Confederate ironclad *Virginia* attacked the fleet of Federal blockading vessels at Hampton Roads, Virginia. At the end of the day the Cumberland was sunk, the *Congress* was burned, the Minnesota had run aground and the rest of the fleet was scattered. The next day the first great battle between ironclads was fought when the Monitor engaged the Virginia in a drawn battle tactically, with strategic victory going to the Monitor.

On the Western front the first really great land battle of the war was fought April 6 and 7 at Shiloh Church, Tennessee. On the sixth Albert Sidney Johnston drove back the Union army under Generals Grant and Sherman and had it in jeopardy, but lost his own life. Before the battle he had urged his men to show themselves "worthy of the women of the South whose noble devotion in this war has never been exceeded in any time." After his death General Beauregard was placed in command. The evening of the sixth large Union reinforcements under Buell arrived and the second day things did not go well for the Confederates. Beauregard withdrew the army to its base at Corinth in northern Mississippi. More than 4,000 men from North and South were killed at Shiloh, and 16,000 wounded; compared with these losses, First Manassas was a skirmish. The waters of Bloody Pond were dyed crimson with blood.

On April 8 the loss of Island No. 10 , the Confederate fort where the Mississippi makes a long S at the Tennessee-Kentucky border, opened the upper stretches of the river to the Union fleet. On the twenty-fourth, after five days of bombardment, Forts St. Philip and Jackson, guarding New Orleans, *were passed by Admiral Farragut and his fleet. That day portended the fall of the greatest port of the Confederacy.*

*In Virginia on April 16 the Confederate Congress passed the first Conscription Act, calling into military service all between eighteen and thirty-five. Martial law was proclaimed in Richmond, Norfolk, parts of South Carolina and other threatened areas.*

*The operations of General George B. McClellan, in command of the Army of the Potomac, constituted the greatest threat. The hazard from his naval attack on Richmond increased with the coming of May. Yorktown had fallen and Williamsburg, and on the ninth Norfolk with its great naval yards was evacuated. Mrs. Davis' levee at the Executive Mansion was interrupted that evening by a message to the President: "The enemy's gunboats are ascending the river." While the enemy fleet steamed toward Richmond, Mrs. Davis and the children were hurried off to Raleigh. The advance up the James was repulsed at Drewry's Bluff, eight miles below Richmond, on the fifteenth, and the Confederate capital saved from naval bombardment. But McClellan's mighty army kept working its slow way up the Peninsula between the York and the James rivers. Stonewall Jackson's First Valley Campaign was in progress—but what Cornelia McDonald saw of that is reserved for Section IV.*

## 1. ALICE READY—"THE DARING, RECKLESS CAPTAIN MORGAN VISITS MURFREESBORO"

*Alice Ready was the younger daughter of Charles Ready, sometime Member of Congress from Murfreesboro, Tennessee. After graduating from Patapsco Institute, near Baltimore, she came home in the summer of 1860, and took her place in Murfreesboro and Nashville society. That year also she began a diary. "Whoever reads a single line without the writer's permission forfeits her love and friendship forever," she wrote in a childish scrawl.*

*War brought both Confederate and Federal troops to Murfreesboro, and the Ready house was intermittently the scene of gay social activities and a place of drawn blinds and heartsickness. After the Battle of Murfreesboro or Stone's River (De-*

*cember 31, 1862-January 2, 1863) the Ready family was sepa-
rated. Alice accompanied her sister Mattie, lovely bride of
dashing John Hunt Morgan, in flight from the occupied town,
and for the next two years she was her devoted companion in
Tennessee, Virginia and Georgia. Finally she wrote the bitter
entry: "I am growing thin hating the Federals."*

*The diary, which she kept for some three years, with lapses
of many weeks, began as the hurried, headlong, hit-or-miss,
spelling-punctuation-syntax-go-hang record of a wide-eyed,
keenly observing girl. It is filled with dramatic excitement and
with romance yielding to tragedy as the shadows lengthened
over the fair world she knew.*

*After the fall of Nashville, General Albert Sidney Johnston's
army encamped near Murfreesboro. The Ready family—father, mother and the young-lady daughters, Mattie (the "Sister"
of the diary) and Alice—offered hospitality to the officers.*

> Murfreesboro, Tennessee,
> Monday March 3, 1862

On last Thursday we all went out to witness a review of
Gen. [William J.] Hardee's troops, or at least a portion of
them. While there we saw Gen [John C.] Breckinridge who
told us he would have a review in a day or two, and invited us
out, we promised of course to go, we invited the two Generals
with Hardee's "staff" to spend the evening with us. They accepted, Gen H——came into town with us, we have seen a
great deal of him, a day has not passed without our seeing him
and some member of his staff—his evenings are always spent
with us, and we have found him charming—he is a tall, fine
looking man, quite militarie between 45 & 50 years of age, he
is very unassuming and affable in his manners, perfectly at
home here calls for whatever he wants, pets Ella and me a
good deal seems to regard me as a child—Sister as a young
lady. After digressing to describe the General, I will say they
were all here to spend the evening except Gen B——as soon
as they came told they had orders to leave next day. It sent a
chill to my heart, for besides bidding them, whom I had
known to like so well, farewell, Brother must now leave us
with greater surrounding dangers than ever before. I was sad
and quiet all evening. . . .

The next day the General came around with one of his aids,
just as we finished dinner, had not left the table, so they took

their seats and dined with us. After dinner we had the carriage after they had insisted very much, and drove out to the Generals Camp. The army was moving and had only stopped for the night. I think the Generals was the only tent pitched, we drove up to it, found Major Shoup and Capt White there to receive us, though not intentionally as they were not expecting us. There was a large log fire in front of the door; we went in the tent to see how things were arranged, found a goods box inverted for a table, with dishes on it, the Generals bed rolled up in a bundle—and one large arm chair completed the furniture. We took our seats by the fire and had a delightful time, the scene was picturesque in the extreme. Whilst we were there Col Adams' Cavalry regiment passed—the band playing a beautiful, heart stirring piece. It was just dark or growing dark, all around far as we could see were bright camp fires, with figures standing round, distinguishable as men from the light thrown out from the fires. The effect of the whole was equal to the most beautiful picture ever painted by my imagination.

The General went to his trunk and brought forth, as a trophy of our visit to his Camp, an elegant blue satin Mouchoir case with his initials embroidered in white, we only waited then for a cup of thin coffee, which I must confess was not worth waiting for. We concluded we should find some better at home, so the General and Capt White came in with us. We found Brother and Hugh[1] all waiting supper for us. The General and Aid only remained until half past nine. Brother retired, I went to the dining room to assist Mama in packing provisions for her "pets" to eat on their march, which must begin in the morning. General gave Brother leave to remain with us until 10 or 11 oclock, said perhaps he would come in and breakfast with us. . . .

Saturday morning after we had bid our *Brothers* a sad sad farewell, the General came, we had breakfast for him, he staid until 2 oclock. Whilst here the already celebrated Capt. John H. Morgan came to see him, with Col Wood,[2] both of whom had just returned from a scout near Nashville, when they came upon a party of Federals, killed a Captain and five or six

[1]Hugh Gwyn, friend of Alice's brother Horace; a young lieutenant who had escaped from Donelson.

[2]Lieutenant-Colonel Wood belonged to Wirt Adams' cavalry regiment.

others—we saw the sword belonging to the Capt, there were many valuable papers found on his person, which were of course given to the General. Morgan is an extremely modest man, but very pleasant and agreeable, though one to see him would scarcely imagine him to be the daring reckless man he is. An immense crowd collected at the front door to see him, two or three actually came in and stood before the parlor door to see him. He and Col Wood, who is a grandson of Gen Taylor's, will be left here with a few cavalry probably until they are driven back by the enemy. Col W——has promised to make Sister and I his confidants of military matters, so long as he remains. Before the General left he took the comfort from his neck, which he had worn during the bombardment of Bowling Green and tied it around my neck, asking me to "wear a Soldier's comfort." Bless his old heart.[1] I love him dearly. Yesterday morning soon after breakfast a courier came from the General with a note to me, very sweet of course. I replied to it immediately. . . . We returned from Church and found a note from Brother, also one from Hugh—which is very sweet and precious. . . .

The Minister made a most touching appeal to the congregation to provide for the sick soldiers, at the Hospital, who were greatly in need of attention. I was under the impression that the sick had all been removed. But came home had some chicken water made and Sister and I went to the Hospital with it and other little delicate things nourishing for the sick. I was shocked to find the place in such a condition men dying all around and no more notice taken of them than if they had been dogs—as if they had neither feeling or soul. . . . I came home with a heavy sad heart, to see human creatures, suffering. . . .

We have done nothing today except think and talk of the absent Soldiers. How it rained on them last night. Gen. Hardee says "The Heavens have been weeping at our misfortunes." There is very great dissatisfaction among the troops against Gen Johnston. Officers and all censure him very severely for the course he has taken. Some accuse him of not being true, that I think is a gross slander.

I must stop my writing for the present Albert has just

---

[1] General Hardee was in his forty-seventh year—so Alice had made a good guess.

brought me several from "headquarters" brought by Col Wood and Capt Morgan who are down stairs, and I must see them. . . .

## Wednesday, March 5th 1862

Monday night after I laid my journal aside sat up until two oclock writing notes—the courier left next morning at nine, so every thing had to be done that night. I was much surprised to find among my notes or "dispatches" as Papa calls them one from Capt White enclosing one to Alice Martin in N—— which he wanted me to send. The one from the General was like all of his very sweet and precious. Sister had one from Brother. They are near Shelbyville and will be for several days. The General said I need not be surprised to see him some night at 11 oclock. We all thought he would be here tonight, but were doomed alas! to disappointment, owing perhaps to the fact that the "Feds" have commenced pursuit—they are 12 or 13 miles from N——in this direction. Mama has been packing up *from* them ever since our army left. . . .

Yesterday the Texan Rangers, which Gen. Hardee had sent back to support Morgan, arrived. . . . We were at the Hospital again yesterday, met Col Wood who would not allow us to go in the wards. . . . I am really disappointed at not receiving a single note today—was sure the General would come, and he did not, Wood returned from his Camp today said they were all well. Tonight there was quite a number of soldiers around the house who said they had orders to guard it. . . . I am tired scribbling Oh! that the soldiers were back again.

## Thursday March 6th 1862

Awoke this morning and found the ground covered with snow. My first thought was of the Soldiers exposed to the bitter cold. This has been a dreadful day for them, cold and gloomy with the sharp March winds, and many of the Soldiers I have no doubt with insufficient clothing. . . .

## Friday March 7th 1862

. . . This evening, young Mr Buckner of Nashville came for a letter which he had given Papa to send to N——for him, there was a young man with him who intended going down tomorrow. I availed myself of his offer, to send Major White's letter to his "ladye love." It has lain like a weight upon my mind ever since it has been in my possession. While the gentlemen were waiting, the bell rang and a "dispatch" was handed me from the General. He does not forget his young friend, although so much harrassed with business. . . .

### Saturday March 8th 1862

. . . My first act after breakfast was to reply to the General's letter, which of course gave me pleasure. I sent him a geranium leaf with some violets. . . . Sister and I went out to walk this afternoon. It was delightful to breath the fresh air once more. We met White Jetton, and asked him to carry some letters for us to Shelbyville, leaves in the morning. There is a good deal of anxiety felt this evening for Col Wood and Capt Morgan, who went out yesterday with 30 men to make a reconnoissance. At first I did not attach much importance to it, remembered how seriously "the Captn" (as his men all call him) said to the General, "Sir, it would be an impossibility for them to catch me," and I was willing to trust to Woods luck, of which he thinks he possesses a pretty good share.

After supper Mr Wallace a Texan Ranger called to see me, and expressed his fears of the safety of our Marion, and his comrades, giving some very good reasons, one was that they had not been gone an hour before every body, for 8 or 9 miles knew where they had gone, and for the purpose of catching a General to exchange for Buckner. I think by morning we must hear something of them. The loss of Morgan the best scout in the service, the Marion of the war, would be an irreparable loss, it is such men as he is that we want, bold, daring and fearless.

### Sunday March 9th 1862

. . . The feeling and anxiety for Morgan and Wood had reached the highest pitch this morning, about nine oclock one of Morgans men came in and said he was afraid he had been taken, that Wood was safe. Papa was very anxious yet said he knew they were all safe. White Jetton called for our letters just before we started to Church. Had not been seated in Church more than a very few minutes, when a lady came in and took her seat just behind us, whispered to me that Morgan was safe with 10 prisoners, there was of course great rejoicing. I sent a silent prayer of thanksgiving, to a kind and merciful God. Just before the minister commenced reading the first lesson, the

Sexton brought a note and handed it to me, from Capt Morgan and Col Wood, who said "in accordance with their promise they would present us in about an hour with thirty eight Yankee prisoners." It excited us very much, we felt it would be mockery to remain in Church and pretend to hear the sermon, so we left, something which I do not remember ever to have done before, had we been in any condition to listen to a sermon, we might have remained, as they did not come until some time after Church was over. We stopped a good many coming from Church and told them so there was quite a crowd collected at our door, to witness the triumphal entrance of Morgan and Wood into town, with their 38 prisoners. The first signal of their approach was a number of Texan Rangers, galloping by here on horseback to the first street crossing this one below. In a much shorter time than I can write it the grand cavalcade appeared from that street, there was I suppose 60 or 70 horsemen including prisoners and all, with Morgan and Wood at the head. As soon as they came in sight, it seemed impossible for any one to restrain their enthusiasm. There was heart felt cheers and waving of handkerchiefs. They moved on until about the middle of the procession were opposite our door, when they were halted, and the two braves rode back to the stepping stone, without dismounting they raised their hats, and said to Sister and me, "Ladies I present you with your prisoners, what disposal shall be made of them?"

We replied, "You have performed your part so well, we are willing to intrust it all to you." I suppose they remained before the door for 15 or 20 minutes. The prisoners were well dressed, most of them Germans. One old grey haired fellow rode up with his guard and asked for a glass of water, while the servant was getting it, he made quite a little speech, asked the ladies to interceed with Captain Morgan to have him released, said he was not fighting, but was a teamster, was compelled to do it, to keep his family in Cincinatti from starving. When the water came he raised it to his lips, saying "ladies here is to your health in water."

I have not attempted a description of the two "great men," nor shall I for it would be worse than useless. I only know that in my admiration and pride for them, I lost control of myself, and must have acted almost as a crazy person. Papa invited them to come back and dine with us. The Captain was too unwell, and fatigued. Col Wood however came, just before dinner. Puss

Ready came in to spend the night with us, regreted very much not being here to see the Yankees, was speaking of it after dinner, when Col W——proposed we should go to the Court House, where they were—said he would go up and see if things were arranged so that we could go. I did not think it by any means proper, though he seemed to think it was and of course I did not say anything. Just before he left the old man who made the speech came down with his guard to ask Mama for an old quilt, seemed very grateful that he was not shot which he and all of them fully expected. He said "when the Captain went up to him he so skeered he just liked to have dropped." They all seem to be cowards. I feel assured that [if] the army at Nashville 65,000. would only come out and give our men battle they would be whipped, such material as it is composed of could never stand before our army, which embraces all the chivalry and worth of the entire south, who if they have the proper leaders must be successful.

Wood was very much engaged getting information from one of the prisoners, and could not come back for us himself, so he sent young Buckner, who seemed happy as possible that the Capt'n had returned, all of his men are equally delighted. I never saw such devotion to a leader in my life. . . . Buckner had a Yankee pistol, which the "Captn" had given him, and a pair of spurs which he said "he gave them a quarter for."

Papa received a note from Gen Hardee asking for information of the absent scouting party, he was very anxious about them, I wanted Papa to allow me to reply to it, which he would not consent to, so I wrote a short note myself, and told the Courier to tell him to open it first. I wanted to be the first to give him the good news. . . .

Tuesday March 11th 1862

I did not write yesterday because I was really quite unwell, and then there was nothing to write. Except in the morning Capt Morgan sent us the Louisville Journal to read the first newspaper I have seen for three weeks. . . . Papa told us last night that Morgan and Wood would leave this morning for Shelbyville to confer with Gen Hardee, respecting that expedition to Gallatin, they go in person, hoping to gain his consent. The Capt' called this morning for any letters we might have to send. . . .

The troops have almost all left Shelbyville—the General

goes tomorrow, and so far that we can hold no communication. . . . My heart is so full and sad tonight that I can scarcely write at all. . . . With that army went all whom I held dear. . . .

I hear they are making men, women and children take the oath in Nashville. I dont think it would be binding, and should feel no scruples in breaking it, when I had the opportunity. . . .

## Wednesday March 12th 1862

. . . I expected to have had a ride of horseback this afternoon with Cousin Kate but was disappointed, and very fortunately too or I would have missed Col Wood and Capt Morgan who had just returned from Shelbyville and came down to ask us to make them a flag of truce, which they wanted to go for their four men who are missing. . . .

## Thursday March 13th 1862

Last night just after I had retired—Sister was still writing —the front door bell was pulled very hurriedly. Margret went down and found a servant waiting with a letter from our darling Brother, which was written from Fayettville. When I discovered what it was I jumped out of bed very quickly—but Sister got the letter first. I was too impatient to wait until she had finished it, and wanted her to tear it in two, so I could read one half, while she read the other—however she would not consent to this, and I had to wait. . . .

The last troops left Shelbyville today for Huntsville. Morgan leaves here Saturday. The Rangers left this morning. . . .

Col Wood called, they were going to leave at 2 o'clock with the flag of truce. He spoke very feelingly and indignantly about Gen Johnston—said he had defended him as long as he could, but believed now that he was either a fool or a traitor, left Gen Hardee to bring up the rear of the retreat blindfolded, took no notice of the many and important dispatches which were sent to him, said that it was not the silence of wisdom, but the wisdom of silence. . . .

## Saturday March 15th 1862

. . . Capt' Morgan called last night and remained quite late, so late that I prefer seeking the bed, rather than my pen to make a record in my journal. He returned yesterday after a successful trip with his flag of truce his four men taken prison-

ers two of them wounded—shot after they were taken. Had it
not been for that flag of truce our town might now have been
in ashes with Morgan and his men prisoners, or killed. About
fourteen miles from here they met 3,000 Federals commanded
by Gen Mitchell[1] coming up to attempt his capture, which
must have been certain, 50 men brave and daring as ours are
could but poorly have coped with 3000 cravens as they
are. . . .

Captain Morgan was more agreeable last night than ever before. I think all of his powers were called into play to be as
charming as possible—related a number of amusing incidents
that occured on Green river Ky. when he would be out scouting—he would become excited, his eyes flash, and cheek flush
he is very modest and personally, is truly appreciated only after an acquaintance of some length. He spoke highly of the
Federal officers except Col Kennet[2]—said they were all nice
gentlemen. . . .

Miss Putnam reached this place last night from Nashville
where she says exists a most complete military despotism. The
houses are all being searched. they entered one for that purpose, the lady was sick, quite so, regardless as usual of the
sanctity of a lady's chamber, they went in and striped the bed
where she lay of each piece of covering, looking for Texan
Rangers and arms. The former with Morgans squadron they
hold in perfect terror, say M has 5,000 men here numbering
each of his men as 100, Capt Morgan and Col Wood called
just before they left town, their hopes in regard to taking
Andy Johnson are disappointed, he has already reached N——
with his 100 body guard. No one knows of the expedition
on foot except our family. Papa went out of town several
miles to show them the way. As he was shaking hands with
Capt Morgan he said "tell the young ladies I will bring them a
trophy on my return"—O! for a dozen Morgan's. . . .

Monday March 17th 1862

. . . I was seated in my own quiet room reading when some
of the servants came rushing in, "The Yankees have come."
What an excitement ensued, my first thought was of the gallant

[1]General Ormsby M. Mitchel.
[2]Colonel H. G. Kennett, who became Chief of Staff to General
Rosecrans.

Morgan, and then to have all the front window blinds closed. . . . We all went to the windows to *peep* through the closed blinds. There were not more I think than 100, who came into town, though they are said to be in force at the river they were a fine looking body of men well mounted and uniformed—the 4th Ohio Regiment, the same from which those prisoners brought into town last week were taken. . . . Papa thinks it may not be safe for him to remain here for a day or two. He is going tonight with some of the negro men & horses, to the Country. . . .

Wednesday March 19th 1862—

. . . Cousin Kate and Puss were spending the night with us, sometime, after supper, we were all sitting around the fire in my room, when Ella came in and announced that Morgan was safe in Shelbyville, having accomplished his object in Gallatin, taken 18 prisoners a Colonel among the number. . . .We had just retired. . . . All at once I scarcely know how I found myself in Sisters room, where she and Cousin K and Puss had their heads out the window talking to a solitary horseman, who wanted he sad to see Mr. Ready, upon Sisters suggestion he dismounted to come in and communicate his intelligence to her, we had quite a scene then to get her dressed and a candle, for her to go down. We had burnt ours till there was not a piece of wick left in the socket. We all felt he was a courier from Morgan nor were we disappointed, he was the bearer of a note from Capt. Morgan asking if it would be safe for him to pass through town, he was then at Lascasses about 8 or 10 miles from here, Papa was not at home, Mama asleep, so we had to act on our own responsibility. Sister wrote "They are eight miles from here, come in haste." . . .

After the courier left and Mama who had been aroused by the noise, had learned the cause of it and been informed of our reply, she became very much excited, said "we were sacrificing the lives of some of our best men—that now the town would certainly be shelled, the enemy were not so far as we supposed." . . . Sister and I still sat up. In the lone hour of the night when nothing was heard save the roaring of the fire in the grate and my own breathing, Sister and I sat before the fire. . . . Sister hastened into the other room and raised the window. I jumped up, and away she and I flew down stairs—for the horseman whom she had spoken to from the window was no other than our gallant Morgan himself. We reached the front door and found him there with Col Wood. Both dismounted and stood on the steps talking for at least a half hour. . . . While we were talking Puss came down, said she must see Capt Morgan. We talked until day began to dawn and then came the sad goodbye. . . . Both mounted their horses and joined the men on the square, when they all stood and sang in the sweetest tones I ever heard, "Cheer boys, cheer." I think it must have been "little Tom Morgan" who sang the solo, in the chorus all joined heartily—and clearest above the other voices was heard the Captains. . . . It was so thrilling and sad that the tears were only restrained by an effort. We watched them till there was none to be seen, and with them went a blessing from true southern womans heart—and a prayer that God would bless them. . . . We have the pleasant, yet melancholy satisfaction of having seen the last, of the gallant Morgan, who endears himself to all, and the last of our Army. . . .

## 2. LOULIE GILMER—"WRITE ME WHAT YOUR HORSE IS NAMED"

*Loulie was ten when she wrote this letter to her father, Major Jeremy F. Gilmer, who had escaped from Fort Henry and Fort Donelson and was somewhere in Tennessee with Albert Sidney Johnston. Later on he was to be chief of the Engineer Bureau in Richmond, with the rank of major-general. We have met Loulie's mother, Louisa F. Gilmer.*

March 16, 1862
Savannah, Georgia

My Dear Dear Father

I do want to see you so much. I do miss you so much in the evenings, when I come in and no one is in, and I am so lonesome by myself and if you were here you would tell me stories and so I would not be so lonesome. I wish you would tell one in your letter to me for I want you to write to me what your horse is named. Give my love to James and tell him I hope he is well. Auntee sends her love and hopes you are well and I hope so too. The Yankees have not got near the city yet. The other day some heavy firing was heard and it was them firing

into one of our Boats. . . . Mother and Auntee had the headache day before yesterday and they got up yesterday. . . .

I go almost every morning to Mr. H.'s printing office but I
have no more to say. I am your loving child

LOULIE GILMER

## 3. CORNELIA PEAKE McDONALD—WINCHESTER
### IS OCCUPIED BY THE ENEMY

*Mrs. Cornelia Peake McDonald, the daughter of Hum-
phrey Peake and Anne Linton Lane Peake, was born in Alexandria, Virginia, on June 14, 1822. The family moved to Missouri and lived for a while in Palmyra and in Hannibal. As a
young lady Cornelia visited at Jefferson Barracks in St. Louis
where she met and danced with Ulysses S. Grant, James
Longstreet and other officers. In 1847 she married Angus
McDonald, a lawyer of Winchester, Virginia.*

*At the outbreak of war Mrs. McDonald was the mother of
seven children: Harry, thirteen; Allan, twelve; Kenneth, nine;
Ellen, seven; Roy, five; Donald, two; and Hunter, born June
12, 1860. She was described by one who knew her well as tall
and slender, with dark hair always simply dressed; a lady of
great dignity, courage and intelligence.*

*The night before he rode off with the Stonewall Brigade in
the spring of 1862 Colonel McDonald urged his wife to keep a
diary. "With the expectation that the town would be immediately occupied by the enemy," she said, "he wished to be informed of each day's events." He was prescient. No town
changed hands so suddenly and so often as Winchester.*

*Winchester, March, 1862.*—On the night of March 11th,
1862, the pickets were in the town; part of the army had already gone, and there were hurried preparations and hasty fare-
wells, and sorrowful faces turning away from those they
loved best, and were leaving, perhaps forever. At one o'clock
the long roll beat, and soon the heavy tramp of the marching
columns died away in the distance.

The rest of the night was spent in violent fits of weeping at
the thought of being left, and of what might happen to that
army before we should see it again. I felt a terrible fear of the

coming morning, for I knew that with it would come the much
dreaded enemy.

I laid down when the night was almost gone, to sleep, after
securing all the doors, and seeing that the children were all
asleep. I took care to have my dressing gown convenient in
case of an alarm, but the night passed away quietly, and when
the morning came, and all was peaceful I felt reassured,
dressed and went down.

The servants were up and breakfast was ready. The children
assembled and we had prayers.

I felt so thankful that we were still free, and a hope dawned
that our men would come back, as no enemy had appeared.
We were all cheerfully despatching our breakfasts, I feeling
happy in proportion to my former depression; the children
were chatting gaily, Harry and Allan rather sulky at not having been permitted to leave with the army, as they considered
it degradation for men of their years and dimensions to be left
behind with women and children. Suddenly a strain of music!
Every knife and fork was laid down and every ear strained to
catch the faint sounds. The boys clap their hands and jump up
from the table shouting, "Our men have come back!" and
rushed to the door; I stopped them, telling them it must be the
Yankees. Every face looked blank and disappointed.

I tried to be calm and quiet, but could not, and so got up
and went outside the door. Sure enough that music could not
be mistaken, it was the "Star Spangled Banner" that was
played. A servant came in. "They are all marching through the
town, and some have come over the hill into our orchard."

I made the children all sit down again, and began to eat my
breakfast, but felt as if I should choke with anger and mortification.

Tears of anger started from Harry's eyes, while Allan
looked savage enough to exterminate them if he had the
power. Kenneth looked very wretched, but glanced occasionally out of the window, as if he would like, as long as they had
come, to see what they were like. Nelly's face was bent in the
deepest humiliation on her plate, as if the shame of defeat was
peculiarly hers. Roy's black eyes were blazing, as if he scented
a fight but did not exactly know where to find it. While Donald, only two and a half years old, turned his back to weep silently, in sympathy I suppose with the distress of the rest.
Presently a trampling was heard around the house, loud voices

and the sounds of wheels and horses' hoofs. Suddenly a most unwonted sound! A mule braying; Nelly looked up from her plate where her eyes had been fixed in shame and distress: "Even their very old horses are laughing." That was irresistible. I was compelled in spite of all to join the horses in their laugh.

I was obliged to attend to my household affairs, and in passing to and fro on the porch and through passages, encountered them often, but took no notice, just moved on as if they were not there. Donald was sitting on a step very disconsolate looking, when one blue coat passed near him, and laying his hand on his head, said "How d'ye do Bub." He did not look up, but sullenly said, "Take your hand off my head, you are a Yankee." The man looked angry, but did not try to annoy us because the small rebel scorned him.

Ten o'clock had come, and we were still undisturbed. Only men passing through the yard to get water from the spring; so I put on my bonnet and went to town to see what had befallen my friends, and to attend to some necessary business. As I approached Mrs. Powell's house, I saw a group of officers standing at the gate, brilliantly dressed men who, as I could not help seeing as I advanced, were regarding me very curiously. I was obliged to pass very near them, but did so without being, or seeming to be aware of their presence. When I had gone by, I heard behind me a "Whew" and a little quiet laugh. I knew they were laughing at my loftiness, but tried to smother my resentment.

As I came near the town I encountered throngs of soldiers of different parts of the army. The pavements were lined with them, the doorsteps and front yards filled, and they looking as much at home, and as unconcerned as if the town and all in it belonged to them, and they were quietly enjoying their own.

Conspicuous above the rest were Banks'[1] bodyguard. A regiment of Zuaves, with scarlet trousers, white leather gaiters, and red fez. I would not look at them, though I saw them distinctly.

As I passed Mrs. Seevers' beautiful house that was her pride and delight, I saw an unusual stir. More Zuaves were on the

[1]Major-General N. P. Banks, commanding the Union forces in the Shenandoah.

pavement in front, many stretched on the beautiful lawn or smelling the flowers that were just budding out. Two stood, straight and upright at each side of the door, while sentinels walked back and forth outside the gate. That I afterwards heard was Banks' headquarters.

I passed some friends who looked at me with unspoken mortification and distress. All houses were shut, and blinds down.

Occasionally at a door might be seen an excited woman talking resentfully to one, or a group of men. I hated the sight of the old town, as it looked with strangers meeting me at every step, their eyes looking no friendliness; only curiosity or insolence. I finished my business, and without exchanging a word with any one, set out for home.

As I turned in at the gate at the end of the avenue, I beheld a sight that made my heart stand still. A number of horses were tied on the lawn, and in the porch was a group of men. I went straight up to the house, as I came near saw they were U. S. officers. There they stood in all the glory of their gold lace and epaulettes, but I felt neither awed by their martial appearance, or fascinated by their bravery of apparel. I walked deliberately up the steps until I reached the top one, as I felt that I could be less at a disadvantage in an encounter if on a level with them. When there I stood still and waited for them to speak. One took off his cap and came towards me colouring violently. "Is this Mrs. McDonald," said he. I bowed stiffly, still looking at him.

He handed me a card, "De Forest, U. S. Army."[1] I bowed again and asked if he had any business with me, knowing well that he had, and guessing what it was. Another then came forward as if to relieve him, and said that they had been sent by General Williams[2] to look at the house, with a view to occupying it as headquarters, and asked if I had any objection to permitting them to see the rooms. I told him that I had no objection to them seeing the rooms, but that I had very many objections to having it occupied as headquarters. (This was said very loftily.) But that as I could not prevent it, they must, if they chose do it. This was meant to be indignant, but at the

---

[1] John William DeForest, brevetted major in July 1863; author of *Miss Ravenel's Conversion* and *Kate Beaumont*.
[2] General Alpheus S. Williams.

end, angry tears would come. One or two seemed sorry for me, but the others looked little moved. I went and opened a room for their inspection, but they declined looking in, and asked what family I had, and how many rooms the house contained. I told them there were seven children, and that the two youngest were ill.

They bowed themselves out but Maj Wilkins, the one who was the second to speak, turned back and coming close to me said, "I will speak to Gen. Williams and see if they cannot be accommodated elsewhere." Then they all left, but in a few hours a note came from Maj. Wilkins, saying that in consideration of sickness in my family, Gen. Williams would not inconvenience me. I was very grateful at being left to myself, but not glad to be obliged to feel grateful to these intruders.

For a week or more I was annoyed but little, though every day would hear tales of the arrest of citizens, and occupation of houses belonging to them, while their families were obliged to seek quarters elsewhere, so of course there was nothing like quietness or peace of mind. These outrages roused all our indignant feelings, but when we had a closer acquaintance with war, we wondered how such things could have disturbed us so much.

One morning, very early I observed a U. S. flag streaming over Mr. Mason's house. Found out that it was occupied as headquarters by a Massachusetts regiment. . . .

*March, 1862.*—The *Baltimore American*, the only paper we see, is full of the amazing success of the "National Army" over the rebels. "The traitor Jackson is fleeing up the valley with Banks in hot pursuit. The arch rebel suffers not the grass to grow under his flying feet. There is perfect confidence in his speedy downfall."

Gen. Shields[1] is in command; Banks has gone—with nearly two-thirds of the army. Those that are here make a great display of their finery, and the grandeur of their equipments, but the people take no notice of them. I meet the gorgeous officers every day in our hall, but I never raise my eyes.

As I came up the avenue a few days since, I noticed one of the beautiful ornamental trees cut down for fuel. I was greatly disturbed by it; and as I entered the hall, still angry and excit-

[1]Brigadier-General James Shields.

ed, I met rather a fine looking officer coming out. He was a
large man, handsomely dressed, and seemed inclined to be
courteous. He raised his cap, and held the door open for me to
pass, but remained standing after I had entered. I took the opportunity to speak of the trees and asked that no more be allowed to be destroyed. He said he would do his best to prevent
it and as he still stood and wished to say something else, I
waited to hear what it was. First he said he was astonished to
see so much bitterness manifested toward them by the people,
especially by the ladies of Winchester. "I do not think," he
said, "that since I have been here I have seen a pleasant coun-
tenance. I always notice that the ladies on the street invariably
turn away their faces when I look at them, or if they show
them at all, have on all their sour looks. Do they always look
sour and do they always dress so gloomily in black?" "As for
the dress," said I, "many of them are wearing black for friends
killed in battle, and others are not inclined to make a display
of dress when those they love are in hourly danger; and they
cannot look glad to see those they would like to have drowned
in the sea, or overwhelmed with any calamity that would take
them from our country." He said no more but passed on.

One day Maj. Wilkins called to bring me a written protection for the house and ground, consigning to death any who
should violate it. Gen. Shields had given it. He also offered to
take for me any letters to friends in the Stonewall Brigade, as
he was to set out that day for the upper valley, and could communicate by flag of truce. I soon wrote one or two while he
waited, putting nothing in them but that we were well, and in
quiet, but anxious for intelligence of their well-being.

He sealed them in my presence, and when I asked him if it
would not occasion him trouble he only laughed and said care-
lessly that it might cost him his commission, but that he would
see that it did not.

I expressed great concern lest it should be a cause of trouble
to him, and felt so grateful for his kindness, that I told him if
he was ever sick or otherwise in need of a kind office to apply
to me; he thanked me, and mounting his horse, galloped off to
join Banks in his advance up the valley.

The *Baltimore American* still continues to publish flaming
accounts of the advance of the Union Army up the valley, and
having no means of knowing their resources, or ability as a
military body, except from their own boastful accounts, I was

filled with apprehension. A feeling of utter despair would take possession of me when I saw their great army moving, or marshalled in all its pomp for parade or review. My heart would be filled with indignation and even rage, all the more violent because of its impotence.

Had I forgotten the gallant array and brave appearance of Gen. Johnston's army as they passed our house on their march to their great victory at Manassas? The exulting strains of "Dixie" or the "Bonnie Blue Flag" almost giving wings to their feet as they moved triumphantly on, keeping step to the joyous music.

I could not recall any triumph of a former time in the humiliation of the present, and the apprehensions for the future which their power and strength would awaken. To hear their bands playing, as they constantly did, in our streets as if to remind us of our captivity and insult our misery was distracting, but Oh! the triumph of their faces when they had a slight advantage! It was maddening to see.

Though their papers were so noisy and boastful, it was observable that they continued to hover near Winchester, and as we could every day hear the sound of cannon not very far off, it was not easy to persuade us to believe that our troops were frightened away altogether.

For two or three weeks, on successive Sundays there was brisk cannonading near the town, and an evident commotion among the troops. One bright Sunday morning I was standing on the porch listening to the sounds of the cannon in the distance, when a Yankee approached and asked me if I expected "Old Jack" that day, saying that "Sunday was the day he usually selected to come."

But a day came, a Sunday, when the cannonading did not cease after the usual annoyance of the enemy in the distance, but as the day wore on it thundered louder and louder, and came nearer and nearer. All the troops left the town, and we soon became aware that a battle was being fought very near us. An intervening hill shut out the sights but not the fearful sounds, which, as the right of the enemy met our left, became more and more dreadful and deafening till two o'clock in the afternoon; then the cannon ceased, and in its place the most terrible and long continued musketry firing, some said, that had been heard since the war began, not volley after volley, but one continued fearful roll, only varied in its distinctness by the swaying of the battle, now nearer and now farther away, as each combatant seemed to gain or lose ground. Harry and Allan had begged me to let them go to the top of the hill early in the morning to see what was going on. I had given permission, thinking of no danger other than occurred every day; but now, how I repented having let them go, and sat all that fearful afternoon in terror for fear my boys had come to harm.

I remained during all those miserable hours with my baby on my lap, and the four little ones clustered round, listening to the dreadful storm of battle, and feeling, Ah! how bitterly, that at each shot some one of the flower of our youth was perishing (for that Stonewall Brigade comprised the very pride and flower of the upper counties of Virginia), that they were being cut down like the grass. Oh, the anguish of those hours! My little boys! How could I have suffered them to go away from me so thoughtlessly when nearly every moment brought danger?

At last the gloomy hours had all rolled by, and with the darkness came silence. All the turmoil had ceased, and in its place a dreary pattering rain was the only sound I heard.

As I sat there in the darkness my imagination painted the scenes behind that hill. The dead, the dying, the trampling horses, the moans, the ghastly forms of those that some of us loved, the cries for help when no help was near. I cried out in my terror, "Where are my boys?" and ran down to the kitchen in the hope of seeing some face that looked natural and reassuring. Aunt Winnie sat there by the fire with Tuss. He was the picture of terror. His poor ugly face was ghostly, his eyes and mouth wide open and his hands clasping each other nervously. He looked up at me and asked in a husky voice, "Whey is dem boys?" I could not answer but went back and sat in the dining room with the little children and poor little Kenneth, who was grieving about the boys. About nine o'clock they came in, very grave and sad looking. Indeed they seemed not like the same boys, so sad and unnatural was their expression. Everything that fearful day seemed unreal. I felt as if a new and terrible existence had begun, as if the old life was over and gone, and one had opened, from the threshold of which I would if I could, have turned away, and lived no longer.

All the careless happiness had gone from the faces and manner of the boys, and though there was no sign of fright or of excitement, they were very grave and sorrowful; disappoint-

ed, too, as we had lost the battle, and they had been compelled
to see the Southern troops sullenly withdraw after the bloody
struggle. I could see that they had comprehended the situation
of the contending forces, and had given a correct account of
what had transpired under their observation.

They told of the prolonged fight behind the stone wall, of
the repeated onsets of our men, and the rolling back of the
blue columns, as regiment after regiment was repulsed by the
Confederates, till at last, outnumbered and borne back, they
had retired from the field, leaving behind the dead and dying,
and even their wounded. When the boys told of the retreat
their anger and mortification found relief in tears, but they
were tears of pity when they told of the wounded. They remained for a while to give water to some, and would have
gladly done more, but were hurried away by the sentinels. "I
was mortified all the time," said Allan, "because we had to stay
on the Yankee side."

They had a position in the beginning of the battle near
where a body of the Federals were awaiting an attack, and
they, the boys, were perched on a fence for a better view, but
the attack was made, and a man's head rolled close to where
they were, and they prudently retreated to a more secure position.

Next morning, a worn and weary, ragged and hungry train
of prisoners came in town under a strong guard. Throngs of
ladies and poor women greeted them and cheered them with
comforting words. Mothers at the doors of elegant houses
waited to give these poor boys food. They were not allowed to
stop, but were hurried out of sight without a word to the parents whose darlings they were. No one had been allowed to go
to the battlefield the night before, though many had begged to
be permitted to carry relief to the wounded.

No one knew who was dead, or who was lying out in that
chilly rain, suffering and famishing for the help that was so
near, and would have been so willingly given but for the bar-
barous order that no relief should be sent from the town. No
eyes closed during those nights for the thought of the suffering
pale faces turned up under the dark sky, or for the dying
groans or helpless cries of those they were powerless to relieve.

Not until the Federal dead were all buried on the field, and
their wounded brought in, which occupied nearly two days,
were our people allowed to go to the relief of their wounded.

Then, no doubt, many had perished who could have been saved had timely relief been given. Our people buried their own dead. Though, as we had no conveyances, the authorities had our wounded brought in. .

Every available place was turned into a hospital, the courthouse was full, the vacant banks, and even the churches. I went with some refreshments as soon as I heard they were coming in. I first went to the Farmer's Bank, where I saw some ladies standing by several groaning forms that I knew were Federals from their blue garments. The men, the surgeon said, were dying, and the ladies looked pityingly down at them, and tried to help them, though they did wear blue coats, and none of their own were there to weep over or help them.

I went from there to the courthouse; the porch was strewed with dead men. Some had papers pinned to their coats telling who they were. All had the capes of their great coats turned over to hide their still faces; but their poor hands, so pitiful they looked and so helpless; busy hands they had been, some of them, but their work was over.

Soon men came and carried them away to make room for others who were dying inside, and would soon be brought and laid in their places. Most of them were Yankees, but after I had seen them I forgot all about what they were here for. I went on into the building intending to find our own men and give them what I had brought.

A long line of blue clad forms lay on each side as I passed up the room. I had not gone far before I saw a pair of sad looking eyes intently regarding the pitcher the servant carried. I stooped and offered him some: it was lemonade; he could not raise his head to drink, so I poured it into his mouth with a tablespoon. He looked up at me so thankfully. "It is a beautiful drink," he said, "for a thirsty man," and the poor fellow looked after me as I walked away.

The next day when I went he was past all succor in this world; he still lay in the same place and in the same position, with his head bent far back; he was breathing painfully and heavily, and after I had spent some time in another part of the room and was going out, I saw them carrying his corpse towards the door.

Many, many poor sufferers were there, some so dreadfully mutilated that I was completely overcome by the sight.

I wanted to be useful, and tried my best, but at the sight of one face that the surgeon uncovered, telling me that it must be washed, I thought I should faint. It was that of a Captain Jones, of a Tennessee regiment. A ball had struck him on the side of the face, taking away both eyes, and the bridge of his nose. It was a frightful spectacle. I stood as the surgeon explained how, and why he might be saved, and the poor fellow not aware of the awful sight his eyeless face was, with the fearful wound still fresh and bleeding joined in the talk, and raising his hand put his finger on his left temple and said, "Ah! if they had only struck there, I should have troubled no one." The surgeon asked me if I would wash his wound. I tried to say yes, but the thought of it made me so faint that I could only stagger towards the door.

As I passed my dress brushed against a pile of amputated limbs heaped up near the door. My faintness increased, and I had to stop and lean against the wall to keep from falling. Just then Mrs. Magill stopped by me on the way in, and asked me what was the matter. I told her about the poor man whose wound I could not wash. "I'll wash him," she said, and with her sweet cheerful face she went in, and I saw her leaning over him as he laid propped up by a bench.

Another poor man I saw who was well known to my family. Townes was his name. He told me his wife was away in Missouri and he should not see her ever again, as the doctor had told him that he could not live till night. It seemed dreadful to hear him say that when his face was full, and his eyes bright as if in health. His wound was in his neck or spine. He shook my hand as I left him and begged me to give his regards to my husband and family.

The regards of a dead man! But he was so polite, and such a gentleman he must send a message of remembrance even though when it could be delivered he would be in another world. He did not like me to see how he suffered, but tried to talk pleasantly, never mentioning his wound. He said he would love to hear some of the church prayers, but there was no book at hand, and it would have been impossible to read among all those sounds of war, for all the amputations were being performed in the room where the wounded lay.

The afternoon of the next day I went by the courthouse, the scene of so much anguish and despair. I could not believe my own eyes when I saw a flaming banner flying from the porch gaily painted and inscribed with the words, "Theatre here to-night." A gentleman told me that they had spent the night before removing the wounded and dying to make way for the theatre, as they said the men must be amused.

Soon after, the *Baltimore American* contained a paragraph to the effect that the ladies of Winchester evinced a very great unconcern for their people and the army as well as for their own situation as prisoners, as the theatre was nightly thronged. It was thronged with negro women and Yankee soldiers.

Some days after the battle of Kernstown[1] I noticed unusual preparations going on by the officers in the house, and soldiers outside. Sleek, splendid horses were brought from the stables, and gorgeously dressed officers came out and mounted them. The band was playing "Hail Columbia" on the lawn. I felt curious to know what was the occasion of so much parade, and raised the windows to ask a soldier.

The Col. saw me, and after the patriotic strain was ended spoke to a soldier to play "Dixie," which was done, but always spoiled by introducing parts of other pieces, for fear that we, I suppose, should enjoy our rebellious pleasure unalloyed. So as the strains of "Dixie" floated on the air, the Col. and his officers rode down the avenue, their horses curvetting and prancing, as if to keep time to the music.

About sunset the bright cavalcade returned, and after dismounting, seated themselves on the front porch. I went and stood in the door, as I was consumed with anxiety to know the occasion of their gay expedition in the afternoon. Col. Candée, after saying good evening, soon remarked that they had had a most delightful time. Mr. Seward and his daughter had come from Washington to see the battlefield, that all the troops had been ordered out to meet them at the depot, and escort them to the scene of their great victory.

The thought of their triumph, and of the glee of the heartless old schemer whose intrigues and falsehoods had done so much for our undoing, was more than I could bear. "Ah!" said I, forgetting prudence, "we can well excuse him for rejoicing as it is the first time he has had occasion to do so, but I must tell you what crossed my mind as you told me of his visit to

---

[1] The Confederates suffered a slight repulse at Kernstown on March 23, 1862.

the battlefield. It was a short poem of Lord Byron's wherein he relates how Mr. Seward's great prototype once visited a battlefield:

> "Then next he paused upon his way
> To look upon Leipsic plain,
> And so sweet to his eyes was the sulphury glare,
> And so soft to his ears was the cry of despair,
> That he perched on a mountain of slain
> And gazed with delight on its growing height
> Not often on earth had he seen such a sight,
> Or his work done half so well."[1]

Some of them laughed, but the Col., with a very red face, sat silent for some time. I began to repent what I had done, as I felt that I might have to pay a severe penalty for my rashness, but soon the Col., addressing the Major, said, "Did the General give the order concerning the hospitals today?" And turning to me, "You will probably have to seek other quarters, Madam, for whenever I leave this house as I may do in a few days, it is quite likely it will be occupied as a hospital."

My courage had all oozed out by that time, so I silently withdrew into the hall, and standing by the window tried, tried to realize the probable consequences of what I had done.

Two days afterwards, preparations were on foot for a march, and the Col. asking to see me for a moment after breakfast, I went out and found them all waiting to take leave of me before mounting their horses. All were politely and smilingly standing, and offered their hands which I was not quite sure I ought to take, but could not be rude enough to refuse.

The Col. thanked me for the civility I had shown him during his stay under my roof, regretting being obliged to leave his pleasant quarters, but they had orders to push on up the valley with the rest of their army. After they had mounted and were touching their caps gallantly as they turned their horses, I spoke to the Col. "I shall be very glad to see you Col. Candée on your way back if you have time to stop."

That last piece of impudence was cowardly, as he could not, as I thought, reply, but he did, saying, "Madam, Jackson is

[1] "The Devil's Drive," quoted from memory.

now pushed to extremities—three columns are now converging to crush him." My heart sank, and as usual my courage melted away in a fit of weeping.

## 4. MARGARET LEA HOUSTON—"MY BOY IS GONE FROM ME"

*A schoolgirl with violet eyes, Margaret Lea had seen the heroic General Houston when New Orleans greeted the victor of San Jacinto. They met in 1839 when he called on her brother-in-law William Bledsoe at Spring Hill near Mobile; fell passionately in love and were married on May 9, 1840.*

*Strongly attached to the Union and bitterly opposed to secession, the general was deposed as Governor of Texas. Sam, Jr., eldest of the seven children, enlisted as a private in Ashbel Smith's company of the 2nd Texas.*

*After the death of her husband on July 26, 1863, Mrs. Houston moved with her children to Independence, Texas. During a yellow-fever epidemic in 1867 she volunteered as a nurse, was stricken and died. Her grave is at Independence.[1]*

Cedar Point [Texas]
March 17th 1862

My beloved Mother,

Since Gen'l Houston's return, I have had no spirit to write to any of you, on account of my deep affliction from my dear boy being sent to Missouri. My heart seems almost broken. . . . I left nothing undone that was in my power, to prevent his going, but my weakness gave him an opportunity of displaying traits of character that made his father's heart swell with pride. . . . When I first heard the news, I thought I would lie down and die, but it is strange how life will cling to such a poor emaciated frame as mine. I want one of the girls to write a letter for you and just give me your words. Reprove me as sharply as you please. It will do me good. I deserve it all. I find now that I had really enshrined an idol in my heart. I did not love him more than the rest of my children, but he absorbed all my anxiety, all my hopes and fears. . . . I believe

[1]See *The Raven*, by Marquis James, p. 457 (Indianapolis: The Bobbs-Merrill Company, Inc., 1929).

it is a settled thing now, that Galveston is not to be attacked. I am teaching the little ones at home. They are all learning very well. Beg my Christian friends all to pray for Sam. Tell Bro. Ross, when the sun is setting, it is my custom to pray for those who are near and dear to me, and I want him and his wife to meet me at that time at a throne of grace, and plead for my poor boy.

Gen'l Houston and the children unite with me in love to all the kindred and friends.

> Ever. thy affectionate daughter
> M. L. HOUSTON

## 5. KATE CUMMING—THE AFTERMATH OF SHILOH

*In her childhood Kate Cumming came from Scotland with her family to Mobile, Alabama. When the war started, her brother enlisted in the famous 21st Alabama. Kate, then twenty-eight, espoused the Confederate cause with equal enthusiasm. On the second day of Shiloh she and other women from Mobile who had volunteered for service in the hospital division of the Army of Tennessee left for Corinth, the Confederate base some twelve miles from the battlefield. She carried with her comforts and delicacies of all kinds, provided by the good people of her home town.*

*Kate Cumming's journal is an astute, authoritative account of events and conditions.*

Corinth, Mississippi

April 11 1862. Miss Booth and myself arrived at Corinth to-day. It was raining when we left Mrs. Henderson's, and as her carriage was out of repair, she sent us to the depot in an open wagon. We enjoyed the novel ride, and began to feel that we were in the *service* in reality. My heart beat high with expectation as we neared Corinth. As I had never been where there was a large army, and had never seen a wounded man, except in the cars, as they passed, I could not help feeling a little nervous at the prospect of now seeing both. When within a few miles of the place, we could realize the condition of an army, immediately after a battle. As it had been raining for days, water and mud abounded. Here and there were wagons hopelessly trying to wade through it. As far as the eye could reach, in the midst of all this slop and mud, the white tents of our brave army could be seen through the trees, making a picture suggestive of any thing but comfort. . . .

The crowd of men at the depot was so great that we found it impossible to get to our place of destination by ourselves. Mr. Miller was not there to meet us. I met Mr. George Redwood of Mobile, who kindly offered to pilot us. We found Mr. Miller and all the ladies busy in attending to the wants of those around them. They had not been assigned to any particular place, but there is plenty for them to do. We are at the Tishomingo Hotel, which like every other large building, has been taken for a hospital. The yellow flag is flying from the top of each. Mrs. Ogden tried to prepare me for the scenes which I should witness upon entering the wards. But alas! nothing that I had ever heard or read had given me the faintest idea of the horrors witnessed here. I do not think that words are in our vocabulary expressive enough to present to the mind the realities of that sad scene. Certainly, none of the glories of the war were presented here. But I must not say that; for if uncomplaining endurance is glory, we had plenty of it. If it is that which makes the hero, here they were by scores. Gray-haired men—men in the pride of manhood—beardless boys—Federals and all, mutilated in every imaginable way, lying on the floor, just as they were taken from the battle-field; so close together that it was almost impossible to walk without stepping on them. I could not command my feeling enough to speak, but thoughts crowded upon me. O, if the authors of this cruel and unnatural war could but see what I saw there, they would try and put a stop to it! To think, that it is man who is working all this woe upon his fellowman. What can be in the minds of our enemies, who are now arrayed against us, who have never harmed them in any way, but simply claim our own, and nothing more! May God forgive them, for surely they know not what they do.

This was no time for recrimination; there was work to do; so I went at it to do what I could. If I were to live a hundred years, I should never forget the poor sufferers' gratitude; for every little thing, done for them—a little water to drink, or the bathing of their wounds—seemed to afford them the greatest relief.

The Federal prisoners are receiving the same attention as

our own men; they are lying side by side. Many are just being brought in from the battle-field. The roads are so bad that it is almost impossible to get them moved at all. A great many ladies are below stairs; so I thought that I had better assist them. The first thing which I did was to aid in giving the men their supper, consisting of bread, biscuit, and butter, and tea and coffee without milk. There were neither waiter, nor plates; they took what we gave them in their hands, and were glad to get it. I went with a lady to give some Federal officers their supper, who were in a room by themselves; only one or two of them were wounded. One, a captain from Cincinnati had a broken arm. Before I went in, I thought that I would be polite, and say as little as possible to them; but when I saw them laughing, and apparently indifferent to the woe which they had been instrumental in bringing upon us, I could not help being indignant; and when one of them told me he was from Iowa, and that was generally called out of the world, I told him that was where I wished him, and all like him, so that they might not trouble us any more.

April 12—I sat up all night, bathing the men's wounds, and giving them water. Everyone attending them seemed completely worn out. Some of the doctors told me that they had scarcely slept since the battle. As far as I have seen, the surgeons are very kind to the wounded, and nurse as well as doctor them.

The men are lying all over the house, on their blankets, just as they were brought from the battle-field. They are in the hall, on the gallery, and crowded into very small rooms. The foul air from this mass of human beings at first made me giddy and sick, but I soon got over it. We have to walk, and when we give the man any thing kneel, in blood and water; but we think nothing of it at all. There was much suffering among the patients last night; one old man groaned all the time. He was about sixty years of age, and had lost a leg. He lived near Corinth, and had come there the morning of the battle to see his two sons, who were in the army, and he could not resist shouldering his musket and going into the fight. I comforted him as well as I could. He is a religious man, and prayed nearly all night.

Another, a very young man, was wounded in the leg and through the lungs, had a most excruciating cough, and seemed to suffer awfully. One fine looking man had a dreadful wound in the shoulder. Every time I bathed it he thanked me, and seemed grateful. He died this morning before breakfast. Men who were in the room with him told me that he prayed all night. I trust that he is now at rest, far from this dreary world of strife and bloodshed.

Other ladies have their special patients, whom they never leave. One of them, from Natchez, Miss., has been constantly by a young man, badly wounded, ever since she came here, and the doctors say that she has been the means of saving his life. Many of the others are doing the same. Mrs. Ogden, and the Mobile ladies are below stairs. I have not even time to speak to them. Mr. Miller is doing much good; he is comforting the suffering and dying; and has already baptised some.

This morning when passing the front door, a man asked me if I had any thing to eat, which I could give to some men at the depot awaiting transportation on the cars. He said that they had eaten nothing for some days. Some of the ladies assisted me, we took them hot coffee, bread, and meat. The poor fellows ate eagerly, and seemed so thankful. One of the men, who was taking care of them, asked me where I was from. When I replied Mobile, he said that Mobile was the best place in the Confederacy. He was a member of the Twenty-first Alabama Regiment. I have been busy all day, and can scarcely tell what I have been doing; I had not taken time even to eat, and certainly not time to sit down. There seems to be no order. All do as they please. We have men for nurses, and the doctors complain very much at the manner in which they are appointed; they are detailed from the different regiments, like guards. We have a new set every few hours. I can not see how it is possible for them to take proper care of the men, as nursing is a thing that has to be learned, and we should select our best men for it—the best, not physically, but morally—as I am certain that none but good, conscientious persons will ever do justice to the patients.

Sunday, April 13—Enjoyed a very good night's rest upon some boxes. We all slept below stairs, in the front room—our baggage separating us from the front part of it, which is the clerks' office, and sleeping apartment of some dozen men. It was a laughable sight to see Father Miller fixing some beds for us. Poor man! He tried so hard to make us comfortable. Some slept on shelves. I slept so soundly that I did not even dream, as I was completely worn out with the labor of the day. I could realize how, after a hard days' marching or fighting, a soldier can throw himself upon the ground, and sleep as soundly as if he was on a bed of down. A number of persons arrived last night, looking for their relations. One very pretty lady, with her parents, is in search of her husband, a colonel, who is reported badly wounded. I have since heard that she has found him at a farm-house, and he is much better off than she had been informed. Her mother, on leaving, presented me with some very nice sperm-candles.

I have just seen my brother. He looks rather the "worse for wear." But, thank God, he is safe. This was his first battle, and I have been told that "he was brave to a fault." The company distinguished itself on that eventful day; and Mobile may well be proud of the gallant men who compose it.

I have been told by a friend that the night of the first day's battle he passed by a wounded Federal, who requested him to bring him some water from a spring nearby. On going to it, he was much shocked to see three Federals lying with their heads in it. They had dragged themselves to the spring to slake their thirst, and there they had breathed their last. There is no end to the tales of horror related about the battle-field. They fill me with dismay.

The confusion and want of order are as great as ever. A great many doctors are here, who came with the men from the different regiments. The amount of good done is not near what it might be, if things were better managed. Some one is to blame for this state of affairs. Many say it is the fault of Dr. Foard, the medical director. But I suppose that allowance must be made for the unexpected number of wounded. I trust that in a little time things will be better.

One of the doctors named Little of Alabama, told me to-day that he had left his young wife on his plantation with more than a hundred negroes upon it, and no white man but the overseer. He had told the negroes, before he left, if they desired to leave, they could do so when they pleased. He was certain that not more than one or two would go.

I have conversed with some of the wounded prisoners. One of them, quite a young man, named Nott, is very talkative. He says that he dislikes Lincoln and abolitionism as much as we do; declares that he is fighting to save the Union, and nothing more. All of them say the same thing. What a glorious Union it would be!

Quite a number of bunks arrived today, and we are having the most severely wounded placed on them. I am so glad, as we can have some of the filth taken off the floors. A doctor requested me to go down stairs and see if there was a bunk with a Federal upon it, and if so have him taken off, as he had a badly wounded man that needed one. I went and asked Mrs. Royal, from Mobile, whom I had heard talk very bitterly. She knew of one, but would not tell me where it was. Her true woman's nature showed itself, in spite of her dislike. Seeing an enemy wounded and helpless is a different thing from seeing him in health and in power. The first time that I saw one in this condition every feeling of enmity vanished at once. I was curious to find out who the Federal was, and, as Mrs. R. would not tell me, I went in search of him. I found him with but little trouble; went to the men who were upon the bunks, and asked them where they were from. One, quite a youth, with a childish face, told me he was from Illinois. I knew in a moment that he was the one. I asked him about his Mother, and why he had ever left. Tears filled his eyes, and his lips quivered so that he was unable to speak. I was deeply moved myself, spoke a few words of comfort, and left him. I would not have had him give up his bunk for the world. Poor child! there will be a terrible day of reckoning for those who sent you on your errand, and who are the cause of desolating so many hearts and homes.

As I was passing one of the rooms, a man called me, and begged me to do something for him and others who were with him. No one had been to see them that morning, and they had had no breakfast. I gave them something to eat, and got a nurse to take care of them. About eight were in the room, among them Mr. Regan of Alabama and Mr. Eli Wasson of Texas, both of whom had lost a leg. I paid these special attention as they were worse than the others. They were very grateful, and thanked me all the time. Mr. W. said that he knew that he would get well now. They are both unmarried, and talk much of their mothers and sisters, as all men do now. "Home, sweet home," is the dearest spot on earth to them, since they are deprived of its comforts. Mother, wife, and sister seem to be sweeter to them than any words in the English language.

We eat in the kitchen, surgeons and all. It is not the cleanest place in the world, and I think, to use a Scotch phrase, would make even Mrs. McClarty "think shame." Hunger is a good antidote for even dirt. I am aware that few will think so except those who have tried it.

April 15.—Enjoyed a very good night's rest in a crowded room. Had part of a mattress upon the floor, but so many were upon it that for half of the night I was under a table.

My patients are doing well. My own health is excellent. While I was down stairs this morning a gentleman requested me to give him something to eat for some fifty or sixty wounded men whom he had in his care. He had nothing for them, but was expecting something from his home in Tennessee. It would be some days before he could get it. Mrs. Ogden gave him what she could. He informed us that his name was Cannon; that he was a doctor and a clergyman of the Episcopal Church. He said that if our men were not better treated than at the present time, it would be the means of demoralizing them more than the enemy's cannon balls.

Mr. Wasson is cheerful, and is doing well; tells me much about his home in Texas and the nice fruit there; says that I must go home with him, as his family would be so glad to see me.

Mrs. Lyons is sitting up day, and night, attending to some eight or nine patients. One of them is shot in the face, and has it covered with a cloth, as it is so lacerated that it presents a most revolting aspect. Mrs. L. is also taking care of some prisoners. There is a Federal surgeon named Young waiting on them. I have been told that Dr. Lyle, one of our surgeons, refused to attend them, as he had just lost two brothers in the war, and has heard that his father is a prisoner. His feelings are such that he is fearful he might not do justice to the sufferers. If there were no other surgeons here, he would endeavor to do his duty by them.

April 16.—Mrs. Miller, Mrs. Ogden, and nearly all the ladies from Mobile left for Columbus, Miss. I remained, with Mrs. Glassburn, from Natchez. My brother is here, and I have become so much interested in some of the wounded that I could not leave them. Mrs. Ogden was completely worn out; and it is not much to be wondered at, as she, with the rest of us, has had to sleep in any and every place; and as to making our toilet, that was out of the question. I have not undressed since I came here.

I dislike very much to see some of the ladies go, as they have been very kind to the sufferers, and I know that they will miss them very much. They go to Columbus, Miss., where are a great many of the wounded. I daily witness the same sad scenes—men dying all around me. I do not know who they are, nor have I time to learn.

April 17.—I was going round as usual this morning, washing the faces of the men, and had got half through with one before I found out that he was dead. He was lying on the gallery by himself, and had died with no one near him. These are terrible things. . . . I thought that my patients were all doing well. Mr. Wasson felt better, and knew that he would soon go home. I asked the surgeon who was attending him about his condition, and was much shocked when I learned that neither he nor Mr. Regan would live to see another day. This was a sad trial to me. I had seen many die, but none of them whom I had attended so closely as these two. I felt toward them as I do toward all the soldiers—as if they were my brothers. I tried to control my feelings before Mr. W., as he was so hopeful of getting well, but it was a hard task. He looked at me once and asked me what was the matter; was he going to die? I asked him if he was afraid. He replied no; but he was so young that he would like to live a little longer, and would like to see his mother and father once more. . . . I could not muster courage to tell him that he was going to die. Poor Mr. Regan was wandering in his mind. I managed to get him to tell me of his mother's address. He belonged to the Twenty-second Alabama Regiment. . . .

April 18.—I remained with Mr. Wasson all night. A child could not have been more composed. . . . About 4 o'clock A.M. he insisted that I should leave him, as I required rest. He begged so hard that I left him for a little while. When I returned he had breathed his last. One of his companions was with him, and was very attentive—told me that he died as if he was going to sleep. . . .

Mr. Regan died this morning; was out of his mind to the last. . . .

Mrs. Lyons left this morning for home. She was very sick;

and one of the doctors informed her, if she did not leave immediately, she would certainly die. I know the men whom she has been nursing will miss her very much, as she has been so attentive to them.

Dr. Smith has taken charge of this hospital. I think that there will be a different order of things now. He is having the house and yard well cleaned. Before this, it was common to have amputated limbs thrown into the yard, and left there.

Mrs. Glassburn and myself started to go to College Hospital, when we met the doctor who spoke to my patient last night, and he went with us. His name is Hughes—is from Lexington, Ky. The walk was very pleasant. Met a general and his staff. The doctor thought it was General Polk[1]—our bishop-general, as he is called. We called at a shed on the way; found it filled with wounded, lying on the floor; some men attending them. All were in the best of spirits. Mrs. G. promised to send them some of our good things. When we arrived at the hospital, we were charmed with the cleanliness and neatness visible on every side. The Sisters of Charity have charge of the domestic part, and, as usual with them, everything is *parfait*. We were received very kindly by them. One was a friend of Mrs. G. She took us through the hospital. The grounds are very neatly laid out. Before the war it was a female college. I saw, as his mother requested, Mr. John Lyons, who is sick; he is a member of Ketchum's Battery. The wounded seem to be doing well. One of the surgeons complained bitterly of the bad management of the railroad, and said that its managers should be punished, as they were the cause of a great deal of unnecessary suffering. They take their own time to transport the wounded, and it is impossible to depend upon them. That is the reason why we see so many sick men lying around the depot. Crossing the depot upon our return, we saw a whole Mississippi regiment sick, awaiting transportation. They looked very badly, and nearly all had a cough. . . .

April 22.—All the patients are being sent away on account of the prospects of a battle; at least, those who are able to be moved.

[1] Leonidas Polk, Bishop of Louisiana and major-general, C. S. A., had been called in with his garrison from Columbus, Ky., to General A. S. Johnston's concentration before Shiloh and fought bravely there.

We have had a good deal of cold, wet weather lately. This is the cause of much sickness. Dr. Hereford, chief surgeon of Ruggles'[1] brigade, has just informed me, that nearly our whole army is sick, and if it were not that the Federals are nearly as bad off as ourselves, they could annihilate us with ease. . . .

Everyone is talking of the impending battle with the greatest indifference. It is strange how soon we become accustomed to all things; and I suppose it is well, as it will do no good to worry about it. Let us do our duty, and leave the rest to God.

April 23.—A young man whom I have been attending is going to have his arm cut off. Poor fellow! I am doing all I can to cheer him. He says that he knows that he will die, as all who have had limbs amputated in this hospital have died. It is said that the reason is that none but the very worst cases are left here, and they are too far gone to survive the shock which the operation gives the frame. The doctors seem to think that the enemy poisoned their musket balls, as the wounds inflame terribly. Our men do not seem to stand half so much as the Northerners. Many of the doctors are quite despondent about it, and think that our men will not be able to endure the hardships of camp-life, and that we may have to succumb on account of it, but I trust that they are mistaken. None of the prisoners have died; this is a fact that can not be denied; but we have had very few of them in comparison with the number of our own men.

April 24.—Mr. Isaac Fuquet, the young man who had his arm cut off, died to-day. He lived only a few hours after his amputation. . . .

It is reported that an engagement is going on at Monterey. A wounded man has just been brought in.

The amputating table for this ward is at the end of the hall, near the landing of the stairs. When an operation is to be performed, I keep as far away from it as possible. To-day, just as they had got through with Mr. Fuquet, I was compelled to pass the place, and the sight I there beheld made me shudder and sick at heart. A stream of blood ran from the table into a tub in which was the arm. It had been taken off at the socket,

[1]Brigadier-General Daniel Ruggles of Louisiana.

and the hand, which but a short time before grasped the musket and battled for the right, was hanging over the edge of the tub, a lifeless thing. . . .

## 6. BETTY HERNDON MAURY—ABRAHAM LINCOLN WAS IN FREDERICKSBURG

*Betty was in Fredericksburg when Confederate forces evacuated the town in the early spring of 1862. With her were little Nannie Belle, her sister Sally and her mother. Will was in Richmond, and so was Betty's father Commodore Maury, now heading the Confederate naval laboratories. Betty longed to be with them. She didn't like Will's leaving her to the oncoming Yankees one bit. Her brothers Johnny and Dick were with their regiments in the field. A cousin, Ellen Herndon, had married Chester A. Arthur, inspector-general and quartermaster-general of New York troops, and so was in disgrace with the family. The young Yankee officer whom Betty met on the street with exclamation points of scorn was to be President of the United States from 1881 to 1885.*

Fredericksburg, Virginia
Good Fri. April 18—62

While we were dressing, we saw great columns of smoke rising from the river and soon learned that the enemy were in strong force, that our troops had retreated to this side of the river and fired the bridges.

I went down to the river and shall never forget the scene there. Above were our three bridges all in light blaze from one end to the other and every few minutes the beams and timbers would splash into the water with a great noise. Below were two large steamboats, the *Virginia* and the *Nicholas*, and ten or twelve vessels all wrapt in flames. There were two or three rafts dodging in between the burning vessels containing families coming over to this side with their negroes and horses.

The streets have been filled with waggons and drays and men and women in carriages and buggies leaving the town. But all have gone now and the streets are deserted. The stars and stripes are floating in Falmouth about five miles North.

Some say the enemy is eight and some say ten thousand
strong. . . .

No cars came up this morning of course. It will be dreadful
to be cut off from all tidings of those that are nearest and
dearest to us. . . .

### Easter Sunday April 20

. . . We can see the Yankees and their tents across the river. They received a reinforcement of ten thousand last night.
One can scarcely realize that the enemy is so near and that we
are in their hands. I heard the Yankees this evening with their
full brass band playing "Yankee Doodle" and "The Star Spangled Banner." I could not realize that they were enemies and
invaders. The old tunes brought back recollections of the old
love for them. It was a sad and painful feeling.

### Friday April 25th 1862

Five steamboats and twenty canal boats came up here this
evening. We suppose the canal boats are to make a bridge of.

The negroes are going off in great numbers and are beginning to be very independent and impudent. We hear that our
three are going soon. I am afraid of the lawless Yankee soldiers, but that is nothing to my fear of the negroes if they
should rise against us.

Nanny came back yesterday. She left Farley Vale with Mr.
Corbin on Friday and went to Richmond. Papa and Mr. Cor-
bin induced her to come back here and stay with Mamma. Mr.
Corbin had been ordered to Norfolk. His arm is still in a sling.

Ten of Mr. Corbin's servants ran off last Friday. The farm,
servants, stock, and all are now in the hands of the enemy.

### Wed. April 30th

Went down yesterday evening to see the bridge of canal
boats that the Yankees are building at the lower wharf. The
boats are laid close together side by side. The length of the
boat being the width of the bridge. Eight boats are in place
and it already reaches more than half way across the river.
The soldiers on the bridge and the surrounding boats were
shouting and talking to the colored men and women on the
wharf. There are several artillery companies stationed on the
hill above the bridge to protect it.

May 1st. 1862

Just before dusk, as we were all seated around the fire in Mamma's room, we heard a light tap at the door, and in walked Johnny, my dear brother Johnny. Cousin Dabney has applied for him as his aide de camp. He expects to start for the West in a day or two—and came to tell us good bye. He looks so handsome. It was a precious visit but at such a risk. The enemy have had guards out for the last few days in search of stragglers. He came in with five others, but they stopped on the outskirts of town. One can realize what the enemy is and how near he is, when our own dear ones are in danger of their lives when they come to their *homes* and have to hide around corners and steal away after dark like guilty wretches.

Sunday May 4, 1862

Gov. Seward, Secretary Stanton[1] and two or three Senators were in town yesterday evening with several Generals. McDowell among the number. The enemy are building a second pontoon bridge above the old Chatham bridge.

General Van Rennselaer was at church today. He sat in the Mayor's pew and the Mayor sat in the gallery.

Mr. Randolph has omitted the prayer for our President and for the success of our cause ever since the enemy have been here. Papa and Will say that such time serving is unworthy of the place and the people. I think there is something to be said on both sides.

Received letters yesterday. Johnny has gotten back safe. . . .

Tuesday May 13th, 1862

. . . I am much struck by the superior discipline of these Yankee soldiers over ours. I have not seen a drunken man since they have been here. They are much healthier too and are not coughing constantly during drill as our Dixie boys used to do.

[1]William H. Seward, Lincoln's Secretary of State, had been Governor of New York. Edwin M. Stanton of Pennsylvania had succeeded Simon Cameron of the same state as Secretary of War on January 15, 1862.

Friday May 16th, 1862

Matters are getting worse and worse here every day with regard to the negroes. They are leaving their owners by the
hundreds and demanding wages. The citizens have refused to
hire their own or other peoples slaves, so that there are numbers of unemployed negroes in town. Old Doctor Hall agreed
to hire his servants, but the gentlemen of the town held a
meeting and wrote him a letter of remonstrance telling him
that he was establishing a most dangerous precedent, that he
was breaking the laws of Virginia and was a traitor of his
state. So the old man refused to hire them and they all left
him. Ours have gone except one girl about 15—Nanny's Molly. We clean up and take it by turns to assist and direct the
cooking. It is a great relief to get rid of the others. They were
so insolent and idle, and Jinny was a dangerous character. She
*boasted* that she had brought the soldiers here to get the
swords and threatened to tell that our name was Maury and
that we brought things here from the Observatory.

Sat. May 17th, 1862

General!!! Arthur, Ellen Herndon's husband, was in town
yesterday. I met him in the street, but did not speak to him. I
could not shake hands with a man who came as an invader to
desolate our homes and kill our brothers and husbands. Besides the soldiers, there are many Yankee citizens and Dutchmen in town.

Sun. May 18th, 1862

This afternoon we saw a Confederate officer on horseback
blindfolded, led by a mounted Federal officer and surrounded
by a guard on his way to headquarters. He came under a flag-
of-truce. We cannot hear what for. It was so refreshing to see
him and to see our gray uniform again. Mamma wanted to say
"God Bless you," but was afraid to venture.

Thursday May 22, 1862

Received a long letter from my dear husband yesterday of
the 14th telling me of Tom's safe arrival in Richmond and of
his adventures while in the enemy's lines. After the battle of
Williamsburg Tom went with several other surgeons, under a
flag of truce to attend to our wounded that had fallen into the

enemy's hands. He was treated with great courtesy and took several juleps with General McClelland who sent his love to cousin Dabney Maury. A Yankee General (Hancock)[1] told Tom that immortality ought to be inscribed upon the banners of the 24th (Dick's) and the 5th North Carolina for their great bravery in that charge at Williamsburg.

Nannie Belle was playing on the pavement yesterday evening when a soldier accosted her and asked if she would not go down the street with him and let him buy her some candy. She replied "No I thank you, Yankee candy would choke me." He seemed much amused.

Sunday, May 25th, 1862

Abraham Lincoln was in town on Friday. Our Mayor did not call on him and I did not hear a cheer as he passed along the streets. The streets are full of wagons and soldiers. A large portion of the army advanced towards Richmond this afternoon. They came over different bridges and advanced over different streets. The Yankees are building their fifth bridge across the Rappahannock. . . .

## 7. SARAH MORGAN—ENEMY SHIPS PASS THE FORTS BELOW NEW ORLEANS

*Sarah, one of Judge Thomas Gibbes Morgan's nine children, was born in Baton Rouge, in 1841. Her father died in '61. Of her several brothers: Henry was killed in a duel in the early days of secession. Philip, a judge in New Orleans, adhered to the Union. Thomas Gibbes, Jr., married Lydia, daughter of General A. G. Carter and a cousin of Mrs. Jefferson Davis; he was a captain in the 7th Louisiana, serving under Stonewall Jackson. George was a captain in the 1st Louisiana, also with Stonewall. He and Gibbes lost their lives in '64. James, the youngest, resigned from Annapolis and hurried home to enlist in the Confederate Navy.*

*Sarah began her diary on March 9, 1862. When she wrote*

[1] Winfield S. Hancock, brigade commander in McClellan's army.

*the following entry her sister Eliza or "Lilly"—wife of J.
Charles La Noue—with her five children was with Sarah in
Baton Rouge. Miriam was the other sister.*

Baton Rouge, Louisiana
April 26th, 1862

There is no word in the English language that can express
the state in which we are, and have been, these last three days.
Day before yesterday, news came early in the morning of
three of the enemy's boats passing the Forts, and then the excitement began. It increased rapidly on hearing of the sinking
of eight of our gunboats in the engagement, the capture of the
Forts, and last night, of the burning of the wharves and cotton
in the city [New Orleans] while the Yankees were taking possession. To-day, the excitement has reached the point of deliri-
um. I believe I am one of the most self-possessed in my small
circle; and yet I feel such a craving for news of Miriam, and
mother, and Jimmy, who are in the city, that I suppose I am
as wild as the rest. Nothing can be positively ascertained, save
that our gunboats are sunk, and theirs are coming up to the
city. Everything else has been contradicted until we really do
not know whether the city has been taken or not. We only
know we had best be prepared for anything. So day before
yesterday, Lilly and I sewed up our jewelry, which may be of
use if we have to fly. I vow I will not move one step, unless
carried away. Come what will, here I remain.

We went this morning to see the cotton burning—a sight
never before witnessed, and probably never again to be seen.
Wagons, drays,—everything that can be driven or rolled,—
were loaded with the bales and taken a few squares back to
burn on the commons. Negroes were running around, cutting
them open, piling them up, and setting them afire. All were as
busy as though their salvation depended on disappointing the
Yankees. Later, Charlie sent for us to come to the river and
see him fire a flatboat loaded with the precious material for
which the Yankees are risking their bodies and souls. Up and
down the levee, as far as we could see, negroes were rolling it
down to the brink of of the river where they would set them
afire and push the bales in to float burning down the tide.
Each sent up its wreath of smoke and looked like a tiny steamer puffing away. Only I doubt that from the source to the
mouth of the river there are as many boats afloat on the Mis-

sissippi. The flatboat was piled with as many bales as it could hold without sinking. Most of them were cut open, while negroes staved in the heads of barrels of alcohol, whiskey, etc., and dashed bucketsful over the cotton. Others built up little chimneys of pine every few feet, lined with pine knots and loose cotton, to burn more quickly. There, piled the length of the whole levee, or burning in the river, lay the work of thousands of negroes for more than a year past. It had come from every side. Men stood by who owned the cotton that was burning or waiting to burn. They either helped, or looked on cheerfully. Charlie owned but sixteen bales—a matter of some fifteen hundred dollars; but he was the head man of the whole affair, and burned his own, as well as the property of others. A single barrel of whiskey that was thrown on the cotton, cost the man who gave it one hundred and twenty-five dollars. (It shows what a nation in earnest is capable of doing.) Only two men got on the flatboat with Charlie when it was ready. It was towed to the middle of the river, set afire in every place, and then they jumped into a little skiff fastened in front, and rowed to land. The cotton floated down the Mississippi one sheet of living flame, even in the sunlight. It would have been grand at night. But then we will have fun watching it this evening anyway; for they cannot get through to-day, though no time is to be lost.

Hundreds of bales remained untouched. An incredible amount of property has been destroyed to-day; but no one begrudges it. Every grog-shop has been emptied, and gutters and pavements are floating with liquors of all kinds. So that if the Yankees are fond of strong drink, they will fare ill. . . .

### April 27th

What a day! Last night came a dispatch that New Orleans was under British protection, and could not be bombarded; consequently, the enemy's gun-boats would probably be here this morning, such few as had succeeded in passing the Forts; from nine to fifteen, it was said. And the Forts, they said, had *not* surrendered. I went to church; but I grew very anxious before it was over, feeling that I was needed at home. When I returned, I found Lilly wild with excitement, picking up hastily whatever came to hand, preparing for instant flight, she knew not where. The Yankees were in sight; the town was to be burned; we were to run to the woods, etc. If the house had to

be burned, I had to make up my mind to run, too. So my
treasure-bag tied around my waist as a bustle, a sack with a
few necessary articles hanging on my arm, some few unnecessary ones, too, as I had not the heart to leave the old and new
prayer books father had given me, and Miriam's, too;—pistol
and carving-knife ready, I stood awaiting the exodus. I heaped
on the bed the treasures I wanted to burn, matches lying ready
to fire the whole at the last minute. . . . People fortunately
changed their minds about the *auto-da-fé* just then; and the
Yankees have not yet arrived, at sundown. So, when the excitement calmed down, poor Lilly tumbled in bed in a high fever in consequence of terror and exertion.

## 8. JULIA LeGRAND—NEW ORLEANS HAS FALLEN

"The Journal of Julia LeGrand," *wrote Dr. Freeman in
his delightful book* The South to Posterity,[1] *"was kept by a
woman of thirty-two who embodied all the elements of romance that an early Victorian novelist would have desired for a
heroine." Her grandfather, of the* petite noblesse, *had come to
Maryland not long before the French Revolution. Her father,
educated in France, a wealthy planter in Maryland, bought a
large estate in Louisiana and moved his family there when
Julia was a child. He surrounded his daughters Julia and Virginia—Ginnie—with every luxury. He would take them with a
staff of servants to the St. Charles in New Orleans for the opera season, and in summer to the Virginia springs. A contem-
porary portrait of Julia reveals a lovely girl in a long white
gown, a big dog at her side. She played the harp and was "full
of romantic fancies." A lover, too poor to press his suit, was
killed in a wagon train somewhere in the west of Mexico, pre-
sumably by Indians. Julia made him the hero, under the name
of Guy Fontenoy, of an unpublished novel.*

*Colonel LeGrand lost all his money and all his estate. When
he died the destitute girls sought a modest competence by
keeping a "select school for girls" in New Orleans. Their only
brother, Claude, left them there when he went off to Virginia*

[1]Charles Scribner's Sons, New York, 1939, 1951.

*with the first Louisiana volunteers. There they stayed until a few months after the city was occupied. Julia refused to take the oath of allegiance, "but," she wrote, "how can an outsider ever know what a temptation it was to take that oath?" They became refugees—in various parts of Louisiana, in Mississippi, Georgia and Alabama—and nursed the sick and wounded of Joe Johnston's army. Their journeys ended in Galveston, Texas, where in 1867 Julia married a young German, Adolph Waitz, "a gentleman of fine ability and attainments."*

*Her diary was written without expectation of publication. Much of it was destroyed. What survives covers succinctly the period from December 1861 through December 1862 and fully the early spring season of 1863. It ends abruptly in the middle of a sentence.*

*All the details of her life, as Dr. Freeman says, would make the reader expect a slushy, sentimental diary—"which is distinctly what it is not. It is an intelligent, direct and honest narrative . . . the story of neighbors' woes, of personal hardship stoically endured . . . of hopes raised one day and dashed the next by reading the newspapers."*

*New Orleans, May 9th, 1862.* . . . Lovell,[1] a most worthless creature, was sent here by Davis to superintend the defense of this city. He did little or nothing and the little he did was all wrong. Duncan,[2] the really gallant defender of Fort Jackson, could get nothing that he needed, though he continually applied to Lovell. Only a few guns at the fort worked at all, but these were gallantly used for the defense of the city. The fort is uninjured and could have held out till our great ram, the *Mississippi*, was finished, but a traitor sent word to the commander of the Federal fleet to hasten, which he did, and our big gun, our only hope, was burned before our eyes to prevent her from falling into Federal hands. First and last then, this city, the most important one in the Confederacy, has fallen, and Yankee troops are drilling and parading in our streets. Poor New Orleans! What has become of all your promised greatness! In looking through an old trunk, I came across a letter to my father from my Uncle Thomas, in which,

[1]Major-General Mansfield Lovell.
[2]General J. K. Duncan.

as far back as 1836, he prophesied a noble future for you. What would he say now to see you dismantled and lying low under the heel of the invader!

Behold, what has now come to the city! Never can I forget the day that the alarm bell rang. I never felt so hopeless and forsaken. The wretched generals, left here with our troops, ran away and left them. Lovell knew not what to do; some say he was intoxicated, some say frightened. Of course the greatest confusion prevailed, and every hour, indeed almost every moment, brought its dreadful rumor. After it was known that the gunboats had actually passed, the whole city, both camp and street, was a scene of wild confusion. *The women only* did not seem afraid. They were all in favor of resistance, *no matter how hopeless* that resistance might be.

The second day matters wore a more favorable aspect, and the Mayor and the City Council assumed a dignified position toward the enemy. Flag Officer [David] Farragut demanded the unconditional surrender of the town. He was told that as brute force, and brute force only, gave him the power that he might come and take it. He then demanded that we, with our own hands, pull down the flag of Louisiana. This I am happy to say, was refused.

Four days we waited, expecting to be shelled, but he concluded to waive the point; so he marched in his marines with two cannons and our flag was taken down and the old stars and stripes lifted in a dead silence. We made a great mistake here; we should have shot the man that brought down the flag,[1] and as long as there was a house-top in the city left, it should have been hoisted. The French and English lay in the Gulf and a French frigate came up the river to protect French subjects.

Farragut allowed the women and children but forty-eight hours to leave the city, but the foreign consuls demanded a much longer time to move the people of their respective nations. If we had been staunch and dared them to shell, the Confederacy would have been saved. The brutal threat would

---

[1]As a matter of fact, a man named William B. Mumford did tear down the flag that was raised over the U. S. Mint. Governor Ben Butler had him hanged for it, and perhaps nothing except his famous—or infamous—"women's order" contributed so much to "Beast" Butler's ill fame in New Orleans and throughout the South.

never have been carried out, for England and France would never have allowed it. The delay would have enabled us to finish our boat, and besides a resistance would have showed the enemy and foreign nations too, what stuff we were made of and how very much we were in earnest. I never wished anything so much in my life as for resistance here. I felt no fear —only excitement.

The ladies of the town signed a paper, praying that it should never be given up. We went down to put our names on the list, and met the marines marching up to the City Hall with their cannon in front of them. The blood boiled in my veins—I felt no fear—only anger. I forgot myself and called out several times: "Gentlemen, don't let the State Flag come down," and, "Oh, how can you men stand it?" Mrs. Norton was afraid of me, I believe, for she hurried me off.

I have forgotten to mention—at first, the Germans at the fort mutinied and turned their guns on their officers. In the first place, several gunboats had passed the fort at night because a traitor had failed to give the signal. He was tried and shot, and Duncan telegraphed to the city that no more should pass—then came a report that the Yankee vessels were out of powder and coal and they could not get back to their transports which they had expected to follow them. We were quite jubilant at the idea of keeping them in a sort of imprisonment, and this we could have done but for the German mutineers. The wives of these men were allowed to visit the fort, and they represented the uselessness of the struggle, because the city had already surrendered. They were told, too, that Duncan intended to blow up the fort over their heads rather than surrender. So they spiked their cannon and threatened the lives of their officers and then the Yankee fleet poured up.

These people have complimented us highly. To quell a small "rebellion," they have made preparations enough to conquer a world. This is a most cowardly struggle—these people can do nothing without gunboats. Beauregard in Tennessee can get no battle from them where they are protected by these huge block steamers. These passive instruments do their fighting for them. It is at best a dastardly way to fight. We should have had gunboats if the Government had been efficient, wise or earnest.

We have lost our city, the key to this great valley, and my opinion is that we will never, never get it more, except by treaty. Many think otherwise.

The most tantalizing rumors reach us daily (though the papers are not allowed to print *our* news, we hear it). We have heard that Stonewall Jackson has surprised and taken Washington City; that Beauregard has had a splendid victory in Tennessee; and our other generals have annihilated the enemy in Virginia. Sometimes we are elated, but most generally depressed. . . .

This is a cruel war. These people are treated with the greatest haughtiness by the upper classes and rudeness by the lower. They know how they are hated and hang their heads. Shopkeepers refuse to sell to them, and the traitor who hurried them up the river has to have guard. Public buildings have been seized by the troops, but so far the civil government has not been interfered with. I think their plan is to conciliate if possible. The cotton and sugar have been burned; that is one comfort, and the work of destruction still goes on on the plantations. I shall never forget the long, dreadful night when we sat with our friends and watched the flames from all sorts of valuables as the gunboats were coming up the river. . . .

I am told that a stand will be made at Vicksburg. They are working hard at batteries there. They will at least delay the gun-boats until we can do something that we wish. About their having the whole river, that is of course only a question of time. Fort Pillow will fall, if it has not already done so. Our only hope now is from our soldiers in the field, and this brings me to my dear brother again and all he will have to endure. Sometimes I feel that nothing is worth such sacrifice. These States may divide and fight one another, too, sometime. This war has shaken my faith. Nothing is secure if the passions and follies of men can intermeddle. Often, though, I feel that these insolent invaders with their bragging, should be conquered—come what will. Better to die than to be under their rule.

The Yankees have established strict quarantine. The people of the town are frightening them terribly with tales about the yellow fever. We are compelled to laugh at the frequent amusing accounts we hear of the way in which they are treated by boys, Irish women, and the lower classes generally. Mr. Soulé[1] refused General Butler's hand (they were old friends), remarking that their intercourse must now be purely official. Our

---

[1] The Hon. Pierre Soulé, a leading citizen and member of the Committee of Safety.

Mayor[1] has behaved with great dignity. Butler says he will be revenged for the treatment he and his troops have received here—so he will, I expect, if matters go against us in other places. There is some fear that the city will need provisions very much. The country people won't send in anything; they are so angry about the surrender. The Texas drovers who were almost here as soon as they heard of it, sold their cattle for little or nothing just where they were and went home again. I wish we were all safe back there again. I don't think Texas will ever be conquered

## 9. SARAH MORGAN—THE ENEMY COMES
### TO BATON ROUGE

*Sarah gave as a reason for keeping a diary "I had to find some vent for my feelings, and I would not make an exhibition of myself by talking, as so many women did." She turned to this outlet when Baton Rouge was occupied. She had the pen of a ready and accustomed writer and more and more disclosed her independence of judgment. Naturally these qualities were suspended at this time by the strength of her feeling, which led her into some extravagances of expression. But it was just as well that the carving knife had been abandoned.*

Baton Rouge, Louisiana
May 9th 1862

Our lawful (?) owners have at last arrived. About sunset day before yesterday, the *Iroquois* anchored here, and a graceful young Federal stepped ashore, carrying a Yankee flag over his shoulder, and asked the way to the Mayor's office. I like the style! If we girls of Baton Rouge had been at the landing, instead of the men, that Yankee would never have insulted us by flying his flag in our faces! *We* would have opposed his landing except under a flag of truce; but the men let him alone, and he even found a poor Dutchman willing to show him the road!

He did not accomplish much; said a formal demand would be made next day, and asked if it was safe for the men to

[1] John T. Monroe.

come ashore and buy a few necessaries, when he was assured
the air of Baton Rouge was very unhealthy for Yankee soldiers at night. He promised very magnanimously not to shell
us out if we did not molest him; but I notice none of them
dare set their feet on *terra firma,* except the officer who has
now called three times on the Mayor, and who is said to tremble visibly as he walks the streets.

Last evening came the demand: the town must be surrendered immediately; the Federal flag Must be raised; they
would grant us the same terms they granted New Orleans. Jol-
ly terms those were! The answer was worthy of a Southerner.
It was, "The town was defenseless; if we had cannon, there
were not men enough to resist; but if forty vessels lay at the
landing,—it was intimated we were in their power, and more
ships coming up,—we would not surrender; if they wanted,
they might come and Take us; if they wished the Federal flag
hoisted over the Arsenal, they might put it up for themselves,
the town had no control over Government property." Glorious! What a pity they did not shell the town! But they are
taking us at our word, and this morning they are landing at
the Garrison.

"All devices, signs, and flags of the Confederacy shall
be suppressed." So says Picayune Butler. *Good.* I de-
vote all my red, white, and blue silk to the manufacture of
Confederate flags. As soon as one is confiscated, I make another, until my ribbon is exhausted, when I will sport a duster
emblazoned in high colors. "Hurra! for the Bonny blue flag!"
Henceforth, I wear one pinned to my bosom—not as duster, but
a little flag; the the man who says take it off will have to pull it
off for himself; the man who dare attempt it—well! a pistol in
my pocket fills up the gap. I am capable, too. . . .

May 10th

Last night about one o'clock I was wakened and told that
mother and Miriam had come. Oh, how glad I was! I tumbled
out of bed half asleep and hugged Miriam in a dream, but
waked up when I got to mother. They came up under a flag of
truce, on a boat going up for provisions, which, by the way,
was brought to by half a dozen Yankee ships in succession,
with a threat to send a broadside into her if she did not stop
—the wretches knew it *must* be under a flag of truce; no boats
leave, except by special order to procure provisions.

What tales they had to tell! They were on the wharf, and saw the ships sail up the river, saw the broadside fired into Will Pinckney's regiment, the boats we fired, our gunboats, floating down to meet them all wrapped in flames; twenty thousand bales of cotton blazing in a single pile; molasses and sugar thrown over everything. They stood there opposite to where one of the ships landed, expecting a broadside, and resolute not to be shot in the back. I wish I had been there! And Captain Huger[1] is not dead! They had hopes of his life for the first time day before yesterday. Miriam saw the ball that had just been extracted. He will probably be lame for the rest of his life. It will be a glory to him. For even the Federal officers say that never did they see so gallant a little ship, or one that fought so desperately as the *McRae*. Men and officers fought like devils. Think of all those great leviathans after the poor little "Widow Mickey"! One came tearing down on her sideways, while the *Brooklyn* fired on her from the other side, when brave Captain Warley[2] put the nose of the *Manassas* under the first, and tilted her over so that the whole broadside passed, instead of through, the *McRae*, who spit back its poor little fire at both. And after all was lost, she carried the wounded and the prisoners to New Orleans, and was scuttled by her own men in port. Glorious Captain Huger! Brave, dare-devil Captain Warley is prisoner, and on the way to Fort Warren, that home of all brave, patriotic men. We'll have him out. . . .

And this is WAR! Heaven save me from like scenes and experiences again. I was wild with excitement last night when Miriam described how the soldiers, marching to the depot, waved their hats to the crowds of women and children, shouting, "God bless you, ladies! We will fight for you!" and they, waving their handkerchiefs, sobbed with one voice, "God bless you, Soldiers! Fight for us!"

We, too, have been having our fun. Early in the evening, four more gunboats sailed up here. We saw them from the corner, three squares off, crowded with men even up in rig-

---

[1] Thomas B. Huger, in command of the Confederate steamer *McRae*, was mortally wounded by fire from the U. S. S. *Iroquois*.

[2] Alex F. Worley fought his Confederate ram *Manassas* until she was helpless, then drove her into the swamp and abandoned her.

gings. The American flag was flying from every peak. It was received in profound silence, by the hundreds gathered on the banks. I could hardly refrain from a groan. Much as I once loved that flag, I hate it now! I came back and made myself a Confederate flag about five inches long, slipped the staff in my belt, pinned the flag to my shoulder, and walked downtown, to the consternation of women and children, who expected something awful to follow. An old negro cried, "My young missus got her flag flyin,' anyhow!" Nettie[1] made one and hid it in the folds of her dress. But we were the only two who ventured. We went to the State House terrace, and took a good look at the *Brooklyn*[2] which was crowded with people, who took a good look at us, likewise. . . .

*May 11th*

I—I am disgusted with myself. Last evening, I went to Mrs. Brunot's,[1] without an idea of going beyond, with my flag flying again. They were all going to the State House, so I went with them; to my distress, some fifteen or twenty Federal officers were standing on the first terrace, stared at like wild beasts by the curious crowd. I had not expected to meet them, and felt a painful conviction that I was unnecessarily attracting attention, by an unladylike display of defiance, from the crowd gathered there. But what was I to do? I felt humiliated, conspicuous, everything that is painful and disagreeable; but —strike my colors in the face of the enemy? Never! Nettie and Sophie[1] had them, too, but that was no consolation for the shame I suffered by such a display so totally distasteful to me. How I wished myself away, and chafed at my folly, and hated myself for being there, and every one for seeing me. I hope it will be a lesson to me always to remember a lady can gain nothing by such display.

I was not ashamed of the flag of my country,—I proved that by never attempting to remove it in spite of my mortification,—but I was ashamed of my position; for these are evidently gentlemen, not the Billy Wilson's crew we were threatened with. Fine, noble-looking men they were, showing refinement and gentlemanly bearing in every motion. One cannot

[1] Nettie, Sophie and Mrs. Brunot were neighbors.
[2] One of Farragut's frigates. Opposite the forts the *Manassas* had torn a great hole in her side.

help but admire such foes! They come as visitors without either pretensions to superiority, or the insolence of conquerors; they walk quietly their way, offering no annoyance to the citizens, though they themselves are stared at most unmercifully, and pursued by crowds of ragged little boys, while even men gape at them with open mouths. I came home wonderfully changed in all my newly acquired sentiments, resolved never more to wound their feelings, who were so careful of ours, by such unnecessary display. And I hung my flag on the parlor mantel, there to wave, if it will, in the shades of private life; but to make a show, make me conspicuous and ill at ease, as I was yesterday,—never again!

There was a dozen officers in church this morning, and the psalms for the 11th day seemed so singularly appropriate to the feelings of the people, that I felt uncomfortable for them. They answered with us, though.

*May 17th*

Four days ago the Yankees left us, to attack Vicksburg, leaving their flag flying in the Garrison without a man to guard it, and with the understanding that the town would be held responsible for it. It was intended for a trap; and it succeeded. For night before last, it was pulled down and torn to pieces.

Now they will be back in a few days, and will execute their threat of shelling the town. If they do, what will become of us? All we expect in the way of earthly property is as yet mere paper, which will be so much trash if the South is ruined, as it consists of debts due father by many planters for professional services rendered, who, of course, will be ruined, too, so all money is gone. That is nothing, we will not be ashamed to earn our bread, so let it go.

But this house is at least a shelter from the weather, all sentiment apart. And our servants, too; how could they manage without us? The Yankees, on the river, and a band of guerrillas in the woods, are equally anxious to precipitate a fight. Between the two fires, what chance for us? They say the women and children must be removed, these guerrillas. Where, please? Charlie says we must go to Greenwell.[1] And have this house pillaged? For Butler has decreed that no unoccupied house

[1] The Morgans' summer cottage.

shall be respected. If we stay through the battle, if the Federals are victorious, we will suffer. It is in these small cities that the greatest outrages are perpetrated. What are we to do?

A new proclamation from Butler has just come. Butler says, whereas the so-called ladies of New Orleans insult his men and officers, he gives one and all permission to insult any or all who so treat them, then and there, with the assurance that the women will not receive the slightest protection from the Government, and that the men will all be justified. These men our brothers? Not mine! Come to my bosom, O my discarded carving-knife, laid aside under the impression that these men were gentlemen. . . .

*May 21st*

I have had such a search for shoes this week that I am disgusted with shopping. I am triumphant now, for after traversing the town in every direction and finding nothing, I finally discovered a pair of *boots* just made for a little negro to go fishing with, and only an inch and a half too long for me, besides being unbendable; but I seized them with avidity, and the little negro would have been outbid if I had not soon after discovered a pair more seemly, if not more serviceable, which I took without further difficulty. Behold my tender feet cased in crocodile skin, patent-leather tipped, low-quarter boy's shoes, No. 2! "What a fall was there, my country," from my pretty English glove-kid, to sabots made of some animal closely connected with the hippopotamus! *A dernier ressort, vraiment!* for my choice was that, or cooling my feet on the burning pavement *au naturel;* I who have such a terror of any one seeing my naked foot! And this is thanks to war and blockade! Not a decent shoe in the whole community! *N'importe!* "Better days are coming, we'll all"—have shoes—after a while—perhaps!

*May 27th*

The cry is "Ho! for Greenwell!" Very probably this day week will see us there. I don't want to go. If we were at peace, and were to spend a few months of the warmest season out there, none would be more eager and delighted than I; but to leave our comfortable home, and all it contains, for a rough pine cottage seventeen miles away even from this scanty civilization, is sad. It must be! We are hourly expecting two regi-

ments of Yankees to occupy the Garrison, and some fifteen
hundred of our men are awaiting them a little way off, so the
fight seems inevitable. . . .

*May 30th, Greenwell*

After all our trials and tribulations, here we are at last, and
no limbs lost! How many weeks ago was it since I wrote here?
It seems very long after all these events; let me try to recall
them.

Wednesday the 28th,—a day to be forever remembered,—as
luck would have it, we rose very early, and had breakfast
sooner than usual, it would seem for the express design of becoming famished before dinner. I was packing up my travel-
ing-desk with all Harry's little articles that were left to me, and
other things, and I was saying to myself that my affairs were
in such confusion that if obliged to run unexpectedly I would
not know what to save, when I heard Lilly's voice downstairs,
crying as she ran in—she had been out shopping—"Mr. Castle
has killed a Federal officer on a ship, and they are going to
shell—" Bang! went a cannon at the word, and that was all
our warning.

Mother had just come in, and was lying down, but sprang to
her feet, and added her screams to the general confusion. Miriam, who had been searching the libraries, ran up to quiet her;
Lilly gathered her children, crying hysterically all the time,
and ran to the front door with them as they were; Lucy saved
the baby, naked as she took her from her bath, only throwing
a quilt over her. I bethought me of my "running-bag" which I
had used on a former case, and in a moment my few precious
articles were secured under my hoops, and with a sunbonnet
on, I stood ready for anything.

The firing still continued; they must have fired half a dozen
times before we could coax mother off. What awful screams! I
had hoped never to hear them again, after Harry died. Charlie
had gone to Greenwell before daybreak, to prepare the house,
so we four women, with all those children and servants, were
left to save ourselves. I did not forget my poor little Jimmy; I
caught up his cage and ran down. Just at this moment mother
recovered enough to insist on saving father's papers—which
was impossible, as she had not an idea of where the important
ones were. I heard Miriam plead, argue, insist, command her
to run; Lilly shriek, and cry she should go; the children

screaming within; women running by without, crying and moaning; but I could not join in. I was going I knew not where; it was impossible to take my bird, for even if I could carry him, he would starve. So I took him out of his cage, kissed his little yellow head, and tossed him up. He gave one feeble little chirp as if to ascertain where to go, and then for the first and last time I cried, laying my head against the gate-post, and with my eyes too dim to see him. Oh, how it hurt me to lose my little bird, one Jimmy had given me, too!

But the next minute we were all off, in safety. A square from home, I discovered that boy shoes were not the most comfortable things to run in, so I ran back, in spite of cannon-ading, entreaties, etc., to get another pair. I got home, found an old pair that were by no means respectable, which I seized without hesitation; and being perfectly at ease, thought it would be nice to save at least Miriam's and my tooth-brushes, so slipped them in my corsets. These in, of course we must have a comb—that was added—then how could we stand the sun without starch to cool our faces? This included the pow-der-bag; then I must save that beautiful lace collar; and my hair was tumbling down, so in went the tucking-comb and hair-pins with the rest. By this time, Miriam, alarmed for me, returned to find me, though urged by Dr. Castleton not to risk her life by attempting it, and we started off together

We had hardly gone a square when we decided to return a second time, and get at least a few articles for the children and ourselves, who had nothing except what we happened to have on when the shelling commenced. She picked up any little things and threw them to me, while I filled a pillow-case jerked from the bed, and placed my powder and brushes in it with the rest. Before we could leave, mother, alarmed for us both, came to find us, with Tiche.[2] All this time they had been shelling, but there was quite a lull when she got there, and she commenced picking up father's papers, vowing all the time she would not leave. Every argument we could use was of no avail, and we were desperate as to what course to pursue, when the shelling recommenced in a few minutes. Then moth-er recommenced her screaming and was ready to fly anywhere; and holding her box of papers, with a faint idea of saving

[1] A neighbor.
[2] Mrs. Morgan's maid, Catiche.

something, she picked up two dirty underskirts and an old cloak.

As we stood in the door, four or five shells sailed over our heads at the same time, seeming to make a perfect corkscrew of the air,—for it sounded as though it went in circles. Miriam cried, "Never mind the door!" mother screamed anew, and I stayed behind to lock the door, with this new music in my ears. We reached the back gate, that was on the street, when another shell passed us, and Miriam jumped behind the fence for protection. We had only gone half a square when Dr. Castleton begged us to take another street, as they were firing up that one. We took his advice, but found our new street worse than the old, for the shells seemed to whistle their strange songs with redoubled vigor.

We were alone on the road,—all had run away before,—so I thought it was for our especial entertainment, this little affair. I cannot remember how long it lasted; I am positive that the clock struck ten before I left home, but I had been up so long, I know not what time it began, though I am told it was between eight and nine. We passed the graveyard, we did not even stop, and about a mile and a half from home, when mother was perfectly exhausted with fatigue and unable to proceed farther, we met a gentleman in a buggy who kindly took charge of her and our bundles. We could have walked miles beyond, then, for as soon as she was safe we felt as though a load had been removed from our shoulders; and after exhorting her not to be uneasy about us, and reminding her we had a pistol and a dagger, she drove off, and we trudged on alone, the only people in sight on foot, though occasionally carriages and buggies would pass, going towards town. One party of gentlemen put their heads out and one said, "There are Judge Morgan's daughters sitting by the road!"—but I observed he did not offer them the slightest assistance. . . .

While we were yet resting, we saw a cart coming, and, giving up all idea of our walking to Greenwell, called the people to stop. To our great delight, it proved to be a cart loaded with Mrs. Brunot's affairs, driven by two of her negroes, who kindly took us up with them, on the top of their luggage; and we drove off in state, as much pleased at riding in that novel place as though we were accustomed to ride in wheelbarrows. Miriam was in a hollow between a flour barrel and a mattress; and I at the end, astride, I am afraid, of a tremendous bundle, for my face was down the road and each foot resting very near the sides of the cart. These servants were good enough to lend us their umbrella, without which I am afraid we would have suffered severely, for the day was intensely warm.

Three miles from town we began to overtake the fugitives. Hundreds of women and children were walking along, some bareheaded, and in all costumes. Little girls of twelve and fourteen were wandering on alone. I called to one I knew, and asked where her mother was; she didn't know; she would walk on until she found out. It seems her mother lost a nursing baby too, which was not found until ten that night. White and black were all mixed together, and were as confidential as though related. All called to us and asked where we were going, and many we knew laughed at us for riding on a cart; but as they had walked only five miles, I imagined they would like even these poor accommodations if they were in their reach.

The negroes deserve the greatest praise for their conduct. Hundreds were walking with babies or bundles; ask them what they had saved, it was invariably, "My mistress's clothes, or silver, or baby." Ask what they had for themselves, it was, "Bless your heart, honey, I was glad to get away with mistress's things; I didn't think 'bout mine."

It was a heart-rending scene. Women searching for their babies along the road, where they had been lost; others sitting in the dust crying and wringing their hands.

Presently we came on a guerrilla camp. Men and horses were resting on each side of the road, some sick, some moving about carrying water to the women and children, and all looking like a monster barbecue, for as far as the eye could see through the woods, was the same repetition of men and horses. They would ask for the news, and one, drunk with excitement or whiskey, informed us that it was our own fault if we had saved nothing, the people must have been——fools not to have known trouble would come before long, and that it was the fault of the men, who were aware of it, that the women were thus forced to fly. In vain we pleaded that there was no warning, no means of foreseeing this; he cried, "*You* are ruined; so am I; and my brothers, too! And by —— there is nothing left but to die now, and I'll die!" "Good!" I said. "But die fighting for us!" He waved his hand, black with powder, and shouted, "That I will!" after us.

Lucy[1] had met us before this; early in the action, Lilly had sent her back to get some baby-clothes, but a shell exploding within a few feet of her, she took alarm, and ran up another road, for three miles, when she cut across the plantations and regained the Greenwell route. It is fortunate that, without consultation, the thought of running here should have seized us all.

*May 31st*

I was interrupted so frequently yesterday that I know not how I continued to write so much. First, I was sent for, to go to Mrs. Brunot, who had just heard of her son's death, and who was alone with Dena.

To return to my journal.

Lucy met mother some long way ahead of us, whose conscience was already reproaching her for leaving us, and in answer to her "What has become of my poor girls?" ran down the road to find us, for Lucy thinks the world can't keep on moving without us. When she met us, she walked by the cart and it was with difficulty we persuaded her to ride a mile; she said she felt "used" to walking now. About five miles from home, we overtook mother. All the talk by the roadside was of burning homes, houses knocked to pieces by balls, famine, murder, desolation; so I comforted myself singing, "Better days are coming" and "I hope to die shouting, the Lord will provide"; while Lucy toiled through the sun and dust, and answered with a chorus of "I'm a-runnin', a-runnin' up to glory!"

[1] A servant.

# IV

## THEY CALLED THEM "GREAT DAYS"

### May-September, 1862

*Now in the face of danger the Confederate military genius was afire.*

*Stonewall Jackson and his incredible "foot cavalry" of some nineteen thousand men fought five battles, defeated four separate commands and marched nearly four hundred miles within a month. He defeated Milroy at McDowell on May 8; routed Banks's army at Front Royal on May 23—Belle Boyd helped there—defeated him again at Winchester on the twenty-fifth and drove him out of the Shenandoah Valley the next day; held off Frémont on June 8 at Cross Keys and repulsed Shields at Port Republic on the ninth. Now he held firmly all the upper Valley. On the twenty-first he could leave the scene to confer with General Lee near Richmond.*

> "Ah! Maiden, wait and watch and yearn
> For news of Stonewall's band!
> Ah! Widow, read, with eyes that burn,
> That ring upon thy hand.
> Ah! Wife, sew on, pray on, hope on;
> Thy life shall not be all forlorn;
> The foe had better ne'er been born
> That gets in "Stonewall's way."[1]

*McClellan had pushed his campaign up the Peninsula until his advance could see the church spires and hear the church bells of Richmond. On May 31 and June 1 Joe Johnston*

[1] From "Stonewall Jackson's Way," by John Williamson Palmer (1825-1906). *The Home Book of Verse*, ed., Burton Egbert Stevenson. New York: Henry Holt and Company, 1912.

*struck him at Seven Pines, a clump of trees near Fair Oaks Station. On the second day of fierce struggle General Johnston was wounded, and Robert E. Lee was placed in command.*

Lee's victories in the Seven Days' fighting, from June 26 at Mechanicsville to dark on July 1 at bloody Malvern Hill, raised the siege of Richmond. McClellan—a great organizer and always immensely popular with his men, but a timid offensive leader always overestimating the number of his foes—was forced back to the protection of his gunboats on the James.

The whole South rejoiced over the deliverance, except Lee who had not accomplished what he sought—the destruction of the enemy army; it was still intact, and mighty. The whole South rejoiced, but many women wept. The losses amounted to over 20,000, including 3,286 dead, whom the South could not afford to lose.

Then Lee's genius shone again. On the last days of summer, with valiant help from Stonewall Jackson and James Longstreet, he gave the boastful General John Pope, McClellan's successor, a grand licking at Second Manassas. But more than 7,200 Confederates were killed or wounded.

The early summer had seen the first of General J. E. B. ("Beauty") Stuart's cavalry raids around the entire Union army.

In the Central South it was mostly an affair of cavalry. John Hunt Morgan, another beau sabreur, made his first Kentucky raid, with fights in July at Tompkinsville, Lebanon, Cynthiana and at Gallatin, Tennessee. The Ready family were breathlessly happy over his successes. Nathan Bedford Forrest, natural genius, master of skill and bluff, captured the Union garrison at their city of Murfreesboro on July 13, and rode on to scare the daylights out of the large Union garrison at Nashville.

In the Mississippi Valley Beauregard skillfully evacuated his army from Corinth at the end of May and drew back to Tupelo. Braxton Bragg took over from the ailing Beauregard and, making Chattanooga his new base, assembled there a noble army. From Chattanooga he marched on August 28 to the invasion of Kentucky.

An attempt by General John C. Breckinridge to recapture Baton Rouge by land and river in early July failed—a fact of decided interest to Sarah Morgan.

*The blockade continued its slowly strangling coils, while the diplomats of the Confederacy were seeking recognition by England and France.*

## 1. CORNELIA PEAKE McDONALD—STONEWALL DEFEATS BANKS AT WINCHESTER

*In occupied Winchester Cornelia had had no news from her husband since he left home in March. She did not know that Stonewall had opened his First Valley Campaign on May 4, defeated Banks at Front Royal on the twenty-third and at Middletown and Newton on the twenty-fourth, and was now rapidly driving the "huge mass of blue" toward Winchester in confusion.*

*Winchester, May, 1862.* May had come, and the trees were showing their young leaves, the lawn was a bright, vivid green, and the flowers were all out in the garden, and but for marching troops, and strains of martial music from the regimental bands, we might have felt like ourselves again.

One rainy afternoon, I was looking from my chamber window at the lovely fresh green of the grass and the dripping trees, and thinking how beautiful everything was, and how they seemed to rejoice at the refreshing rain. Smooth as velvet was the turf, and neat and trim the walks and drive.

As I stood by the window, the large gate opened and troop after troop of cavalry entered and wound along through the cedars that lined the drive. They did not keep to the drive, but went on over the grass in any direction they saw fit to take. Fifteen hundred horsemen rode into the grounds and dispersed themselves, tying their horses to the trees and pouring out grain for them to eat. As I looked a party tore off the light ornamental wooden railing on top of the stone wall to kindle their fires. A crowd soon collected around the house demanding admittance.

I told the servants to close every door and bolt it, and to answer no knocks or calls, that no one must go to a door but myself. For some time I took no notice of any knock or summons to open the door, but at last the calls became so imperative, that I, fearing the front door would be broken in, went and

opened it. I only opened it a very small space, but saw three
men holding another up between them, they requested permission to bring in a sick comrade. I suspected a trick and closed
the door again. They retired, but soon another party came,
and more earnest and determined than the other, as their man
was hurt, and was their Captain. His horse had fallen down a
stone wall with him as he rode to the stables, and had broken
his leg. It was no use to refuse permission as I was sure they
would take it. So I had to open the door, and they brought
him in and laid him on a lounge in the dining room.

From that moment such confusion reigned that it was impossible for me to do anything to stem the tide of those crowd-
ing in. The hall, the rooms and even the kitchen was thronged. I
tried to get into the kitchen to get some supper for the children, but had to give it up. So Mary and I took our little ones
and went up stairs for the night, leaving the invaders possession of the lower floor.

The next morning I went down, determined at all hazards to
have some breakfast for my family. My heart sunk as I beheld
the scene that waited me down stairs. Mud, mud, mud—was
everywhere, over, and on, and in everything. No colours were
visible on the carpets, wet great coats hung dripping on every
chair and great pools of water under them where they hung. I
went to the hall door and looked out at the lawn. I would never have recognized it; a sea of deep mud had taken the place
of the lovely green—horses and mules were feeding under the
trees, many of which had been stripped of bark as far up as
the animals could reach; wagons were tilted up with lazy men
around them laughing and joking. I turned from the sight and
went into the dining room where was a scene almost as irritat-
ing and wretched.

Stretched on a lounge, pale and ill, lay the man who had
been hurt; the lounge was drawn close to the fire, and seated
around were several more men who never moved or looked up
at my entrance. One had hung his great coat on the back of a
large rocking chair before the fire to dry, and another was
scraping the mud from his boots over the handsome bright
carpet, or what had been so the day before.

I knew it would not do to give them quiet possession, so I
took the great coat, and threw it out on the back porch, turned
the chair around and seated myself in it by the fire.

The men, upon this, got up one after the other and left the room.

After a moment's silence the man on the sofa spoke and attempted to express his regret at my being so incommoded; saying that after his own admittance he tried to keep the others out, but that he could do nothing with them as they did not belong to his own company.

After some days we became accustomed to the condition of things around us, and began to pick up a few crumbs of comfort in a state of existence that at first seemed unbearable. Pratt was still there, though his regiment had left. The surgeons said he ought not to be moved, and for fear he would be too comfortable, I would not give him a chamber up stairs, but still permitted him to occupy the lounge in the dining room.

He was therefore present at the family gathering around the fireside, and as our talk was unreserved, he acquired some knowledge of our feelings for Yankees in general, though he hoped we did not entertain the like kindly sentiments for him in particular. We gave him to understand, however, that though as a man we might show him kindness, as a Yankee we would feel it our duty to withhold from him our mercy, should an occasion arise when we had the opportunity so to do.

One morning in May, Pratt rode away to join his regiment. He took leave very politely, and hesitatingly offered me a crisp bank note. It had "United States" on it very conspicuously, as I could see at a glance, but I proudly ignored the note and the offer also, and merely shook hands with him.

The town was now emptied of troops, all having pushed on up the valley after Jackson, but in a few days a regiment from Maine, very fresh and clean, with perfect neatness displayed in all their appointments, occupied the town.

Comparative quiet reigned, and but for the separation from our friends and family, and the remembrance that those in the army were hourly surrounded by dreadful dangers we might have had some happiness. Our church, Christ's, was occupied by Yankee preachers, so we went to the Kent Street Presbyterian Church, where we could have the comfort of hearing God's word from the lips of a friend, and of knowing that every heart there joined in the prayers for the safety of our army, and the success of our cause, though their lips must be silent on that subject.

Of our army we knew nothing except what we could learn from the papers of our enemies, and they with exulting joy and great flourishing of trumpets published flaming accounts of the advance of their conquering hosts, and of our poor, ill-clad rabble, humbled, flying, disheartened, and in a short time to be wiped off the face of the earth.

But though sometimes our hearts sickened, they did not altogether fail for we believed in our people, and trusted in God to deliver us.

On the evening of May 22nd, 1862, a guard of soldiers from that triumphant army rode into town at a gallop.

Orders were hurriedly given, and preparations for something important set on foot. I had been in town on business and was hurrying home when I first saw the commotion. As I came up to Mr. Patrick Smith's house, an officer was dismounting at the gate. I do not know what prompted me to do it, but I stopped and asked him where Gen. Banks was. He looked at me for a moment very angrily and suspiciously, but in a little while said that he was near the town and would be in that night. I never could imagine why he told me unless he thought I was a Union woman. His information was sufficient. I knew from it that they were retreating because they were beaten, and I went on home quietly, and slowly, with an air sad and subdued, but those I passed could see the triumph of my heart in my face and manner. I got home, whispered it to Mary, and quietly sat down to supper without a word of what I had heard to the boys and children.

Soldiers were constantly passing about near the house as if to observe what went on.

I sent all the children to bed early, put out the lights, and fastened the doors in the lower story, then took my seat up stairs by my chamber to await whatever might come. . . .

At dawn the next morning we were awakened by cannon close to the town.

Through the early morning hours the din of the musketry and cannon increased and came nearer and nearer. Federal troops were moving in all directions, some scudding over the hills toward a point opposite to the place where the battle raged.

Mr. Mason's house had been long occupied as headquarters by the Maine Regiment, and their camp was in the grounds. Those gallant fellows had fled early in the morning, leaving

their breakfasts cooking on the stoves, savory dishes that the
hungry rebels enjoyed greatly. Harry and Allan ran in to say
that they could see our flag coming up from behind the hill to
the south, from the top of the house, where they had posted
themselves.

I could see from the front door the hill side covered with
Federal troops, a long line of blue forms lying down just behind its crest, on the top of which just in their front a battery
spouted flame at the lines which were slowly advancing to the
top. Suddenly I saw a long even line of grey caps above the
crest of the hill, then appeared the grey forms that wore them,
with the battle flag floating over their heads! The cannon
ceased suddenly, and as the crouching forms that had been
lying behind the cannon rose to their feet they were greeted by
a volley of musketry from their assailants that scattered them.
Some fell where they had stood but the greatest number fled
down the hill side to swell the stream of humanity that flowed
through every street and by way, through gardens and over
fences, toward the Martinsburg turnpike, a confused mob of
trembling, fainting objects that kept on their mad flight till
they were lost in the clouds of dust their hurrying feet had
raised. Nothing could be distinguished, nothing but a huge
moving mass of blue, rolling along like a cloud in the distance.

At different points the battle continued, and through the
streets the hurrying masses still rushed. Occasionally a few
would pause to fire at their pursuers, but all were making
frantically for the one point of egress that was left open to
them. Arms, accoutrements, clothes, everything was thrown
away as they sped along, closely followed by their victorious
foes, who never paused except to give a word or smile to the
friends who were there to greet them.

I put on my bonnet and went in town, and the scenes I
there witnessed I could not describe to do them justice. Old
men and women, ladies and children, high and low, rich and
poor, lined the streets. Some weeping or wringing their hands
over the bodies of those who had fallen before their eyes, or
those who were being brought in by soldiers from the edge of
the town where the battle had been thickest, and others shouting for joy at the entrance of the victorious Stonewall Brigade,
and exultation at the discomfiture of the flying enemy. All
were embracing the precious privilege of saying what they
chose, singing or shouting what they chose.

My husband did not come. He wrote saying that he was on duty in Richmond and could not leave then; but if our army held the lower valley he could come in a few weeks. . . .

## 2. CONSTANCE CARY—IN RICHMOND DURING AND AFTER SEVEN PINES

*Constance the Witty and the other young ladies of the threatened Confederate capital had no time for tableaux, private theatricals or any other form of gaiety as May ended and June began in 1862. These were grave days. While the Battle of Seven Pines, or Fair Oaks, was raging outside Richmond they prepared to receive the wounded and the dead.*

And now we come to the 31st of May, 1862, when the eyes of the whole continent turned to Richmond. On that day General Joseph E. Johnston assaulted the portion of McClellan's troops which had been advanced to the south side of the Chickahominy, and had there been cut off from the main body of the army by the sudden rise of the river, occasioned by a tremendous thunder-storm. In face of recent reverses, we in Richmond had begun to feel like the prisoner of the Inquisition in Poe's story, cast into a dungeon with slowly contracting walls. With the sound of guns, therefore, in the direction of Seven Pines, every heart leaped as if deliverance were at hand. And yet there was no joy in the wild pulsation, since those to whom we looked for succor were our own flesh and blood, standing shoulder to shoulder to bar the way to a foe of superior numbers, abundantly provided as we were not with all the equipments of modern warfare, and backed by a mighty nation as determined as ourselves to win. Hardly a family in the town whose father, son, or brother was not part and parcel of the defending army.

When on the afternoon of the 31st it became known that the engagement had begun, the women of Richmond were still going about their daily vocations quietly, giving no sign of the inward anguish of apprehension. There was enough to do now in preparation for the wounded; yet, as events proved, all that was done was not enough by half. Night brought a lull in the cannonading. People lay down dressed upon their beds, but not to sleep, while their weary soldiers slept upon their arms. Early next morning the whole town was on the street. Ambulances, litters, carts, every vehicle that the city could produce, went and came with a ghastly burden; those who could walk limped painfully home, in some cases so black with gunpowder they passed unrecognized. Women with pallid faces flitted bareheaded through the streets, searching for their dead or wounded. The churches were thrown open, many people visiting them for a sad communion-service or brief time of prayer; the lecture-rooms of various places of worship were crowded with ladies volunteering to sew, as fast as fingers and machines could fly, the rough beds called for by the surgeons. Men too old or infirm to fight went on horseback or afoot to meet the returning ambulances, and in some cases served as escort to their own dying sons. By afternoon of the day following the battle, the streets were one vast hospital. To find shelter for the sufferers a number of unused buildings were thrown open.

I remember, especially, the St. Charles Hotel, a gloomy place, where two young girls went to look for a member of their family, reported wounded. We had tramped in vain over pavements burning with the intensity of the sun, from one scene of horror to another, until our feet and brains alike seemed about to serve us no further. The cool of those vast dreary rooms of the St. Charles was refreshing; but such a spectacle! Men in every stage of mutilation lying on the bare boards with perhaps a haversack or an army blanket beneath their heads,—some dying, all suffering keenly, while waiting their turn to be attended to. We passed from one to the other, making such slight additions to their comfort as were possible, while looking in every upturned face in dread to find the object of our search. The condition of things at this and other improvised hospitals was improved next day by the offerings from many churches of pew-cushions, which, sewn together, served as comfortable beds. To supply food for the hospitals the contents of larders all over town were emptied into baskets; while cellars long sealed and cobwebbed, belonging to old Virginia gentry who knew good Port and Madeira, were opened by the Ithuriel's spear of universal sympathy. There was not much going to bed that night, either. There was a summons to my mother about midnight. Two soldiers came to tell her of the wounding of one close of kin; but she was already on duty elsewhere, tireless and watchful as ever. Up to that time the younger girls had been regarded as superfluities in hospital service; but on Monday two of us found a couple of rooms where fifteen wounded men lay upon pallets around the floor, and, on offering our services to the surgeons in charge, were proud to have them accepted and to be installed as responsible nurses, under direction of an older and more experienced woman. The constant activity our work entailed was a relief from the strained excitement of life after the battle of Seven Pines. When the first flurry of distress was over, the residents of those pretty houses standing back in gardens full of roses set their cooks to work, or better still, went themselves into the kitchen to compound delicious messes for the wounded, after the appetizing old Virginia recipes. Flitting about the streets in the direction of the hospitals were smiling white-jacketed negroes, carrying silver trays with dishes of fine porcelain under napkins of thick white damask, containing soups, creams, jellies, thin biscuit, eggs á la crême, broiled chicken, etc., surmounted by clusters of freshly gathered flowers.

From one scene of death and suffering to another we passed during those days of June. Under a withering heat that made the hours preceding dawn only ones of the twenty-four endurable in point of temperature, and a shower-bath the only form of diversion we had time or thought to indulge in, to go out-of-doors was sometimes worse than remaining in our wards.

Day after day we were called to our windows by the wailing dirge of a military band preceding a soldier's funeral. One could not number those sad pageants: the coffin crowned with cap and sword and gloves, the riderless horse following with empty boots fixed in the stirrups of an army saddle; such soldiers as could be spared from the front marching after with arms reversed and crape-enfolded banners; the passers-by standing with bare, bent heads. Funerals less honored outwardly were continually occurring. Then and thereafter the green hillsides of lovely Hollywood were frequently upturned to find resting-places for the heroic dead. So much taxed for time and attendants were the funeral officials, it was not unusual to perform the last rites for the departed at night. A solemn scene was that in the July moonlight, when, with the few who valued him most gathered around the grave, we laid to rest one of my own nearest kinsmen, about whom in the old service of the United States, as in that of the Confederacy, it was said, "He was a spotless knight."

During all this time President Davis was a familiar and picturesque figure on the streets, walking through the Capitol square from his residence to the executive office in the morning, not to return until late in the afternoon, or riding just before nightfall to visit one or another of the encampments near the city. He was tall, erect, slender, and of a dignified and soldierly bearing, with clear-cut and high-bred features, and of a demeanor of stately courtesy to all. He was clad always in Confederate gray cloth, and wore a soft felt hat with wide brim. Afoot, his step was brisk and firm; in the saddle he rode admirably and with a martial aspect. His early life had been spent in the Military Academy at West Point and upon the then northwestern frontier in the Black Hawk War, and he afterwards greatly distinguished himself at Monterey and Buena Vista in Mexico; at the time when we knew him, everything in his appearance and manner was suggestive of such a training. He was reported to feel quite out of place in the office of President, with executive and administrative duties, in the midst of such a war. General Lee always spoke of him as the best of military advisers; his own inclination was to be with the army, and at the first tidings of sound of a gun, anywhere within reach of Richmond, he was in the saddle and off for the spot —to the dismay of his staff-officers, who were expected to act as an escort on such occasions, and who never knew at what hour of the night or of the next day they should get back to bed or a meal.

When on the 27th of June the Seven Days' strife began, there was none of the excitement attending the battle of Seven Pines. People had shaken themselves down, as it were, to the grim reality of a fight that must be fought. "Let the war bleed, and let the mighty fall," was the spirit of their cry.

### 3. LUCY LOWE—"I WANT TO SEE YOU SO BAD"

*Lucy Lowe, wife of John Lowe of Lowndes County, Alabama, gave four sons and a husband to the Confederacy. During their absence she managed the crops, fed and clothed the small children at home and prayed for her husband "nearly every breath she drew."*

Iounds County June 1 1862

Dier husband I know take my pen in hand drop you a few lines to let you no that we are all well as common and I am in about the same helth that I was when you left I hopes these lines may find you the same I received a leter from you the 29 of May and you sed that you had not got many leters from me yet I have sent you fore leters besides this one George has got home he got hear the end of May he is very lo yet the boys has come home to sea me on a furlow and stade 10 days they started yestrday to the camp they dont no whare they wil git to from their they are station at arbon [Auburn] above Mongary [Montgomery] John my corn is out know and I have not drawed any thing yet but I hop I wil my crop is nice but pane hes quit and left my crop in bad fix but the neighbors ses they will help us you sed you wanted me to pray for you as for prayers I pray for you all of the time I pray for you nearly every breth I draw and I want you to pray for yourself I have give the bys 13 dollars and I bought some 9 bushels of corn and that is all that I give him for his work and I have got 20 dolars yet George is very bad yet and he dont no whether he will ever get able to go back the sargent give him furlo to stay at home til he was able to rejoin his company and he ses for you to try to get him a discharge from the head one for he never will be able to go back agane and I want you to get one if you can George ses that you can get one any time you want to Sister ses she wants to sea you and kis you Your baby is the pertyest thing you ever saw in your life She can walk by her self and your little gran son is perty as a pink and growes the fastest in the world you must come home and sea all of your babyes and kis them I have got the ry cut hook sent and cut it for nothing Your old mare is gone blind in one eye and something is the matter with one of her fet so she cant hardly walk your hogs and cows is coming on very wel I want you to come for I want to sea you so bad I dont no what to do I must come to a close by saying I remane your loveing wif until deth You must write to me as soon as you get this leter goodby to you

Lucy lowe to John P. lowe

## 4. BETTY HERNDON MAURY—"JACKSON IS DOING GREAT THINGS"

*Enemy occupation of Fredericksburg did not prevent Betty Maury from paying a brief visit to her husband beyond the lines. Neither did it prevent her mother from attending the twice-postponed wedding of Dick to Sue Crutchfield on July 17. Brother Dick had been wounded at the Battle of Seven Pines and later was again wounded and imprisoned.*

Fredericksburg
Thursday June 12 1862

Jackson is doing great things. He is somewhere between Winchester and Staunton. We got our information from the Yankee papers and they give a very subdued and confused account of things. Say that they were outnumbered five to one. Had to retire, etc. etc. And we interpret it that they were *well whipped.*

When the enemy first came to Fredericksburg we put all of our silver, including the New York service presented to Papa at Mr. Goolrick's, the English Vice Consul, that it might be under the protection of the British flag. Since our new military Governor came, the house has been searched and the flag and several boxes taken away. Fortunately ours escaped them. Nanny and I went there today, opened the box and smuggled the contents away under our shawls and in a basket. They were informed by a negro woman. The Governor! says that Mr. Goolrick is not an authorized Vice Consul.

Sun. June 22nd, 1862

The town is intensely Yankee and looks as though it never had been anything else. Yankee ice carts go about selling Yankee ice. Yankee newsboys cry Yankee papers along the streets. Yankee citizens and Yankee Dutchmen have opened all the stores on Main Street. Some of them have brought their families and look as if they had been born and bred here and intended to stay here until they died. One man has built him a house!

The different currencies are very confusing. A pair of shoes are worth so much in Specie, so much more in Yankee paper, and double their real value in Virginia money.

General Stuart made a most daring dash the other day with two thousand of our Cavalry. They passed *through the enemy lines to their* rear, burnt several loaded transports on the Pamunky and many loaded wagons, took many horses and mules and prisoners. We lost one man killed and two wounded and were gone between two and three days. They were greeted with shouts and cheers by the country people as they galloped along. One old woman rushed out to her gate and shouted out above all the clatter and din, "Hurrah, my Dixie boys, you drive the blue coated varmints away."

Wed. June 25th
At Mr. White's—twelve miles from
Fredericksburg

Monday afternoon Willie White came to our house to say that my dear husband was at his father's and he had come to take me out to him. In less than half an hour Nannie Belle and I were ready to start. When we had gotten about three miles from town we were overtaken by a party of Yankee cavalry that had pursued us to search for letters. They asked my name, where I came from and where I was going. And when I gave my word of honor that we had no letters or papers of any kind they allowed us to go on.

We were out in a dreadful storm and got wet through and through. Had to ford a river. The bridge had been burned by our army on its retreat. The descent to the river was perpendicular. It seems a miracle that we got down safely.

When we arrived I was much relieved to find that Will had gone to Uncle Jourdan Woolfolk's. Mr. White thought he would be running a risk to stay here all night and had persuaded him to go, promising that he would send me down the next day. But the storm of that night has caused such a freshet in the rivers that it will be impossible for us to go for several days yet. All the bridges have been destroyed and we can only cross by fording.

Sat. 28th June
Uncle Jourdan's

Here I am at last safe and sound with my dear husband. Oh! how thankful I am to be with him again once more. Had many difficulties and adventures in getting here. Left Mr. White's Thursday afternoon but when we reached the Matapony—a distance of seventeen miles we found that it was impossible to ford it. Willie White and I concluded that we would have to ask the hospitality of some people in the neighborhood for the night. Mr. Gravitt received us most kindly and hospitably. Found a party of gentlemen there who had been waiting for two days to cross the river. Spent a very pleasant day at Mr. Gravitts and forded the river in the afternoon in the Marylander's wagon. It was higher and safer than our buggy.

Will looks horrid in a dark calico shirt and a heavy beard.

Sunday June 29th

Will has shaved off the beard and looks handsome again. I do not object to the shirt.

Wednesday July 9th

Will has gone back to Richmond to that most disheartening of all occupations, waiting and waiting and trying to get something to do. But I will not complain so many blessings have been granted us lately. We have passed a happy, happy ten days together and ought to feel strengthened and elevated and ready for the work set before us.

Thursday July 10, 1862

Heard yesterday that Mamma and Sue are at Ridgeway. The old woman was determined not to be outdone by her daughters. Bless her heart. I should have liked to see her running the blockade. What a happy meeting they will all have up there. I suppose Dick was married yesterday evening.

July 29, 1862

My husband is thirty years old today. God grant him many happy returns.

Mon. Aug. 18, 1862

Hurrah for domestic manufactures, and a fig for the Yankees. We can do without them. Have just completed a hat of plaited wheat-straw for Mr. Maury. I made it every bit myself and it looks elegant. I've been hard at work on it for the last three days.

Sunday Aug. 31st, 1862

I've been deep in the mysteries of wool dying, spinning and weaving lately. Am trying to have the cloth made for a suit of winter clothes for Mr. Maury. Cousin Anne Morris said she would like to see Mother's shocked look when he makes his appearance in Washington in a homespun hat.

Aunt Betsy replied: "Well she ought n't to look shocked. She ought to think he has a jewel of a wife to be able to turn her hand to such things, when necessary."

## 5. AMIE KELLEY—"WHAT CANNOT BE CURED MUST BE ENDURED"

*Amie Kelly was the mother of four small children and the wife of Samuel Camp Kelly who was fighting with the Army of Northern Virginia. The responsibility of their plantation in Calhoun County, Alabama, rested on her shoulders.*

Calhoun County, Alabama
At home, July 8th, 1862

My dearest S.

. . . Bro. James has sold your corn. There were only 60¼ bu. He paid me yesterday at 1$ a bu. and I paid Stipes. . . . You say I must sell a mule if I am out of money. I had rather buy than sell. I have plenty of money so far, and keep getting a little along. What has become of your Mexican blanket? Have you lost it with your clothes? I should be sorry for you to lose it. I heard before that some of the Reg. were lousy. Is it the case? Do try to keep them off you. I would hate it so bad for you to get lousy. I heard this morning that you were elected Major. Is that so? I do not believe it. I had rather you were a good soldier than Major, there is not so much danger. We are listening for a fight at Chattanooga. Oh, may the God of Battles shield your precious self. How could I bear to hear that you had fallen and no one near to close your eyes or wipe the death damp from your brow. May God sustain us all and keep us in the way we should go. We are needing rain. The weather is dry and hot and I feel like it is for our sins that these things come upon us. Truly these are trying times and who will be able to stand. I will leave half of this sheet for you to write back on. I send it with Mother's. But for this cruel war you would be at home, but be a good soldier and maybe it will not be long till we can sit at home together. Write often, my dear one. Good bye. AMIE

At Home, July 17, 62

My dearest S.

. . . God grant to send us peace on honorable terms and that speedily! All the soldiers write that peace will soon be made. For my part I wish soon, but do not see anything to just-ify the conclusion, for England and France are both uncertain and Lincoln has called for 300,000 more troops. Bro. Smith was here day before yesterday. He looks badly and limps a lit-tle. He says we did not near whip the Yanks at Richmond, they are reinforcing for another fight. We heard that your Reg. was ordered to Richmond, but I did not believe it. . . . I am sorry you dislike your Captain, but it has turned out as I feared. He thinks he knows it all. . . . H. Steel will start back next Monday night. I do not knew whether to send your jeans pants and some shoes or send you the money and let you buy for yourself. I could send the money easier than the things un-less you are on the railroad. I wish it were so I could come and see you or you me! I do want to see you so bad I can scarce-ly bear it, but what cannot be cured must be endured and I will have to wait, as bad as I hate to. The boys are done plowing and the corn looks better than other corn in the neighborhood. We had roasting ears day before yesterday that we got out of the garden. We have a big peach pie every day and how I do wish my dearest had some. I never sit down to eat but I think of you and wish you were here to help us enjoy what we have. . . .

The ambulances and wagons of Van Dorn's[1] army passed this week going to Chattanooga. They had some of the finest mules I ever saw. There were not many men with them. They went by Atlanta. They looked stout and rough, the Yanks may run when they get after them. There is no news now. All quiet at R. and I am afraid the next big fight will be in Tennessee,

[1]Generals Earl Van Dorn and Sterling Price had brought the Army of the West across the Mississippi to Beauregard's concen-tration after Shiloh.

and you will be in it. I have not got any wool yet and will have to pay 75 cents in the dirt when I do, which is rather tough. I sent you some paper and envelopes this morning by Griffin and will send this by B. Pike tonight, and will write again by H. S. next Monday, if I can. You say you have a notion of having 2 teeth pulled but thought you would consult me. I would dislike to have them pulled unless they ached. Could you have them plugged and save them? . . .

I like the plan of your writing back on my letters, particularly when written with ink but when written with pencil, it is hard to make out. Sometimes I think you improve in writing very much. Go on improving and you will make your mark some day. May God help you so to live that you will not be ashamed in a coming day. I want you to be a meek follower of the Savior and a useful one too to your fellow men. I would not do all the work and not study any. I would let the Capt. do his part. May God direct you and keep you from harm.

AMIE

## 6. ELIZABETH McGAVOCK HARDING—"I AM PROUD TO BE YOUR WIFE"

*The Belle Meade plantation near Nashville was famous throughout the South for its hospitality, its fine blooded horses and its many servants. Its mistress, the wife of General William G. Harding, was a woman of beauty and charm, a great lady who put honor first.*

*General Harding was arrested after the occupation of Nashville for refusing to take the demanded oath of allegiance. He was then fifty-four years old. He was sent to Fort Mackinaw in northern Michigan and imprisoned till 1866. Meanwhile Mrs. Harding ran the plantation with the help of the overseer, Mr. Hague. Having bravely and steadfastly done her full duty, she died soon after her husband's return.*

*Her letters to him in the summer of 1862 give a vivid picture of life in Nashville under Yankee possession, and at Belle Meade, with all its problems. She was forty-four, the mother of two daughters, Mary Elizabeth and Selene.*

Belle Meade, Thursday, July 17th 1862

My Dearest Husband,

I wrote you on Sunday last, stating the facts in regard to a skirmish that occurred during the day in Murfreesboro[1]; on Monday I went in, and prevailed on your Father to leave the City, at least until the excitement subsided, and intend using my best efforts to get him to stay here, during my absence. . . .

His health is very good. He looks more robust than in the spring, and if you were only at home, would be perfectly content and happy. I cannot tell you how often he repeats the question, "Daughter, when do you think William will be at home?" and what benefit to the Union cause in Tenn. to be gained by his incarceration in a distant prison, the *policy* is *bad,* and will never result in any good. I am not able to answer either question satisfactorily, but as regards the first, I hope the autumn will find you in the enjoyment of home, and the inestimable blessing of liberty. Surely you will not be overlooked, when a general exchange of prisoners is made. We have political or state prisoners, who are expecting an exchange, and it seems very unjust they should be denied the same consideration accorded prisoners of war; I cannot think it will be so, and many friends agree with me in opinion.

I told you in several preceding letters, I should leave, probably the 22nd, (next Tuesday) and am still determined to go, if possible, but the whole country is in a state of excitement, particularly between this place and Louisville; the trains have been stopped several times this week, and forced to return, each way, after securing the persons, or property desired. John Morgan[2] has created all the disturbance in Ky. so the "Journal" says, and Colonel Forrest commanded at Murfreesboro. To show the state of excitement here, *among certain persons,* on Monday last, John Trimble, Gov. Campbell,[3] Jordan

[1]Colonel N. B. Forrest captured Murfreesboro and its Union garrison on July thirteenth. He was commissioned brigadier-general on the twenty-first.

[2]Colonel J. H. Morgan was on first raid in Kentucky, with fights at Tompkinsville on the ninth, Lebanon on the twelfth, and Cynthiana on the seventeenth.

[3]William Bowen Campbell, elected in 1851, was the last Whig governor of Tennessee. He strenuously opposed secession and was the most distinguished of those in Middle Tennessee who remained Unionists. For a brief period he held a brigadier-generalship in the Union Army.

Stokes and brother, and several others of the same stamp, took the train for Louisville, all having sudden pressing business to transact, not known of on Saturday. They passed through safe, as I saw their names in the list of arrivals in Louisville, en route to New York. What do you think of it?

When Gov. J.[1] heard of Gov. C's. hasty exit, he became furious, and remarked, "Gov. C. has just applied for a Brigadiership, at his solicitation I backed him, now at the first approach of danger he deserts his post. I consider his action indefensible and open to the charge of cowardice." Pretty plain spoken for a politician, was it not? I think he prides himself in his candor and blunt mode of speaking, but tis said he was greatly excited at the time. Gen [Wm.] Nelson and his brigade of five hundred men arrived here from Huntsville night before last, and today left for Murfreesboro. Forrest took two thousand prisoners, fifty wagons, and numerous stores and arms, so the papers say; paroled upwards of nineteen hundred privates, and sent the officers to Chattanooga, among them two Generals, Crittenden and Duffield,[2] of Indiana.

You can understand now why it may not be possible for me to get off the day appointed, though I will strive to do so. I have concluded to take Mr. Hague for an escort, as Brother John finds it impossible to leave home. . . .

If anything occurs to prevent my going at the appointed time, I will write, every few days, until I do start. Farewell, my beloved; I trust we will meet *very soon.*

Your loving wife,

E.

Belle Meade, July 24th, 1862

My Dearest Husband;

I hoped ere this to have been on my road to Mackinaw, but events have transpired *immediately around us,* of a nature to stop all regular communication between this and Louisville. I wrote you on Sunday last to say that we could start on the 22nd as appointed, as Mr. Hague went in town Saturday on some business, and was told to report himself at the Provost's office Tuesday, the very day we were to have started. Of

[1]Andrew Johnson, Military Governor of Tennessee.
[2]The Union force at Murfreesboro was under command of General T. T. Crittenden of Indiana. Duffield was colonel of the 9th Michigan.

course I had no fears of *his* detention *long,* but it prevented our starting that day, and it was well, for the cars were taken above Gallatin by Forrests or Starnes[1] Cavalry, and the passengers forced to return; on the same day ninety-three federal pickets were taken prisoners eight miles from Nashville on the Murfreesboro Pike, and two bridges destroyed on the railroad, thus cutting off communication between Nelson's brigade at Murfreesboro and this place.

Immediate preparations were made to defend Nashville (from some of her own sons) by the Federal forces; cannon planted on Capitol hill; at the mouths of all the streets, and on College hill; some of the principal streets, leading in the direction of Murfreesboro and Lebanon, were barricaded by wagons chained together, and the cannon placed behind them, rendering it perfectly impossible to get in, or out.

Our road too was blocked at the depot in the same manner, and the Charlotte Pike was the only unobstructed passway in this direction, though the cannon on Capitol hill perfectly commanded it; in short, the preparations made proved they expected an attack, and were determined to resist it; some threats were made by the federals to burn the city, though it was understood to be Gen. Buell's order, if they could not hold it, to surrender, as we had done to them; in answer, it is said, Gov. Johnson remarked "No, we will defend it to the last extremity, and if defeated, leave it in a heap of smouldering ruins, not one stone shall remain to mark the spot where our proud Capitol now stands." Whether he said it, or intends carrying out his threat, it is certain he and Gen. Buell do not get on well, as is evidenced by Gov. J's wish to get rid of Gen. B. in Tenn; his popularity here did not please the Gov.

It is certain the officers here, belonging to Buell's staff, do not harmonize at all with the Gov. They all disapprove of the arrests made in direct violation of Gen. Buell's promise, yours among the number and *particularly;* and a gentleman, a Union man, told me, if Buell had been here, he would not have permitted your removal from Tenn. nor indeed your arrest at all, after the assurances given you; if this be so, oh how I wish he had never left, or had the power to rescind Gov. J's. decrees.

It is said, and believed here, Gen. Buell is falling back on Nashville, as his supplies are cut off near Chattanooga; Leba-

[1]Colonel John W. Starnes.

non is in the hands of the Confederates, and day before yesterday a picnic party went to the "Hermitage" and there met with a large body of Forrest's men, who escorted them back to Mount Olivet, taking sixteen Federal pickets on the way, paroled them, and sent them in with the pleasure party. Yesterday Gov. J. had the gentlemen of the company up, to know if they were aware, beforehand, who they would meet, but as some good unionists happened to be among the numbers, and they affirmed their utter ignorance of the proximity of Forrest, he let them off, with a lecture about being found in *bad company.*

You can see from what I have written, we are almost surrounded by the Confederates, and yet, I do not think they seriously intend to attack Nashville now; if so, they could have taken it easily last Thursday, as the federal force was then small and inadequate to hold the city, and a perfect panic prevailed, as news of the approach of the cavalry with artillery was brought in by the pickets, on the Murfreesboro and Lebanon Pikes, to stop the artillery. They left town about five o'clock, had a skirmish in front of Mr. Weaver's residence, near the Asylum, and near Mill Creek Bridge, on the Lebanon Road; they did not succeed in burning either bridge, and came in next morning, paroled by *Forrest.*

The soldiers in Nashville slept on their arms Monday and Tuesday nights, but yesterday reinforcements arrived from Huntsville, and they breathe more freely; I assure you, *we* are made to suffer for all these alarms.—I mean in a petty way.— For instance, on Tuesday morning last, I went in town, not knowing the state of excitement pervading the whole community, to bring Father Harding out, and to see Gov. J. in regard to your being paroled to stay with me at the Hotel, while in Mackinaw; when I arrived on "Capitol Hill" the formidable preparations for war alarmed me, and I determined to write to, instead of seeing Gov. Johnson; did so, he sent word to call at five o'clock, and the *letter* would be *ready.* I sent Miles for the letter at five, and he told him to come in the morning, as he had been too busy to attend to the letter.

Just as I was starting home, Cousin Frank and Amanda Cheatham drove up, both looking much excited and informed me they had been turned back from Cockrill's Spring, because they refused to take the "oath," though they had a "pass" signed by the Provost Marshall; the pickets had not acted so before, and we began to suspect *the new order* was designed to catch all unwary country men then in town. Cousin F. determined to remain all night, and as Mr. Cheatham was in town to take care of Amanda, I hurried on, not dreaming of being stopped, as the children only were with me; as we passed Elliston's, Joe hailed the carriage, and said we could not pass, as Mrs. John Williams had just been turned back, with no gentlemen in, only a small son, and begged we would stay all night with them. I had left Sister entirely alone, of course could not; as we neared the spring, one stood in the middle of the road, and called to Miles to halt; an inferior officer of Johnson's precious body guard stepped up, took the "Pass" from Miles and remarked to me, "I suppose you have read the oath, on the back of this pass, Madam." I replied, "I have, Sir." "Have you any objection to taking this oath." "I have most decidedly." "Pray, what objections?" "They are numerous, and insuperable, Sir, but why do you ask? My pass is correct, and renewed a few days since?" He replied, "My orders are to let no one through, unless they take the oath, or have taken it." I asked him why he did not inform people of that as they went in the city; because he had no orders to that effect, beside they were surrounded with dangers, and must be very strict with both women and men. Just then Miles spoke up and said "I showed Gov. Johnson my pass this evening, and asked him if it would take us home, and he said Yes." The man looked at me earnestly for a moment, and said "Madam, if you will give me your word you will not give any information to any Confederate Cavalry that may visit your house, tonight or tomorrow, detrimental to us?" "I will certainly promise *that,* as I have no information to give." He then called on Selene, to know if she promised also, she answered very coldly, "I know nothing to communicate," then, Mary's turn came; the answer was quite as brief, and we were then permitted to pass; but if Miles had not mentioned the "all powerful name" we would have been turned back, as *every other* was. I knew nothing of his application till just before we left town, he told me not to be uneasy, as "his pass was good sure." I asked why, and he told me Gov. J. had approved it.

Next morning early, I sent in for the promised letter; the servant waited one—two hours, at last the servant that waits on him confessed he was not up, and he did not know what hour he would, as he *sat up late* the night before. The truth is, he was afraid to lie down, lest the rebels should catch him napping. When he did rise, he sent the servant to the Capitol, saying his secretary would give him the letter; he did so, and when I opened the unsealed envelope, it contained the *self same complimentary* letter of introduction to the "Officer Commanding the Post" I referred to in several of my previous letters.

What a bitter *disappointment* it was to me, you can well imagine, after promising so much, and I am at a loss to determine whether he intended it, or, in the excitement of the preceding twenty-four hours it was entirely overlooked; but why not say so, and ask me to call, or send again, instead of enclosing a formal note, "hoping the enclosed will be satisfactory"? "Put not your faith in Princes" sayeth the Bible, but I have almost lost faith in all politicians & Union Governors.

I *will* go to see you *yet*, and tell you what he said to me, when I asked him why you were in a distant prison, and Gov. at liberty to enjoy *home* and *freedom;* his answer made my heart thrill with pride for my husband. Yes, I was proud to be your wife, the loved one of that noble heart,—but I must reserve this until we meet, and it will not be long, I trust, but I must wait patiently until the times are more settled.

One danger I have not hinted at, and that is, John,[1] from going back and forth, as he will be compelled to do, and to get permits, runs the risk of being required to take the —— what he does not wish or intend to do, Since the excitement commenced he has remained close at home, and as yet has not been molested. Well my eighth page is nearly full, and I have said nothing about home affairs. Ask Capt. Wormer to excuse my *war details*, but I have told nothing the newspapers have not published, therefore tis not contraband. . . .

> Farewell my darling husband,
>
> E.

> Belle Meade, Sunday morning, July 27th

My dearest,

I cannot resist slipping in a little scrap to give you a faint

[1]John McGavock, Mrs. Harding's older brother, who inherited Cairnton, her birthplace.

idea of the present state of affairs and account for my detention; Mr. Hague was refused a pass to come home yesterday, unless he took the oath; and David[1] was arrested late last evening, to report at ten o'clock this morning; we fear John's arrest every hour, and tis said they will give no more passes to come and go, unless the person takes "the oath," or is a union man. If I leave *now*, John will be compelled to stay part of his time at home, as it *requires his presence more than usual;* he cannot do so, even if he is not arrested, without a pass,—and then the troops here daily look for Forrest or Starnes to turn up near the city, consequently the reins are tightened with us all.

Tis said the renowned Bull Nelson intends calling on the people of Davidson County to furnish one thousand negroes to work upon fortification *here,* and the newspaper called the "Union," edited by a man named Mercer from Ky., advocated it strongly and *urges* that the negroes shall subsist, while so employed, on the secessionists around. . . . All the regular army officers, almost without an exception, disapprove this, and are the most conservative men we have among us, but our Governor, I fear, will use his influence against us. . . .

Oh, how this state of uncertainty worries me, but the hardest of all to bear is the thought of your *disappointment,* after looking for me to say when I can start, and I fear I cannot be spared long from our dear old home; but let it be long or short, I will assuredly go to see you *if I can,*—but until we know whether John is to be arrested, I cannot leave; if he is not to be taken up, we will know it in a few days.

. . . If you should fail to hear frequently from home, do not be uneasy, as the mails are, and have been, interrupted in *both* Ky. and Tenn.

Your Father is in usual health now, had a little spell this week of a few hours duration, caused by eating too much fruit, but has perfectly recovered. All the rest in usual health. Farewell, my beloved husband, that we may meet soon is my intense desire and prayer.

Yours,<br>E.

---

[1]David Turner McGavock, a first cousin.

Belle Meade, August 5th, 1862

My Beloved Husband,

Again I sit down to chronicle another disappointment about leaving here, after writing you on Sunday last that we would certainly start Thursday, 7th. In your last letter to John (the last recd.) you said you appreciated the slight manner in which he referred to the causes of my detention, and other troubles, but would prefer the *whole facts,* even if it increased your anxiety in regard to us. It is useless for me to dwell on the pain these repeated disappointments give me, but I feel it on your account so much more keenly than my own, for I know you are looking every day to see us, but my dearest, I strive to act as *you* would advise me, if cognizant of the situation of affairs at the present time.

You know, John had consented to stay at Belle Meade until my return, and go back and forth home; unfortunately he has had a good deal of trouble of late about keeping his servants away from town, the camps, and running about generally; of course his presence is required often, and he expected to go up two or three times a week; in order to do so, of course a "pass" is requisite; within the last few days this is denied, unless the person asking one goes up and proves his loyalty by taking the oath.

This deters hundreds from leaving home, and if that were *all,* it could be borne patiently, but arrests *at home* are of hourly occurrence, and they are hurried off immediately, without a hearing, not to the prison, but out of the state, and to a northern place of confinement. *All the ministers,* except Dr. Sehon, are at Jeffersonville, Ind., in the state prison, and the Dr. leaves tomorrow, accompanied by your old friend Jo Edwards, and thirty other prominent citizens from Sumner [County], living near Saunderville. Col. Watson is another you know, and probably all, but I cannot give the list; if you can procure a "Louisville Journal," that will inform you.

I looked for John and family this evening, but rec'd. a note only, begging me not to start *just yet,* and giving the reasons mentioned. . . . It is the intention of Gov. Johnson to get up about one thousand horses in this county for the cavalry, batallion of Col. Jordan Stokes, and in requiring persons to furnish their quota, the men sent wish to choose the horses themselves. David feels very solicitous about your blooded stock, as he well may, and begs me to defer my departure for a time, until this matter be settled, as well as a probable call on us to furnish hands to work on fortifications to be commenced here soon.

I think it is my duty to heed their advice, but, oh my husband, how my heart yearns to be with you, if only for a short time. . . .

I went to Gov. Johnson this day, to get a protection for the place until my return, he promised to send me tomorrow a paper worded somewhat in this wise, *as I understood him,* "No person shall molest or take anything away from Gen. H's plantation, without first coming to me." What this will be worth, I cannot tell. I represented to him how unprotected the place was, and that you had valuable and favorite horses, unfit for cavalry purposes, and yet I feared were in danger. He said when persons were called on to furnish horses, certificates would be given attesting their value, to be paid at a "proper time." I told him your blooded animals were all too valuable to be used for such purposes, and I hoped he would not permit to be molested in my absence.

He asked how long I wished to stay, I replied, "Until my husband returns with me," he smiled, shook his head, and asked me if I knew Col. Guild was coming home? I was never more surprised and scarcely knew how to believe it, yet he assured me it was so; it is spoken of on the streets as a hoax, and few persons credit it.

Have you heard anything of political prisoners being exchanged? I heard the Louisville Journal contained a paragraph, saying, they too, would be, very soon. God grant it may be so.

It is growing very late, and I must close, with the assurance I will do all in my power to insure the safety of your *favorites,* and hope my next will tell you certainly when to expect us. All the family in usual health. Every servant wants to send a present by me, and wish to be remembered. . . .

Farewell,<br>Your loving wife.

Belle Meade, August 29th, 1862

My Dearest Husband,

For seventeen days we have not received a through mail from Louisville; of course, our letters to you cannot reach you, nor can we hear from you. For six weeks I have expected to

visit you. . . . I have at last abandoned the idea, and as Gov.
Johnson seems willing to parole you, that you may come home
and judge for yourself in regard to the present state of affairs,
I deem it best to send Mr. Hague with the parole, as it is impossible to communicate with you by mail.

You know, my dear husband, I would never have applied to
Gov. J. to parole you, if in my own judgment your acceptance
of it could compromise your honor, dearer to you and myself
than life itself; but I have consulted with many of your dearest
friends, and they all agree with me in thinking you should accept, come home and examine the condition of things, with the
distinct understanding that you are at liberty to surrender it,
when you see fit, and place yourself in the same position you
occupy at present.

I tried hard to procure your release on your simple bond,
with security, but Gov. J. said no such paroles were given, and
the one sent only bound you so long as you kept it in possession. I endeavored to procure the release of your companions
on the same terms, but failed, though I think *their friends*
could do if they were to make application.

I understand, through a not perfectly reliable source, that
*our* and every one else's negroes about here, that are now
working on the fortifications, are to be sent to Cairo to work
there. When our men were pressed, the understanding was
they should not be sent out of the county. The runaways are
the negroes to send, and not those who have staid at home and
behaved themselves, as *all ours* have done. . . .

But all this is of small importance to the object of Mr. H's
mission, and only speak of it to show what little control we
have of our property, and it is no better as regards *all* other
kinds. Gov. Johnson told me to write you plainly, so that you
might have a correct idea of the state of things, as they now
exist, and I have told both Randall[1] and Sister to do so.

If you conclude to come home (I pray God you may), you
had best purchase your winter clothing either in Canada or
some of the northern cities. Almost nothing can be procured
here, and what there is, at enormous prices. Mr. Hague has a
little list of things I want that cannot be procured here at all.
If you decide *not to come,* I can only say I will do all in my
power to take your place, as I have done, but I am feeble sub-

[1]Randall M. Southall, Mrs. Harding's nephew.

stitute for you, though I believe your place has suffered less than if you had been here. My unprotected position, as well as the knowledge of your imprisonment, have prevented some encroachments made upon others.

Mr. Hague is waiting to start, and I must close. May God direct you, *but I say come.*

Yours ever,

E.


## 7. LUCY SMITH—"WE APPEAL TO YOU AS OUR FRIEND"

*The son of Mrs. Smith of Oak Hill, Georgia, had recently been killed while fighting under General Magruder before Richmond in the Seven Days' battles. On behalf of all bereaved mothers, she wrote a letter of protest to the officials of the Confederate government in Richmond—criticizing the Conscription Act passed by the Confederate Congress on April 21, 1862, and the conduct of Confederate generals and surgeons.*

*John Bankhead Magruder, of Virginia, was a colonel when he turned back the Federals at Big Bethel. He became a major-general in October 1861. "Prince John" had been most energetic in building defenses against McClellan's advance. On June 29 he attacked gallantly at Allen's Farm and at Savage Station. Of Malvern Hill on July 1, where he marched on the wrong road, General D. H. Hill said, "I never saw anything more grandly heroic than the advance of the nine brigades under Magruder's orders. Unfortunately they did not move together, and were beaten in detail." The carnage was awful.*

*Mrs. Smith is not an elegant writer, but there is no mistaking her meaning.*

Oak Hill, [Georgia]
August the 20 [1862]

To President Davis, Ex President Alex H. Stephens and the War department

Dear Sirs   We appeal to you as our friend   Please read pardon and consider and act accordingly   It is with great emo-

tion that we women of the Southern Confederacy and striving
to maintain ourselves as patriotic mothers are almost driven to
subjugation and almost preferring the tyranny of Lincoln to
the tantalizing inhumane treatment to our soldiers by our head
leading Generals and regimental surgeons  We have born it
long and silently with all the fortitude we could hoping that
they would certainly amend after awhile  what we speak of is
the tyranny of our generals and surgeons. Look at Magruder
when he ordered my poor sons charge when they knew it was
death inevitable under the circumstances but he [was] so
drunk [he] dident have no care as is the case with the drunk
but cursed them and ordered again which proved a failure of
accomplishing anything but dreadful slaughter on one side in
which my poor child fell  the name of Butler is more agreeable in this bereaved neighborhood than Magruder Butler never drove out our sons head long into a slaughter pen Magruder
did it and it is the case with the most of our big generals to
gallop off to the hospitals to drink up the wines that are
sent in for the sick  now dont we have great encouragement
to contribute to the sick when [they] rarely if ever get sight
of the dainties that are sent them    tell us what is more
despotic and more disgusting when they write to us mother
wife or sister you said you sent us jellies fruit and so forth
but we never saw any of it  the head ones eats the dainties sent to the sick themselves  all that is overbearing enough
but next comes something still worse the conscript  now we
have no objections to the conscript and think it a blessed thing
to take some of the stout cowards or lazy men  but here is the
point  they say all under and over such an age  none
excepted all to report themselves well now here and there
is a man that has a big lingering disease  which the least ex-
posure will kill  still he must go out when he could hardly
keep up at home with all the attention of a wife and not half
his time able to cut his own firewood  still he was a great help
to that wife who took all the hardships on herself to prolong
her husbands life to aid her in raising her little family  Still
the conscript (for all it says able boddied men) takes him
along  the surgeon merely thumps his breast and grasp his
arm  tells him he has a good mussle . wishes he had a regiment like him and sends him on through  then he must travel
day and night  perhaps on open cars  take the rain  night
air and heat of the sun as it comes  without a place hardly to

sit down for 3 and 4 or 5 days at a time   then when he lands to walk perhaps 10 or 12 miles   a thing which his constitution never could bear   then camp out without even a tent let the weather be as it may   now the loss of sleep   the fatigue of traveling the damp night are all unaccustomed and diseased lungs or liver to contend with who could stand it   you will admit none but stout sound men   no they dont stand it   we hear directly they are sick   next news they are dead but a trifle over there   but it is a serious damage to us here is a little group of children   a broken hearted mother to maintain and raise   now as little as you may make of this   that is the case in these parts   no less than 10 of our neighbor men taken off by conscript failing to get a discharge when we all knew that the poorest surgeon in the world could tell they were infirm men by the complexion if nothing else are burried over at Richmond after having been there only 3 weeks   10 widows in one neighborhood   made so in the course of 3 weeks when apt as not if the surgeon had rightfully examined them he would have known they couldnt of stood it   if he had of discharged them and let them return home they perhaps would have lived to raised their families by being prudent   that is the main thing   we say conscript and take all the able boddied men but let the infirm remain if you want to abate the distress among the women and children   these lines can be vouched for   Our Surgeons are savage   unprincipled men   especially in Atlanta   they regard not ours as their interest   and tell me what use is a man lying on a couch in a hospital to the government when he carried the disease with him there   do you expect to have a new man made out of him why not let him remain where there is room for him

A patriotic mother and wife

LUCY SMITH

## 8. SARAH MORGAN—"GONE WAS MY SMALL PARADISE!"

*When things in Baton Rouge quieted down, the Morgans moved back home. Acting on General Earl Van Dorn's proclamation of July 10, advising all persons within eight miles of the Mississippi to withdraw into the interior, they fled for the*

*second time. Sarah, her mother and her sister Miriam found
temporary refuge on near-by plantations. Mr. LaRoue established sister Lilly and their five small children in Clinton,
Louisiana. Sarah listened to the guns when General John C.
Breckinridge made an unsuccessful attempt to recapture Baton
Rouge on August 5. She was then on Dr. Nolan's plantation
some seven miles to the east of the city. Enemy shells drove
them to Randallson's Landing and to Linwood, the home of
General A. G. Carter, whose daughter Lydia had married
Thomas Gibbes Morgan, Jr. When she heard reports of property destruction and pillage in Baton Rouge, Sarah wrote on
August 20, "I am determined to see my home. . . . I'll not
cry." Instead she laughed—but there was bitterness in her
laughter.*

*Illness and near starvation were to drive the Morgan family
to the protection of Unionist Judge Philip Morgan in New Orleans. Sarah unwillingly took the oath of allegiance, comforting herself with the thought that "a forced oath is not binding."*

*After the War Sarah married a young Englishman in South
Carolina, Francis Warrington Dawson, who had run the blockade to give his service to the Confederacy. Until his death in
1889 he was the brilliant and influential editor of the Charleston* News and Courier. *Sarah died in Paris in 1912, survived
by a son, Warrington.*

*She wrote the last entry in her dairy on June 15, 1865. It
was never intended for publication. Indeed, Sarah had directed
that it be burned, but at her son's plea it escaped oblivion. The
year after her death it was issued under the Title* A Confederate Girl's Dairy.

[Linwood] *August 28th.* [1862]

I am satisfied. I have seen my home again. Tuesday I was
up at sunrise, and my few preparations were soon completed,
and before any one was awake, I walked over to Mr. Elder's,
through mud and dew, to meet Charlie. He was very much opposed to my going; and for some time I was afraid he would
force me to remain; but at last he consented, and with wet
feet and without a particle of breakfast, at length found myself in the buggy on the road home. . . . Four miles from
town we stopped at Mrs. Brown's to see mother, and after a
few moments' talk, went on our road.

I saw the first Yankee camp that Will Pinckney and Colonel Bird had set fire to the day of the battle. Such a shocking sight of charred wood, burnt clothes, tents, and all imaginable articles strewn around, I had never before seen. The next turn of the road brought us to two graves, one on each side of the road, the resting-place of two who fell that day. They were merely left in the ditch where they fell, and earth from the side was pulled over them. Beyond, the sight became more common. And one poor fellow lay unburied, just as he had fallen, with his horse across him, and both skeletons. Next to Mr. Barbee's were the remains of a third camp that was burned; and a few more steps made me suddenly hold my breath, for just before us lay a dead horse with the flesh still hanging, which was hardly endurable. Close by lay a skeleton, —whether of man or horse, I did not wait to see. Not a human being appeared until we reached the Penitentiary, which was occupied by our men. After that, I saw crowds of wagons moving furniture out, but not a creature that I knew. Just back of our house was all that remained of a nice brick cottage— namely, four crumbling walls. It really seems as though God wanted to spare our homes. The frame dwellings adjoining were not touched, even. The town was hardly recognizable; and required some skill to avoid the corners blocked up by trees, so as to get in at all.

Our house could not be reached by the front, so we left the buggy in the back yard, and running through the lot without stopping to examine the storeroom and servants' rooms that opened wide, I went through the alley and entered by the front door. . . .

I stood in the parlor in silent amazement; and in answer to Charlie's "Well?" I could only laugh. It was so hard to realize. The *papier-machè* workbox Miriam had given me was gone. The baby sacque I was crocheting, with all knitting needles and wools, gone also. Of all the beautiful engravings of Annapolis that Will Pinckney had sent me, there remained a single one. Not a book remained in the parlor, except "Idyls of the King," that contained my name also, and which, together with the door-plate, was the only case in which the name of Morgan was spared. Where they did not carry off articles bearing our name, they cut it off, as in the visiting-cards, and left only the first name. Every book of any value or interest, except Hume and Gibbon, was "borrowed" permanently. I regretted

Macaulay more than all the rest. Brother's splendid French histories went, too; all except "L'Histoire de la Bastille."

The dining-room was *very* funny. I looked around for the cut-glass celery and preserve dishes that were to be part of my "dot," as mother always said, together with the champagne glasses that had figured on the table the day that I was born; but there remained nothing. There was plenty of split-up furniture, though. I stood in mother's room before the shattered armoir, which I could hardly believe the same that I had smoothed my hair before, as I left home three weeks previously. Father's was split across, and the lock torn off, and in the place of the hundreds of articles it contained, I saw two bonnets at the sight of which I actually sat down to laugh. One was mother's velvet, which looked very much like a football in its present condition. Mine was not to be found, as the officers forgot to return it. Wonder who has my imperial? I know they never saw a handsomer one, with its black velvet, purple silk, and ostrich feathers.

I went to my room. Gone was my small paradise! Had this shocking place ever been habitable? The tall mirror squinted at me from a thousand broken angles. It looked so knowing! I tried to fancy the Yankee officers being dragged from under my bed by the leg, thanks to Charles; but it seemed too absurd; so I let them alone. My desk! What a sight! The central part I had kept as a little curiosity shop with all my little trinkets and keepsakes of which a large proportion were from my gentlemen friends; I looked for all I had left, found only a piece of the *McRae*, which, as it was labeled in full, I was surprised they had spared. Precious letters I found under heaps of broken china and rags; all my notes were gone, with many letters. . . .

Bah! What is the use of describing such a scene? Many suffered along with us, though none so severely. All our handsome Brussels carpets, together with Lydia's fur, were taken, too. What did they not take? In the garret, in its darkest corner, a whole gilt-edged china set of Lydia's had been overlooked; so I set to work and packed it up, while Charlie packed her furniture in a wagon, to send to her father.

It was now three o'clock; and with my light linen dress thrown off, I was standing over a barrel putting in cups and saucers as fast as I could wrap them in the rags that covered the floor, when Mr. Larguier sent me a nice little dinner. I had been so many hours without eating—nineteen, I think, during three of which I had slept—that I had lost all appetite; but nevertheless I ate it, to show my appreciation.

As soon as I had finished my task, Charlie was ready to leave again; so I left town without seeing or hearing any one, or any thing, except what lay in my path. I cast many a longing look at the graveyard; but knowing Charlie did not want to stop, I said nothing, though I had been there but once in three months, and that once, six weeks ago. I could see where the fence had been thrown down by our soldiers as they charged the Federals, but it was now replaced, though many a picket was gone. Once more I stopped at Mrs. Brown's, while Charlie went on to Clinton, leaving me to drive mother here in the morning. Early yesterday we started off in the buggy, and after a tedious ride through a melting sun, arrived here about three o'clock, having again missed my dinner, which I kept a profound secret until supper-time.

By next Ash Wednesday, I will have learned how to fast without getting sick! Though very tired, I sat sewing until after sunset. . . .

## 9. MARY FRANCES BROOKS—"THE CHILDREN ALL WANT TO SEE YOU"

*The wife of Rhodam Maxie Brooks of Meriwether County, Georgia, had four small children. While her husband was off fighting Yankees she managed the farm, taught the youngsters, and tried unsuccessfully to hire a "substitute" for him—a practice sanctioned by the Confederate conscript law. One hopes she got the pocketknife.*

Georgia, Meriwether Co.
September 3, 1862

Dear Beloved Husband,

. . . I was very glad to hear from you and to hear that you are well. This leaves me and the family well but I am so tired for I never get any rest night or day, and I don't think I will last much longer, but I will try to write to you as long as you stay there, if I can raise a pen. . . . We have had a very fine rain at last, it came last Saturday, Sunday, and Monday, but we have fair weather now and all hands are pulling fodder. Mr. Andrews sent two hands two days so I reckon if they don't have any bad luck they will get through by frost.

My dear, when I wrote to you last I thought I would get a man in your place, but I have failed. The man I thought of getting had already hired himself to another man, I could get plenty of men if I knew what to do and how much you would be willing to pay. Mr. Brown wants me to hire him, and says he will go for fifty dollars for two weeks, and me to pay his way, but I thought that was more than you would be willing to pay. Lutron has n't been here yet so I got Mr. Brown to take your note . . . and if he gets the money, I will send to you forthwith, for I want you home the worst sort, for I can't get anything attended to with out the money, it is money for every thing so you may know it is getting low with me, and I have got to buy bacon, and have n't any salt, and no one to see to it with out pay.

You wrote that you wanted to know how much the children had learned, they are getting along tolerable well. Henrietta is reading, writing and studying geography, and dictionary, Buddy can spell in three syllables very well, and I do not think I ever saw children grow as fast in my life as they all do, they all want to see you and talk of you very often. I have n't weaned the baby yet but I think I shall soon. My dear, I want you to try to get me a little pocket knife from the Yankees as long as you have got to trading with them.

I must close for want of room to write more. So farewell my dear husband,

MARY F. BROOKS

## 10. BELLE BOYD—"I RECEIVED MY COMMISSION"

*The most sensational of Southern spies, daughter of a well-known family of the Shenandoah Valley, was born at Martinsburg, Virginia (now West Virginia), on May 9, 1843. After attending Mount Washington Female College in Baltimore from twelve to sixteen, she made her debut in Washington so-*

*ciety in the winter of 1860–1861. Belle was an attractive, fair-haired, blue-eyed girl with a tall and charming figure. Prompt-ly she became a favorite. With secession her father Ben Boyd enlisted in the 2nd Virginia and the family returned to Martinsburg. Belle nursed the wounded in Valley hospitals.*

*Inspired by the Manassas exploit of Betty Duvall, Rose Greenhow's assistant, and encouraged by the gallant Turner Ashby, the chief of Stonewall Jackson's cavalry and scouts, Belle Boyd became a Confederate courier. As she moved about on her missions to Jackson, Stuart, Beauregard and oth-er generals, she soon fell under Union suspicion. She was ar-rested at Winchester and sent to Eutaw House in Baltimore, but General Dix kindly released her. Then she went to Front Royal in the Valley where her uncle and aunt kept a small ho-tel, which had been taken over by General Shields. She found this an ideal arrangement for espionage. While a council of war was being held in the dining room, Belle lay in the closet over it, her ear glued to a knothole which she had enlarged in the floor. As soon as the council was over she jumped on her horse, galloped fifteen miles to give her information to Ashby and was back home before dawn.*

*On May 23, 1862, came her opportunity to be of greatest service to the Confederacy. She had gathered all sorts of infor-mation about the several Union forces being concentrated against her "undaunted hero," Stonewall Jackson. By moving quickly he could save the bridges the Federals planned to wreck and keep the road open for an advance on Banks. Jack-son was ten miles from Front Royal. Belle ran over open fields, under a cross fire from pickets of both armies, climbed fences, crawled along the tops of hills, till she drew close to the first line of Confederates. Frantically she waved her sun-bonnet as a signal to advance. They caught on and did so. She succeeded in getting her full message to Jackson. A few days later he wrote her: "I thank you, for myself and for the Army, for the immense service that you have rendered your country."*

*Melodrama always attended Belle when she did not create it. A scout for the 5th West Virginia Cavalry, with whom she had fallen in love, betrayed her to the Union government. She was arrested on July 29, 1862, by order of Secretary of War Stanton, and carried to Old Capitol Prison in Washington. Leslie's Weekly said "the Secesh Cleopatra is caged at last."*

*After a month she was released in an exchange of prisoners and returned to Virginia.*[1]

September, 1862
Martinsburg, Virginia

The very day after my return home I rode out to the encampment, escorted by a friend of my family, in order to pay a visit to General Jackson. As I dismounted at the door of his tent, he came out, and, gently placing his hands upon my head, assured me of the pleasure he felt at seeing me once more well and free. Our interview was of necessity short, for the demands upon his valuable time were incessant; but his fervent "God bless you, my child," will never be obliterated from my memory, as long as Providence shall be pleased to allow it to retain its power.

In the course of our conversation the General kindly warned me that, in the event of his troops being forced to retreat, it would be expedient that I should leave my home again, as the evacuation of Martinsburg by the Confederates would, as on former occasions, be rapidly followed by its occupation by our enemies and that it would be unwise and unsafe for me to expose myself to the caprice or resentment of the Yankees, and run the risk of another imprisonment. He added that he would give me timely notice of his movements, by which my plans must be regulated.

Very shortly after the interview I have just noted, the General rode into the village and took tea with us, and on the very day after his visit I received from him a message to the effect that the troops under his command were preparing for a retrograde movement upon Winchester, and that he could spare me an ambulance, by aid of which I should be enabled to precede the retreat of the army, and thus keep my friends between my enemies and myself.

Acting upon General Jackson's advice, I removed to Winchester; and it was there and then that I received my commission as Captain and honorary Aide-de-camp to "Stonewall"

[1]Belle Boyd's autobiography gives a lavishly detailed account of all her romantic and well-nigh incredible adventures. Indebtedness is acknowledged to *Dictionary of American Biography*, II, 524, for a convenient condensation, and to *Spies for the Blue and the Gray*, by Harnett T. Kane (Garden City: Hanover House, 1954) for a highly entertaining version.

Jackson; and thenceforth I enjoyed the respect paid to an officer by soldiers.

Upon the occasion of the review of the troops in presence of Lord Hartingdon and Colonel Leslie, and again, when General Wilcox's[1] division was inspected by Generals Lee and Longstreet, I had the honor to attend on horseback, and to be associated with the staff officers of the several commands. . . .

I went on to Charlottesville, where I remained some time.

At last, feeling very anxious to rejoin my mother, I determined to write to General Jackson and ask his opinion upon the step I so longed to take. I was prepared to run almost any risk; but, at the same time, I resolved to abide by the General's decision.

It was pronounced in the following note, which I transcribe verbatim:

"Head-Quarters, Army of Virginia,
"Near Culpepper Court-House.

"My Dear Child,

"I received your letter asking my advice regarding your returning to your home, which is now in the Federal lines. As you have asked for my advice, I can but candidly give it. I think that it is not safe; and therefore do not attempt it until it is, for you know the consequences. You would doubtless be imprisoned, and possibly might not be released so soon again. You had better go to your relatives in Tennessee, and there remain, until you can go with safety. God bless you.

"Truly your friend,
"T. J. JACKSON."

I lost no time in acting upon this sound advice, and was soon "on the road" once more.

[1] Major-General Cadmus M. Wilcox, C. S. A.

# V

# HIGH HOPES WANING

*September 1862—May 1863*

    *The armies of the Confederacy launched three offensives in the autumn of 1862.*

    *On September 5 General Lee and the Army of Northern Virginia crossed the Potomac and invaded Maryland. On the sixteenth and seventeenth he fought at Antietam (or Sharpsburg) an indecisive battle with McClellan, who had been restored to command after Second Manassas. The seventeenth was the bloodiest day of the whole war. Out of less than 40,000 men Lee lost 8,000; out of 70,000 McClellan lost more than 12,000. His disproportionate force so hurt, Lee recrossed the Potomac into Virginia.*

    *On September 7 General Braxton Bragg invaded Kentucky. He gave up a good position to go to Frankfort to inaugurate a Confederate Governor of Kentucky, letting General Don Carlos Buell acquire reinforcements at Louisville. Buell marched against Bragg's divided command, part of which he met and fought at Perryville on October 8. In a tactical victory Bragg lost 3,000 men out of 15,000; Buell nearly 4,000 out of more than 25,000 actively engaged. So depleted, Bragg drew back toward East Tennessee.*

    *Early in October General Earl Van Dorn and Sterling Price made a desperate effort to retake the stronghold of Corinth, but were beaten off and driven back in Mississippi by General W. S. Rosecrans.*

    *Lincoln, in his effort to find a general who could cope with the great Virginians, tried Ambrose E. Burnside, but the frightful decimation at Fredricksburg on December 13 proved he was not up to the mark. Betty Maury was one among Southern millions who rejoiced for a great victory. Several weeks before the battle, the message went out from the head-*

*quarters of the Army of Northern Virginia: "General Lee desires me to state, for the information of the Secretary of War, that of barefooted men there are in total 6466."*

*At the Battle of Stone's River, or Murfreesboro, in Tennessee (December 31, 1862-January 2, 1863) Braxton Bragg lost 10,000 men. He withdrew to Tullahoma, and Rosecrans occupied Murfreesboro on January 4.*

*The miscalled "Fighting" Joe Hooker was the next one to try things for Lincoln. He was terrifically outfought and defeated by Robert E. Lee at Chancellorsville, but Lee lost there his right arm—Stonewall Jackson—and more than 10,000 Confederates fell, dead or wounded.*

*So the Union of Southern States was being drained of its vital force, but not of its stanch determination. Undiscouraged, it fought on with hope deferred. Back home or in exile the women gave their thrift and love. Some of them, like young Emma Sansom down in Alabama, had active parts to play.*

## 1. CASSIE SELDEN SMITH—"WHAT SHALL I NAME THE BABY?"

*Cassie, daughter of Samuel S. Selden of Lynchburg, Virginia, met thirty-seven-year-old Edmund Kirby Smith in August 1861 during his convalescence from a wound received at First Manassas. They were married on September 24.*

*Edmund Kirby Smith, born in St. Augustine, Florida, had distinguished himself in the Mexican War and risen rapidly in the Confederate Army from colonel to major-general. Early in 1862 he had been given command of the Department of East Tennessee. In June he invaded Kentucky, won the Battle of Richmond, and occupied Lexington. His force was united with Bragg's after the Battle of Perryville (October 8) and he commanded the rear guard as Bragg retired. Now a lieutenant-general, he was in Middle Tennessee when Cassie wrote him this letter from back home.*

*Some months later she joined him in Tennessee. When in February 1863 he was placed in command of the Trans-Mississippi Department she followed him to Shreveport. In the spring of 1864 she moved to Hempstead, Texas, for the rest of the war. On May 26, 1865, General Smith surrendered the last large military force of the Confederacy and sought refuge in Mexico and Cuba. Cassie went to Washington to secure permission for his return to the United States. He got back in November. For a short while the Kirby Smiths were in Kentucky where Edmund tried his hand running a military school. From 1870 to 1875 they were in Nashville where he was president of the University. From then on they lived happily in Sewanee, Tennessee, where he was professor of mathematics at the University of the South. Edmund died in 1893, Cassie in 1905. She had five sons and six daughters.*

Lunchburg, Virginia Oct. 10th 1862

My dear Husband:

As I am unable to give account of myself, I have employed Nina to be my amanuensis. The day after *the baby* was born Mrs. B. wrote to you. . . . All day Saturday I felt badly, as night grew on the pains grew worse. I thought I had better make known my situation. Until then I kept it to myself, a silent sufferer. I could not *muster* up courage to send for a Dr. so the boy went off post haste for Mrs. B., the ladies' friend in such cases, with the information that if I grew worse Dr. Owens should be sent for & chloroform administered which however was not done, although I suffered great pain all night Saturday and all day Sunday. I walked the floor (when I could) in extreme agony & not until twelve o'clock at night was the baby born—& after such a length of suffering Mrs. B. said I had a *good* time. If mine was good what can the worst be?

At first, I regretted the baby was not a boy—as you were so anxious that it should be so, but she is a dear little girl, & I feel thankful it is all over. She is a little, fat creature, & only weighs six pounds. Her eyes are very dark blue. I think they will be like yours. Her mouth is beautiful, forehead fine, but I can't say much about her nose. Everybody says it is a pity she is not a *Little General.* I have one consolation—she is very good. Sleeps well & gives no one any trouble. Our Mary is with me & is very faithful & kind—nurses me well. Josephine was with me during all my trouble. I am doing very well—am very prudent—dieting myself to try & get rid of dyspepsia. I wish so much that you were with me & trust that you can be relieved from duty sometime this fall.

What shall I name the baby? Can you not think of a pretty fancy name—Spanish names are pretty—something uncom-

mon as I consider her an *uncommon baby*.[1] You must come
on as soon as you can to have her christened. I am glad &
proud of your success in Ky.

I lie in bed, look at your picture & the baby, & think of you
all the time. . . .

I will give you continued assurances of mine & the baby's
good health.

I recd. the letter sent by Genl. Marshall's[2] cousin. I have
written every week since you have been in Ky., sending your
letters to Knoxville. I recd. the box sent from Barboursville—
which was very acceptable. I thank you very much for it.
Write when you can to

Your devoted wife
CASSIE

## 2. CORDELIA LEWIS SCALES—"I NEVER WALK OR RIDE WITHOUT MY PISTOL"

*Delia Scales was born on July 10, 1843, at the family
home "Oakland," eight miles north of Holly Springs in northern Mississippi. Her brothers Dabney and Henry became officers in the Confederate Navy, and Joe was an aide to General
Beauregard. All through the war there were movements of
troops in and about Holly Springs. Oakland was repeatedly
used as headquarters by officers of the invading armies and at
intervals furnished hospitality to Confederates from near-by
encampments.*

*Cordelia carried on a lively, slapdash correspondence with
her old school friend Lou Irby, of Como Depot, some thirty
miles away.*

Home Sweet Home
Oakland Oct. 29 1862

My dear darling Loulie:

I have just received your letter of the 29th of September; &
I do not blame you for thinking I had forsaken you after writing three letters & not hearing a word from me; but before I

[1] They named the baby Frances.
[2] Brigadier-General Humphrey Marshall, C. S. A.

proceed farther, I must clear myself—in the first place I have received only two letters, & you remember the Yankees paid us a visit soon after the reception of the first, & after their departure I was taken very sick very sudden one morning. Oh! Loulie I cannot describe my sufferings, I had three attacks of conjestion. After that I was then taken with inflammation of the stomach. I had three Doctors (enough to kill any common person). They all gave me up. . . . Brother Joe ran the risk of losing his life to save mine by making two trips to Memphis for ice & lemons for me, & I do think the ice was the means of saving my life. . . . And Lou what do you think, they shingled my hair & it was so long & even & I had learned to braid & tuck it up like a grown lady. You do not know how becoming it was. I have enough to make me a beautiful braid. . . . I wish you could see me now with my hair parted on the side with my black velvet zouave on & pistol by my side & riding my fine colt, Beula. I know you would take me for a Guerilla. I never ride now or walk without my pistol. Quite warlike, you see. We have had the house full of our soldiers ever since the Yankees left. I suppose you know our Army is encamped almost in sight of us. I was down at Gen Tilghman's[1] headquarters yesterday & had the pleasure of dining with the officers, enjoyed myself so much. I sent some wine down to them (the General and other officers there) & thought we would brake up with a barn dance. Lou, I do wish you were here. We would have so much fun. Do please come up. I will go home with you. Now please come Loulie. I think we have about fifty soldiers with us every day. They are as thick as the flies used to be in the dining room of the old College. Speaking of the College reminds me to tell you that it is full of Federal soldiers & Dr. C. has taken the *oath*.

I do wish you could see the camps. The tents look so pretty. I must tell you about the Yankees as you are so anxious to know how they behaved. You may congratulate yourself, my dear friend, on being slighted by them. They came & stayed in our yard all the time. The camp was where our soldiers are now. And they use to order the milk to be churned any time & they took corn, fodder, ruined the garden & took everything in the poultry line. Hulberts[2] division, the very worst, stayed

---

[1]Brigadier-General Lloyd Tilghman, C. S. A.
[2]Major-General Stephen A. Hurlbut, U. S. A.

here with us nearly all the time. I never heard such profanity in all my life & so impudent, they would walk around the house & look up at the windows & say, "wonder how many Secesh gals they got up there." I did not have my pistol & Ma would not let me go where they were, but one evening she was so worn out she sent me down to attend to the skimming of some wines & other household matters, when she thought they had all left. Just as I got out in the yard, two Cavalry men & six infantry came up & surrounded me. Pa was not at home. Ma & Sis Lucy were looking on & were frightened very much for they knew I would speak my mind to them if they provoked me. The first Lt. asked me if we had any chickens. I told him, "no," "Any milk?" I said, "no,"—that some of his tribe had been there that morning & got everything in that line. He smiled & said "they did not pay you for them?" I told him a few pretended to pay by giving us federal money, that I preferred leaves to that. He said "why federal money dont seem to be in demand." I said "not down this way sure." The second Lt. a red-haired ugly pert thing commenced to laugh about our men running from Holly Springs & said "our men never run, miss." I told him, no, we all knew what a orderly retreat they made from Bull Run, Manassas, & Leighsburg,[1] that it did their army a great deal of credit & that I hope they felt proud of it. One of the pickets remarked then "Oh! hush Tom you dont know how to talk to Secesh gals." I turned to him & thanked him that we were all ladies in the South. The 2nd. Lt. got very mad at what I said about their men running—said, "I can inform you miss, I was in the battle of Leighsburg & our men did not run far." I told him I knew they did not, they ran as far as they could and then jumped in the river. The first Lt. broke out in a laugh & said "Ah! Tom shes got you now," & turned to me & said, "I admire your candor very much. I had much rather see you so brave than for you to pretend to entertain Union sentiments." I told him that there wasnt a Union man, woman, or child in the state of Mississippi & the first man that he was to shoot him right there for he did it only to protect his property. He said he would & wanted to know if all the ladies were that brave. I informed him they were & if they whipped this part of our army that we had girls & boys enough

---

[1] Battle of Ball's Bluff on the Potomac, near Leesburg, Virginia, October 21, 1861.

to whip them. One of the soldiers said, "I think you had better inspire some of your men with your bravery." I told him that our men needed no inspiration whatever. The Lt. then said to me "Now, Miss, you southern ladies would not fight, you are too good natured." I said we were very good natured but when our soil was invaded & by such creatures as they were it was enough to arouse any one—he wanted to know what I styled them. I told him Yankees or Negro thieves. This made him very mad & he told me they were western men. I told him I judged people by the company they kept, that they fought with them & stayed with them that "birds of a feather would flock together." He remembered & turned & left then. I wish you could have seen me when I walked away just like the very ground was polluted by them. The first Lt. asked me for some water when he saw I was going, I told him there was a spring on the place if he wanted any. He then told me that such bravery should be rewarded—that nothing on the place should be touched. He made all the men march before him & he did not let them trouble anything. . . . I could write you a newspaper about them but I reckon you are tired now & it makes me mad to think about them. Write soon to your true friend,

DELIA

Excuse this scribbling I can get no pens fit to write with. If you read this it is more than I can do.

Your friend,
DELIA

## 3. MARY WILLIAMS PUGH—WE HOPE
### TO REACH TEXAS

*Mary, daughter of John Williams was born at Leighton plantation, Assumption Parish, Louisiana. On February 7, 1861, she married Richard L. Pugh, son of the master of Dixie plantation near Thibodaux in Lafourche Parish. The next year Richard enlisted in the Washington Artillery at New Orleans. He campaigned under General Bragg in Mississippi, Tennessee and Kentucky. When the Federal troops of General Godfrey*

*Weitzel threatened the Bayou Lafourche late in October 1862
Mary joined her father and mother for a journey to Rusk, in
east central Texas. They carried their many slaves with them,
and their household and plantation equipment. It was hard,
month-long travel. They stayed in Rusk till hostilities ceased.*

*Mary had five children. Three sons went to Virginia Mili-
tary Institute. When Richard died in 1885 she bought Live
Oaks plantation in Lafourche Parish and spent the rest of her
days there, living on to a grand old age.*

*(According to Lyle Saxon in* Old Louisiana *"there was an
old Louisiana conundrum: Why is Bayou Lafourche like
the aisle of a church? And the answer was: Because there are
Pughs on both sides of it.")*

Between Opelousas & Alexandria [Louisiana],
Sunday night Nov. 9th 1862

My *dear dear* husband

How little did I dream when I last wrote you that my next
letter would be written so far away from our dear old home
yet here we are in this miserable country feeling very grateful
& happy at our escape from the horrid wretches who are now
doubtless enjoying themselves in that same old home. You will
have heard long before receiving this of the Bayou being in
their possession & I know have suffered great anxiety in not
knowing what had become of us so I will go back two weeks &
try to tell you as well as I can how this thing has all come
about. On Saturday morning (two weeks ago yesterday) we
heard Yankees were at Donaldsonville, but this being a common report caused no alarm. Judge then of our astonishment
Saturday evening when we heard they were coming down the
bayou & that our troops had fallen back twelve miles where
they said they would make a stand. This quieted the people as
they believed our troops would whip them back but no sooner
did the Yankees show themselves again than our troops retreated to the piece of woods just above Mr. Littlejohn's where
they did make a final stand but were badly defeated owing to
miserable management. But for the pretense of Gen. M—[1]
to fight above Napoleon many would have moved their negroes—as it was they were completely sold & caught.

At daylight Sunday morning Pa went up to the camp above

[1]General Alfred Mouton, the Confederate commander.

Mr. L's & returned saying he did not believe our officers had any great desire to fight & thought it more than probable we would have to leave & advised us to begin packing immediately. At twelve oclock we were fully convinced we would have to go & in the evening after a long day spent in packing I rode up to Dixie, sent for all the negroes & told them there was a strong probability of the Yankees coming in which case it was your desire that I should move & take all of them—that you had plenty of money to support them until they could return home (a big story isn't it?) & that you would certainly take care of them as long as possible, &c. They all expressed great regret at leaving their "good fields" but said they were willing to do anything I said. I then sent them off to get their clothes ready in case we were forced to go. When I reached home about dark Pa and David[1] were there & had made up their minds to leave next morning at daylight as the Yankees were by this time nearly down to Mr. Littlejohn's & only waiting for the next morning to begin the fight.

About ten oclock that night Pa & David went up to Dixie & told the negroes they must be ready to start at daylight. They sat up all night cooking & getting ready & I met them all on the road next morning looking bright & happy. They have behaved as well as possible since we started notwithstanding they have had every example to do otherwise. The morning we started about 27 of Pa's had disappeared, amongst them Jim Bynum (Will you ever have faith in one again?), old Mary Nell & her husband, & old David & his family & old Virgil & his family. The first night we camped Sylvester left—the next night at Bayou B. about 25 of Pa's best hands left & the next day at Berwick Bay nearly all of the women & children started —but this Pa found out in time to catch them all except one man & one woman. Altogether he had lost about sixty of his best men. He bears his losses very cheerfully all things considered & says he thinks he was fortunate in saving what he has done. As I wrote you David started with us but turned back at Bayou Boeuf. Twelve of his best hands left him the morning we started & as many more at Bayou B. so this decided him to return as he was afraid of being left with only women & children. Your Mother started little Nathan with David but he left with the last twelve. He told some of the negroes he

[1] Mrs. Pugh's brother.

was going back to your Mother. Now all of this was going on
around & about your negroes & of course they heard all the
talk & had everything to induce them to behave badly & every
opportunity to go if they wished—but they are all here still &
as humble & respectful as possible. I really feel *grateful* to
them for their good behavior & you have every reason to be
proud of them as I have told them you would be. They are the
talk of every neighborhood they pass through as they are such
exceptions to other negroes. Even Aunt Tiby is along. I tried
for some time to persuade her to stay—but she seemed so unwilling that I consented she should come. I thought too her
staying might tempt Sharp to run off & as negroes are so much
like sheep I did not desire any such example. I am very glad
now I brought her as she would certainly have wanted something alone there. She looks ten years younger already & is
*grinning* all the time. She talks a great deal about the sheep
which I think is her only regret. I had cloth enough left from
their clothes to make several cart covers—so they are very
comfortable at night. I brought their winter clothes along in
bundles—as I had not yet given them out I determined if any
of them ran off they should go without any clothes. I will give
them out in a day or two as we now think all danger is past.

Pa has at last determined after a great deal of thought to go
into Texas . . . *he thinks* about Polk county. There provisions can be had in any quantities and at a reasonable rate. We
hear 40 cents a barrel for corn—12 to 18 dollars for beef &c.
& as it is more than likely that we will be kept from home all
winter it is of course very necessary to look to this. The distance from here is about two hundred miles & Pa expects to
reach there certainly in two weeks. The roads & weather are
splendid & we hope to get the negroes in comfortable quarters
before the winter rains. Edward is along with his negroes—
more have left him since he started but he left several families
at home. Mrs. Young is along too & about eighty women &
children which Pa has to look after as all of her men have run
off with the exception of about twelve. Your Mother declined
moving her negroes & said they were too many to attempt it.
She would protect them there or nowhere & I think she was
perfectly right. She was very well when we left. I had a note
from her the day before we left.

We could hear distinctly the firing at Labadia as we drove
from our gate—the fight had just then commenced so you see

how narrowly we escaped as the Yankees were in Thibodaux[1] a few hours after. Oh Wretched[2] you can guess how sad it made me feel to say good-bye to all the things so dear to me. As I rode through the yard as I was leaving Dixie I felt as if I were saying good-bye again to you. Your sheep were quietly feeding with their many beautiful little lambs around them— your pretty colts and our little trees all looked so beautiful & were so dearly associated with you that it was hard to take what I know more than likely my last look at them. David engaged Mrs. Williams brother to look after & stay on the place & he said he would turn the sheep & two small colts in the fields & try & keep them hid until the Yankees left, but they find out everything so we may as well make up our minds never again to see anything left there—if we do find anything it will be an agreeable surprise. Ma brought nothing but her clothes & bedding—not a single piece of furniture—her glass & china are packed & sent to Mrs. S. hoping she might protect them. Pa left old Mr. R. his engineer to stay in the house & look after the place. He left old Uncle Punch & one or two other old negroes to assist him—but I am afraid the Yankees will carry them off.

Pa had sold all of his crop to the government but left your sugar all in his sugar house & some of it in the moulds—he says he could have sold it for sixty thousand dollars—but of course the Yankees will save him that trouble. We have heard all sorts of stories since leaving but don't know what to believe. One is that they have visited & stripped Gen Bragg's place.[3] We saw Mr. Miles Taylor at Mr. Wilson's where we spent two days—they have been to his place & taken off everything that could walk—not even a chicken left. He borrowed a coat & came off with his daughter & they are spending some time with Mr. Wilson. The Yankees did not wait until they reached Thibodaux to begin their work of destruction but commenced as soon as they reached the bayou. I hear they have taken all of Mr. R.'s negroes—killed two who refused to

[2]They reached Thibodaux on October 27.

[3]A pun on her husband's name, Richard, used as a term of endearment.

[4]Braxton Bragg had married Elisa Brooks Ellis of Louisiana in 1849 and bought a plantation in Lafourche Parish after he resigned from the U. S. Army in 1856. He named it "Bivouac." From now on Mrs. Bragg was a refugee.

go with them. Your brother Walter took his negroes off but I have not heard where to. Mr. Dillon, Jr. has overtaken us & says they have taken all of his father's & all of old Mr. Parkins —even old Lucinda. It is said they have made a camp of all of the negroes on Mr. Buxton's place until they can send them off but a great many they have already sent.

Frank poor fellow leaves on tomorrow morning. I have written this tonight to send by him as he promises me faithfully to go to see you if you are anywhere near. He seems much to prefer returning to his old company & I don't wonder at anyone being disgusted with the military doings here. We all feel very sorry to see him go again but God grant that he soon may return to us.

We hear nothing encouraging except rumors of intervention which we are afraid to believe. I have almost despaired of the war ever ending though many persons look for it by Spring & now Wretched that I have told you as well as I can in this hurried way all of our troubles of the past two weeks I must take a little time to pour out my heart to you which has been so full & so sad for the two past months. First of all I have not heard one word from you in all that time. My last letter was dated Sept. 6th. I knew all of this time that you were so situated it was impossible to get letters back to me. I should have been crazy long before now—*no one* has received a letter from Gen. Bragg's army since my last one came—not even Mrs. Bragg. I have kept myself alive from day to day hoping better things for tomorrow—expecting each day to bring up something which would permit me to go at least enough to hear from you. When I look back & think of the long long time spent without news from you I look at myself in astonishment & wonder how I have stood it. . . . I have tried so hard to please you by bearing this patiently & cheerfully dear Wretched that surely now I deserve some reward. All of my cries have been taken in our dear old room so no one but you will ever know of them. Yesterday I must confess I did behave badly but I have been thinking for some time of going to Miss. with Frank & yesterday when he determined to go tomorrow & I knew I could not go with him it was more than I could bear. I expect he will tell you how much I *did* cry—but I know dear Wretched it would be wrong for me to leave the negroes now & I go with them most cheerfully once I knew twould be your wish but my good behavior now is all put on & will soon disappear unless I see something brighter ahead—the truth is Wretched you *must* come home. Pa says your interests demand that you should leave the army & *he* thinks it your duty to come if you possibly can. You can certainly find some way of getting off—either a substitute or this late exemption law which requires one white man to every twenty-five slaves. Many persons have been taking advantage of this & why cannot you?

Mr. Williams,[1] although he is with us now, is very much dissatisfied at having left his family & wishes to return now to see after them but I told him I could not consent to have him go until we arrived at our place of destination & got the negroes a little comfortable & straight—so he has agreed to go on—but of course he will not be contented to stay there & have his family on the bayou & it will be impossible for him to bring them over even if the Yankees would allow it. So I know when I once let him go I may make up my mind not to see him again for some time although he says he will return as soon as he sees that his family is comfortable—but it would be so much better Wretched if you could be yourself with your negroes—they are satisfied now but I don't know how long I can keep them so—besides Pa has more than he can attend to. Mrs. Young has attached herself on to him *for the war* & this with her women is no slight tax. Pa says you *ought* to come Wretched & you know he would never say this unless he believed it. Frank Nicholls & his wife are here. He has a furlough & speaks of resigning to take care of the G. family. I wish he would & relieve Pa. I have told your negroes that I thought as soon as you hear of this you would come & I think it has had a great deal to do with their good behavior. They look so happy at the idea. Surely Wretched you have done enough now to satisfy yourself & every one else so come now if only for the sake of your little wife. . . . You must write to me immediately upon the receipt of this if you are where you can possibly write. We know nothing here except that Gen. Bragg has fallen back & can't even find out where his army is.[1] Direct your letters to Opelousas, La. care "William J. McCulloch, Surveyor General." Pa had made arrangements

[1]The Pughs' overseer.
[1]Bragg and his army had retired to Murfreesboro after the Battle of Perryville.

with him to send my letters on—but heaven grant dear
Wretched you may yourself come. I have lost all hope of letters. I sent you by Frank the shirts I have made for you. I
have been very happy in making them though I have buried
my face in them & taken many good cries. I know *you* will appreciate them & think them nice & will acknowledge for *once*
that you have a sweet little wife—no one else has put a stitch
on them. I did it all myself. Tell Caesar when he washes them
he must pull the *tails long* & the sleeves wide else they will
draw up & be uncomfortable. I have many other little things I
would like to send you & some things for Caesar but Frank is
uncertain about seeing you as he does not know where the
army is & as he may be forced to send the shirts by some one
going I am afraid to make too large a bundle.

It is very late & I am all alone writing this when I know I
ought to be in bed as we start very early tomorrow morning
but it has been such a long time since I have written you & I
have so much to say that I feel as if I would rather never stop.
When you do come Wretched (for you will come, *I know you
will*) how much we will have to tell each other—how many
nights I will keep you awake—but ah when, when will they
come? You must remember me kindly to Caesar. I have taken
a boy to drive me that Mr. Williams calls "Yellow Lewis." He
is a very nice obedient fellow & gets on with the carriage &
horses as well as anyone. I am now driving Champ & Inkey.
Poor old John died at Mr. Nelson's with lock jaw fever stick-
ing a nail in his foot. . . .

I do sincerely pray that Frank will be able to see you my
dear dear Wretched. I know it will be such a satisfaction to
you to see him. You must ask him all you want to know. How
sorry I am that he must go. May we meet him soon at
home. . . .

God bless & take care of you. Yours fondly & devotedly
                                                    MARY

                                        La. Near Sabine City
                                    Tuesday night. Nov. 18th/62

My *dear dear* husband,

We reached this place this morning and will remain here at
a comfortable house until tomorrow by which time the wagons
will all be across Sabine river when we cross & begin our journey again. So far we have got on very well but for the last
week rather slowly owing to bad roads & sometimes bad hills.

However we hear now that these are all over with so we hope we get on more rapidly. We have had no break driving—no sick mules or sick negroes. Pa has only had a few slight breaks with his wagons. Mrs. Young has been in a *stew* from the time we started until now & I am afraid her troubles are not over —her mules all in a wretched condition & not able to haul all of the old plunder she has allowed her negroes to bring. Of course we have all tried to help her as much as possible but she seems to feel so little gratitude that master & overseer are all getting tired—so I think hereafter she will hardly be able to keep up. At first as she started with Pa he felt bound to assist her as she could not possibly get on without it, having been left with only sixteen men—so we all lent her mules & men who have worked hard at her wagons for two weeks *apparently* without her knowledge for not one word of thanks has anybody ever received—on the contrary a stranger would think *we* were the favored party. Her face is nearly a yard long & would give anyone the "horrors" out here in these piney woods when we travel on until day without seeing even a bird. You must not think the troubles have passed me for I *do* feel sorry for the poor woman as who would not? but then her troubles are no greater than other peoples & she ought sometimes to think of this. I often often think as I see her management of her negroes &c. of what you once said of her "that for a woman who prided herself on her common sense she had very little." There are many little scenes which I have stored away for your amusement. At first Mr. Williams at my request did every thing in his power for her—in fact as much almost as if he had been her overseer—but for the last few days he won't do anything & says "I would not mind helping her Madam Pugh if she did not look at me like she thought I was so damned contemptible"—and I must confess I agree with him. . . .

Edward is still with us & in fine spirits. He says camping out has improved his health wonderfully. Mr. Brady serves as his overseer. Pa and all of the gentlemen stay at night with the wagons but we go on in our carriages to the nearest house. We have been living on beef & corn bread so we are almost as much delighted as the negroes are to get a little bacon—which we are beginning to find now at twenty five cents a pound. Pa bought a little for them yesterday & gave them all a treat. I don't think they were particularly well pleased when they first heard they were going to Texas—but I think the prospect of pork has quite reconciled them.

Your negroes continue to behave as well as one could wish & believe that every days travel takes them nearer to you. I often listen to their talk of this with a smile on my face but with a sad heart & wish so fervently I could believe as they do. I often speak to them of your coming as I think it encourages them to good behavior & Frederick says he has already commenced to look up the road for you—& I must tell you that you have one more negro than we started with which is more than every one can say. Two days ago Bill Roads wife Martha was taken sick soon after we started in the morning & in about an hour her son was born. Bill's cart fortunately was one that I had covered so Martha & Mattie took possession of that & got on finely without the cart ever being stopped. I brought all of the hospital beds & blankets of which I gave her a good supply for a bed & then had the cotton cover covered closely with blankets which will prevent her from taking cold. I give her every attention & suitable food & have no fears about her doing well. Bill is delighted & asked me to name the baby. I proposed "Louella" which they all think is splendid. Pa has had two born since we started & Mrs. McFall one & they all got on finely. Ma named one of hers "Tribulation." Pa has taken a great fancy to Jacob who has been invaluable ever since we started. Both of Pa's smiths ran off so Jacob has had his hands full as something or other is always breaking or coming loose.

Pa has not yet decided where he will settle but has decided to go higher up than Polk county as he thinks that too near Galveston & that Leon or some county there would be better —but nothing is decided as yet. Tomorrow he will leave us & go on ahead to look around & find places by the time we reach there. He will try to find some deserted farms if possible so as to have some cabins. At any rate he will get cleared land enough to raise corn, potatoes &c. in case we have to stay next year. Edward & his mother will try and get places in the same neighborhood but Pa will find places adjoining for himself & you. I think that would be much better than to have one large place as I know you would rather your negroes were kept & managed to themselves. Mr. Williams seems much better satisfied & does not seem in such a hurry to get back home although I have told him as soon as we were comfortably settled if he could find a good man to take charge of the negroes during his absence I was perfectly willing for him to go for three or four weeks. We can hear nothing from home except wild exaggerated stories & I suppose will hear nothing reliable until some one goes there. As soon as Pa finds a place & gets us to it he will leave to go to Chattanooga & will hire some man at Port Hudson to go in home & see what is going on there. Pa thinks we will be at the end of our trip in about ten days at farthest—so he will be on his way back in less than two weeks. Ah my dear dear Wretched I do wish the negroes were all comfortably provided for for the winter & that I might give all my thoughts to you & you only.

When you told me three months ago that you would be back Christmas how long the time seemed then—how much longer it has proven itself—but Christmas is about here & will or will it not be a happy one for me? I shall probably not find an opportunity of writing you again until Pa goes. He of course will come to see you when he crosses the river if he can possibly reach you—so you may look for him soon after receiving this.

Pa & Ma send their kindest love & the negroes send their usual "howdy's" & messages. Remember me to Robert & Caesar. I hope Pa will soon take you good news of us all & God grant you may soon bring us good news of yourself. In the meantime be happy & don't forget to love me or how much I love you.

Ten thousand kisses

Yours forever devotedly
MARY

## 4. MARY CAHAL—"ACCEPT MY BEST WISHES FOR YOUR HAPPINESS"

*As a relative of the Ready family, Mary Cahal of Lebanon, Tennessee, had met General John Hunt Morgan when he was camped at Muurfreesboro in the spring of 1862. She was not present at the wedding of twenty-one-year-old Martha Ready and the thirty-seven-year-old general Sunday evening,*

*December 14, 1862. The exigencies of war prevented the sending of invitations far and wide. John's brother Tom was hurt that he had not been asked. But Mary Cahal soon heard about it—from the general himself.*

*It was a brilliant occasion. The Ready house was a two-story building with spacious halls and rooms, just off the public square. With Christmas near, it was decorated with holly and winterberries. Mattie wore a lace dress with a veil. Morgan was in his general's regalia. Bishop Polk performed the ceremony, with his vestments over his lieutenant-general's uniform. Hardee—Alice Ready's friend—Breckinridge and Cheatham, corps commanders, were groomsmen. There was a lavish supper, with wines from Colonel Ready's cellar for toast after toast to the happy couple. The pretty Tennessee girls and the officers danced to a late hour, to the music of two regimental bands.*

*Mary Cahal's fears that marriage might interfere with Morgan's "career of glory" were soon allayed. He rode off on his Christmas raid six days after the wedding.[1]*

Lebanon
Dec. 16th. '62

My Dear Cousin Mattie

I have just received General Morgan's note informing me of your marriage.

I heard Sunday that it was to be on that day but was not certain until a few minutes since.

Tell the General I only excuse him for not sending the courier for the reason he gave, i.e., he was *so much in love* he forgot all but *you.*

Accept my best wishes my dear friend for your happiness and prosperity and present them to General Morgan.

I thought of you much on Sunday and wished that it might be a bright day and thus typical of a bright and happy life.

Uncle Robert wishes to be remembered and says he hopes your fondness for *matrimonal Union* will not make you *union* in a political sense. Also that you must remember your promise not to restrain the General in his career of glory, but encourage him to go forward. Perhaps it will be over soon.

My love to Alice & the General.

[1]See *Morgan and His Raiders,* by Cecil Fletcher Holland. New York: The Macmillan Company, 1942.

May God bless you my dear friend in all relations of life as I feel your affectionate heart deserves.

> Very Affectionately your friend
> MARY CAHAL

## 5. JULIA LeGRAND—"NEW ORLEANS IS FULL OF RUMORS"

*Life in occupied New Orleans brought limitations and hardship to Julia and Ginnie LeGrand. The animosity toward Ben Butler had been largely due to his Order No. 28: "When any female shall, by word, or gesture, or movement, insult or show contempt for any officer or soldier of the United States, she shall be regarded and held liable to be treated as a woman of the town plying her avocation." The general indignation which that created, hardly "pent-up," found expression in a poem written at the time of his departure from New Orleans, "The Ladies' Farewell to Brutal Ferocity Butler." Julia copied it into her diary. It began:*

> We fill this cup to one made up
> Of beastliness alone.

*Banks replaced Butler on December 16.*

*New Orleans, December 20th, 1862.* Butler, after his long, disgusting stay here has been compelled to yield his place, his sword, and much of his stolen property. Banks arrival and Butler's disgrace has created a vent for a long pent-up disgust.

General Banks has, so far, by equitable rule commanded the respect of his enemies. We know him as an enemy, it is true, but an honest and respectable one. Every rich man is not his especial foe, to be robbed for his benefit. Butler left on the steamer *Spaulding*, was accompanied to the wharf by a large crowd, to which he took off his hat. There was not one hurrah, not one sympathizing cry went up for him from the vast crowd which went to see him off—a silent rebuke. I wonder if he felt it!

Heard to-day of the existence of a negro society here called the "vaudo" (I believe). All who join it promise secrecy on pain of death. Naked men and women dance around a huge snake and the room is suddenly filled with lizards and other reptiles. The snake represents the devil which these creatures worship and fear. The existence of such a thing in New Orleans is hard to believe. I had read of such a thing in a book which Doctor Cartwright gave us, but he is so imaginary and such a determined theorist that I treated it almost as a jest. The thing is a living fact. The police have broken up such dens, but their belief and forms of worship are a secret. These people would be savages again if free. I find that no negroes discredit the power of the snake; those who do not join the society abstain from fear and not from want of faith.

*December 31, 1862.* I write, this beautiful last day of December, with a heart filled with anxiety and sorrow; with my own sad history that of others mingles. Our side has gained again. The Confederate banner floats in pride and security, but who can help mourning over the details of that ghastly battle of the Rappahannock.[1] Oh, Burnside! moral coward to lead men, the sons of women, into such a slaughter-pen to gratify a senseless president and a tyrannical giver of orders!

Our town is filled with rumors. There has been a bloody fight at Port Hudson,[2] it is said, and the brazen cannon which we have so often seen dragged through these streets have all been taken by our Confederate troops. Banks has ordered the return of the Federal troops sent up the river so proudly and confidently a short while ago, but it is reported that they are so surrounded by the Confederates that they cannot extricate themselves. It is rumored that we are to have a negro insurrection in the New Year (New Year's Day). The Federal Provost-Marshall has given orders that the disarmed Confederates may now arm again and shoot down the turbulent negroes (like dogs). This after inciting them by every means to rise and slay their masters. I feel no fear, but many are in great alarm. I have had no fear of physical ill through all this dreary summer of imprisonment, but it may come at last. Fires are

---

[1] Fredericksburg, December 13.

[2] Port Hudson and Vicksburg were the only places on the Mississippi then held by the Confederacy.

requent—it is feared that incendiaries are at work. Last night
was both cold and windy. The bells rang out and the streets re-
sounded with cries. I awoke from sleep and said, "Perhaps the
moment has come." Well, well, perhaps it is scarcely human to
be without fear. I wonder my Ginnie and I cannot feel as others do—whether we suffer too much in heart to fear in body,
or whether we lack that realizing sense of danger which forces
us to prepare for it. Mrs. Norton has a hatchet, a tomahawk,
and a vial of some kind of spirits with which she intends to
blind all invaders. We have made no preparations, but if the
worst happen we will die bravely no doubt.

The cars passed furiously twice about midnight, or later; we
were all awaked by sounds so unusual. There are patrols all
over the city and every preparation has been made to meet the
insurrectionists. I indeed expect no rising now, though some of
the Federals preach to the negroes in the churches, calling on
them to "sweep us away forever." General Banks is not like
Butler; he will protect us. The generality of the soldiers hate
the negroes and subject them to great abuse whenever they
can. This poor, silly race has been made a tool of—enticed
from their good homes and induced to insult their masters.
They now lie about, destitute and miserable, without refuge
and without hope. They die in numbers and the city suffers
from their innumerable thefts.

Christmas passed off quietly, and, to us, sadly. The ladies
gave a pleasant dinner to the Confederate prisoners of war
now in the city. Rumors from Lafourche that Weitzel has been
defeated. His resignation was sent on the *Spaulding*, but has
not been received yet by the President. He resigns, they say, to
marry an heiress, Miss Gaskett. She, a creole of Louisiana,
consents to marry one who has spent months in command of
soldiers who have been desolating her country.

# 6. SARAH L. WADLEY—"THE NEGROES
## ARE HAVING A MERRY TIME"

*Sarah was one of the eight children of William Morrill
Wadley of New Hampshire and Rebecca Everingham Wadley
of Cockspur Island off Savannah. Her father was president of
the Vicksburg, Shreveport & Texas Railroad. Sarah got her*

*schooling from a governess who lived with the family—a con-*
*venient arrangement as the railroad man moved from one*
*home to another in Louisiana and Mississippi. In December*
*1862 the Secretary of War nominated him to take supervision*
*and control of transportation for the government on all rail-*
*roads in the Southern states, but the Senate refused to confirm*
*the appointment.[1] After the war he became president of the*
*Central Railroad of Georgia. He built "Great Hill," a house*
*some twelve miles from Macon. Sarah lived there to an ad-*
*vanced age.*

*She was seventeen when she penned these entries in her dia-*
*ry. Her "Oakland" is a different one from Delia Scales's.*

                                        **"Oakland"**
                              **Near Monroe, Louisiana**

Dec. 25/1862. Christmas night.

It has been a sad Christmas to us, Father was not here. We
received a despatch Tuesday night saying that he must return
to Richmond before coming home.

Friday-Dec. 26th/1862

Our turn has come at last. We heard this morning the Yankees had come as far as Delhi (on the railroad) burning everything in their track, and coming four miles an hour. We
know nothing of their force, all suppose that they are coming
to Monroe. I do not know whether our few troops will resist
or not. Willie is gone in at full speed to ascertain the truth of
the matter and to bring back our teams which went in this
morning for corn. Oh if Father was here! I am determined,
come what may, never to renounce my country, but what is
before us!

The negroes are busy barbecueing and cooking for their
party night. They may have to start before day but we shall let
them enjoy themselves while they can.

*Night.* Willie returned this evening, bringing us no further
news. Mr. McGuire thinks that the Yankees e'er this have
gone back to their gunboats. It is true that they laid Delhi in
ashes.

---

[1] See *Victory Rode the Rails,* by George Edgar Turner. Indianapolis: The Bobbs-Merrill Company, Inc., 1953.

General Blanchard[1] has ordered all the men under forty five to meet at Cotton post tomorrow morning early, he purposes to make a stand at Monroe. I hope he will.

We have been watching the negroes dancing for the last two hours. Mother had the partition taken down in our old house so that they have quite a long ball room. We can sit on the piazza and look into it. I hear now the sounds of fiddle, tambourine and "bones" mingled with the shuffling and pounding of feet. Mr. Axley is fiddling for them. They are having a merry time, thoughtless creatures, they think not of the morrow.

I am sad, very sad, tonight. Last Christmas Father watched their dancing with us; where is he now? Where shall we all be next Christmas, and tomorrow Willie[2] must go, perhaps to battle. I do not feel a single complaint in my heart, but I am sad. . . .

## 7. BETTY HERNDON MAURY—"GOD BLESSED US WITH VICTORY AT FREDERICKSBURG"

*Protected by 147 guns on the Stafford hills to the north of the Rappahannock, the attempts of General Burnside's grand army to cross the river, pass through the town of Fredericksburg and storm the Confederate position on Marye's Heights resulted in complete defeat and awful slaughter. Betty Maury overestimates the Union losses; still they amounted to 12,500 killed or wounded. All the great leaders of the Army of Northern Virginia were noble participants in that day of victory— Stonewall Jackson in a splendid new lieutenant-general's uniform, Jeb Stuart with his bright yellow sash and plumed hat. General Burnside was dazed by the defeat and grief-stricken for the loss of life.*

*Writing from Richmond where she was then living, Betty records in her diary what she had heard about the painful scene in the quaint old town she knew so well.*

[1] A. C. Blanchard.
[2] Sarah's brother.

Richmond. December 28, 1862

On the —— of November the whole of the Yankee Army moved down and occupied the heights opposite Fredericksburg. Our forces fronting them on this side of the Rappahannock.

In a few days General Burnside gave notice to the women and children to leave the town, that he would shell it in sixteen hours. Mamma and the children came down to Richmond in a cattle car and were put out at Milford depot, with five hundred others. The sick and aged were brought out of town on beds. Mrs. Randolph had a baby two days old when she was moved. The scene at the cars is described as very touching.

On the 13th of December God blessed us with a great victory at Fredericksburg. Upwards of eighteen thousand of the enemy were killed. We lost but one thousand. Even the Yankees acknowledge it to be a terrible defeat. The battle took place in and around the town. The streets were strewn with the fallen enemy. The houses were broken open, sacked, and used for hospitals and their dead were buried in almost every yard.

Dr. Nichols was there. Came as an Amateur with his friend General Hooker.[1] He occupied Uncle John's house (where his wife had been entertained for weeks at a time), drank up Uncle John's wine, used his flour and ate up Ellen Mercer's preserves.

I cannot find words to express my disgust and horror of the man who is so lost to all sense of delicacy and so cold blooded and heartless as to come—not at the stern call of duty—but for the love of it to gloat over the desolated homes of people whom he once called friends and who are relations and connections of his wife.

Mr. Corbin was here last night and gave us some account of the appearance of things in Fredericksburg. Almost every house has six or eight shells through it. The doors are wide open, the locks and windows broken. Two blocks of buildings were burned to the ground.

Our house was a hospital. He says every vessel in our house, even the vegetable dishes and cups, are filled with blood and water. There are large pools of gore on the floor. The table in

---

[1] General Joseph Hooker commanded at this time one of the three grand divisions of the Federal army.

the parlor was used as an amputating table—and a Yankee (Byron Pearce of N. Y.) is buried at the kitchen door. . . .

## 8. MARTHA READY MORGAN—"COME TO ME, MY DARLING"

*Three exciting weeks had passed since the wedding in Murfreesboro. In his two weeks of Christmas raiding General Morgan, master of the hit-and-run, had fought in Kentucky at Green's Chapel, Bacon Creek, Elizabethtown and Bacon Creek again. With Bragg's retreat Mattie and the lovely Alice had been forced to take flight from home. Under escort by members of General Hardee's staff, they reached the army at Winchester, Tennessee, fifty miles away.*

*This was a foretaste of what was to become habitual for Mattie—flights before the enemy, lonely vigils, brief intervals with her husband. On his most famous raid—into Indiana and Ohio, nearly into Pennsylvania, the Confederacy's "farthest north," in the summer of 1863—the general was captured and imprisoned in Columbus, Ohio. From the dreary old prison he wrote to Mattie two or three times a week in terms of cheer and confidence, but his concern for her steadily increased. Mattie and Alice were in Knoxville, in Augusta, in Knoxville again, in Danville with the Withers family. When they heard that their brother Horace was wounded at Chickamauga, Alice hurried off to take care of him. Alone and desperately anxious, Mattie grew seriously ill. Her baby was born dead.*

*The night of November 27, 1863, Morgan, always sensational, made his sensational escape with several fellow officers who dug through the cell floor into an air chamber, tunneled through a wall into the outer yard and scaled the outer wall. After various adventures he managed to reach Mattie in time for Christmas.*

*She accompanied him to Richmond for a great ovation on January 9, 1864. Mrs. Chesnut was on hand to hear General J. E. B. Stuart praise the hero to the crowd "with all his voice." Mattie told her: "At Covington, after the escape, General Morgan did not know where to turn or whom to trust. He decided upon Mrs. Ludlow. She gave him a warm welcome, and without a moment's hesitation or loss of time ordered two*

*horses saddled for Morgan, and one for her son. She handed
Morgan sixty dollars in gold, all she had in the house. 'Now
go. Ride for your life.' She did not show any fear of the venge-
ance Yankees were sure to wreak upon her and hers if they
knew the part she played in Morgan's escape." Mrs. Chesnut
goes on to say: "Throughout Kentucky it was the same thing.
Men and horses were at his command, and brave women tried
to force their money on him and were mortified when he refused."*

*Her general was with Mattie in Abingdon, Virginia, in the
summer of 1864.*

Winchester [Tennessee] Jan. 6th/63

Come to me my own Darling quickly. I was wretched but
now I am *almost* happy and will be quite when my precious
husband is again with me. I can bear anything Darling when
you are with me, and so long as I have your love—but when
separated from you and I know that you are surrounded by so
many dangers and hardships as you have been on your last expedition I become a weak nervous child. Have I not lived a
great deal, love, in the last three weeks? When I look back
now at the time, it seems three years. But in each hour I have
passed through, there has always been one dear face ever before me—and can you doubt whose face that was! If you do, I
dont intend to enlighten you, at least until you come. So there
is another inducement. I have so much to tell you, and so very
much to hear from you. Although I have heard nothing from
you since you left Glasgow, I *knew* you had accomplished
what you had in view—but oh I was so anxious for your safety.

I had some dark days, dearest, and when the battle was raging around me in such fury, and everybody from the com-
mander-in-chief to the privates were praying for "Morgan to
come," I thanked God in the anguish of my heart that it was
not for me to say where you should be. There was one contin-
ual inquiry at the front door—"When will Genl. Morgan be
here?" Madame Rumor says you attacked Nashville last Monday and as a natural course *captured* it.[1] Genl. Bragg established his head Quarters at this place. We reached here
today . . . and although an entire stranger to the people I am

[1]It was only rumor.

with, they received me, as the saying is, with open arms, because I am your Wife. We are comfortably, but very plainly accommodated. Alice is with me. Papa & Mama remained at home with Ella. I almost dread to hear from them. I am so impatient for tomorrow to come. When the Courier arrived Cols. —— & Johnston of Genl. Bragg's staff were calling upon us. Came with an invitation from the Genl. for us to join his Hd. Qts. but Gen. Hardee had a prior claim. I sent the papers giving an account of your expedition, or part of it, to Gen. B. Everybody is anxious to hear from you, and to see you, but none a thousandth part as much as your little wife.

I am at Mrs. McGee, just in the suburbs of the town, so you will know exactly where to find me. I love to write to you, Dearest, and your *sweet* letters always make me happy. It grieved me that I could send you no word of love from my pen while in Kty. Both because it would have been a relief to pour out my heart to you, and then, Darling, I feared you would forget me. You left me so soon. Genl. Hardee has just arrived, and regrets he will not be here when you come tomorrow. Alice sends love. . . . Good night, my *Hero*. My dreams are all of you.

Your affectionate

MATTIE

## 9. AGNES—"THERE IS NOT A BONNET FOR SALE IN RICHMOND"

*We owe to a lifelong friend the memory of the lively lady who preferred to be known only by her Christian name. When Mrs. Roger A. Pryor published her* Reminiscences of Peace and War *she happily included many of Agnes' letters to her. "Being a lady of the old school," explained Sara Pryor, "she is averse from seeing her name in print." We gather that her husband had been a Member of Congress in Washington at the same time as Roger, and now was a colonel on service with the Confederate army near Richmond, while Agnes, like Mrs. Chesnut, lived at the Spotswood Hotel. Her letters are filled with gossip of the Confederate capital; of White House receptions; of activities of old friends of Washington days. Since*

*paper was no longer available, she wrote on blank sheets torn
from an old album.*

*At this time Mrs. Pryor was a refugee near Suffolk, Virginia. Some of her own writing will appear later on.*

Richmond, January 7, 1863

My Dearie: Have you no pen, ink, and paper on the Blackwater—the very name of which suggests ink? I get no news of you at all. How do you amuse yourself, and have you anything to read? I am sending you to-day a copy of Victor Hugo's last novel, "Les Miserables," reprinted by a Charleston firm on the best paper they could get, poor fellows, pretty bad I must acknowledge. You'll go wild over that book—I did—and everybody does.

Major Shepard must order some copies for the brigade. As he has plenty of meat and bread now, he can afford it. I have cried my eyes out over Fantine and Cosette and Jean Valjean. The soldiers are all reading it. They calmly walk into the bookstores, poor dear fellows, and ask for "Lee's Miserables faintin'!"—the first volume being "Fantine." I've worlds of news to tell you. Alice Gregory is engaged to Arthur Herbert, the handsomest man I know. Alice is looking lovely and so happy. Helen came to see me in Petersburg, and is all the time worried about Ben. Did you know that Jim Field lost a leg at Malvern Hills—or in the hospital afterwards? He was such a lovely fellow—engaged to Sue Bland—I never saw a handsomer pair. Well, Sue thinks as much as I do about good looks, and Jim wrote to release her. She had a good cry, and finally came down to Richmond, married him, and took him home to nurse him.

Do you realize the fact that we shall soon be without a stitch of clothes? There is not a bonnet for sale in Richmond. Some of the girls smuggle them, which I for one consider in the worst possible taste, to say the least. We have no right at this time to dress better than our neighbors, and besides, the soldiers need every cent of our money. Do you remember in Washington my pearl-gray silk bonnet, trimmed inside with lilies of the valley? I have ripped it up, washed and ironed it, dyed the lilies blue (they are bluebells now), and it is very becoming. All the girls intend to plait hats next summer when the wheat ripens, for they have no blocks on which to press the coalscuttle bonnets, and after all when our blockade is raised we may find they are not at all worn, while hats are hats and never go out of fashion. The country girls made them last summer and pressed the crowns over bowls and tin pails. I could make lovely flowers if I had materials.

It seems rather volatile to discuss such things while our dear country is in such peril. Heaven knows I would costume myself in coffee-bags if that would help, but having no coffee, where could I get the bags?

The papers announce that General French[1] reports the enemy forty-five thousand strong at Suffolk. How many men has your General? Dear, dear!

But we are fortifying around Richmond. While I write a great crowd of negroes is passing through the streets, singing as they march. They have been working on the fortifications north of the city, and are now going to work on them south of us. They don't seem to concern themselves much about Mr. Lincoln's Emancipation Proclamation, and they seem to have no desire to do any of the fighting.

Your loving

AGNES

P.S.—I attended Mrs. Davis's last reception. There was a crowd, all in evening dress. You see, as we don't often wear our evening gowns, they are still quite passable. I wore the gray silk with eleven flounces which was made for Mrs. Douglas's[2] last reception, and by the bye, who do you think was at the battle of Williamsburg, on General McClellan's staff? The Prince de Joinville who drank the Rose wine with you at the Baron de Limbourg's reception to the Japs. Doesn't it all seem so long ago—so far away? The Prince de Joinville escorted me to one of the President's levees—don't you remember?—and now I attend another President's levee and hear him calmly telling people that rats, if fat, are as good as squirrels, and that we can never afford mule meat. It would be too expensive, but the time may come when rats will be in demand.

Dearly,

AGNES.

[1]Major-General William H. French, U.S.A.
[2]Wife of Senator Stephen A. Douglas.

## 10. CORDELIA LEWIS SCALES—"I WORE MY PISTOL ALL THE TIME!"

*For the sixth time Northern officers had made headquarters at Cordelia Scales's Oakland!*

*Late in 1862 General Grant's main base was at Columbus, Kentucky. Thence he used the railroad line south to Holly Springs, eight miles below Oakland, and built it up as a great secondary base. His plan was to send his principal army down the railroad while General William Tecumseh Sherman's force would float the winding Yazoo River in a fleet of transports. The objective of the combined operation was the capture of Vicksburg, the Confederacy's great stronghold on the Mississippi.*

*Sherman got started. But Grant had to change all his conceptions in a hurry. On December nineteenth the secretive, indefatigable N. B. Forrest got on his line to Columbus and began tearing up track and creating general havoc. And on the twentieth Earl Van Dorn burst into Holly Springs like a tornado and wrecked all those vast Union stores.*

*Delia writes again to her friend Lou Irby.*

> Destruction Hollow
> Mississippi
> Jan. 27th 1863

My Dear Sweet little Friend:

I really thought some time ago that I never should have the pleasure of writing to you again, & you have no idea how sad it made me feel, to think, that I was in the Federal line, & would never have the pleasure of holding sweet communion with the dearest friend I have on earth. Oh! Lou, I hope you may never experience such feelings as I did the day the Yankee army passed our home—you will think no doubt as I had stood two raids, that I ought to have got use to them & I suppose I would, if I had not seen the manner in which our troops left Holly Springs & I am sorry to say it was shameful; I could not keep from crying to save my life, I felt as though my heart would break—just a few days before I had attended the

"Grand review," & I felt so confident that our army intended making a stand, & that north Mississippi would be defended. But I soon found out it was a stampede instead of a stand, they anticipated making. Our soldiers were ready & anxious for a fight, & it was all owing to the bad generalship of Van-dorn & Pemberton,[1] that we did not drive the last blue devil from the country. When I saw the federals coming in such force, I thought this portion of the country would be held for some time & not like they had formerly done—stay a week or two & then "skeedadle," so you may know how bad I felt.

The first skirmish I witnessed was in front of our house at the pickett stand; our men were surprised by McPherson's[2] Cavalry. They were near enough to use their pistols; I'll tell you what our pickets run like clever fellows, they made rail-road time. After the fight was over three hundred of the Yan-kees came up to our house—one of the officers asked me, "Well, Miss, what made your men Skeedadle so." I told him that our men only wanted to show them that they would beat them at every game they tried, that they had beat them fight-ing so often, they wanted a little variety. Pa was out in the field soon after the skirmish took place & the Yankees on the hill in front of our house fired on him three times. One of the balls passed through his coat under his left arm, one by his ear, and the other through his hat—they knew he was an un-armed citizen too, Lou. I'll tell you what the cowardely rascals have no respect whatever, for age, nor sex.

The day the army came to Holly Springs, & when the wag-gon trains were passing thirty & forty of the Yankees would rush in at a time, take everything to eat they could lay their hands on, & break, destroy & steal everything they wanted to —all of our mules, horses & waggons were taken, 42 waggons were loaded with corn at our cribs, & a good many more after. I'll tell you what I thought we would certainly starve. One thousand black republicans, the 26th Ill., camped in our groves, for two weeks. We did have such a beautiful grove & place too, but you ought to see it now, it looks like some "ban-quet hall deserted"—all the gates and pailings are torn down & burnt & as for a rail it is a curiosity up here. Col. Gilmore was

---

[1]General John C. Pemberton, who had been in command of the Department of South Carolina and Georgia, was sent west by the government to supersede Van Dorn in November 1862.

[2]General James B. McPherson, U.S.A.

in command of the 26th. He made our house headquarters; he
use to let his men go out foraging every day & one day while
some of them were out stealing chickens & hogs about four
miles from here at Thompsons' place, a company of our
"guerillas" overhauled them—killing two & wounding two. I
never saw such enraged men in my life as they were when
those that were taken prisoners & paroled came in camp with
the news.

The Col. took Pa's room for a hospital; when they were
bringing the wounded in, I never heard men groan as they did
in my life; all our sick & wounded in the hospital did not make
as much noise as those two did. Gilmore searched our house
for arms & I wore my pistol (a very fine six shooter) all the
time & stood by my saratoga, would not permit them to search
it. One said, "She's a trump."

I met with an old school mate of Dabney's from Annapolis,
his name was Meriman, a first cousin of Meriman, the jewell-
er, in Memphis. I liked him as well as I could a Yankee; &
surprising to say he was a gentleman. . . . They had a large
flag waving in our grove & you could not see anything but blue
coats & tents. The Col. made the band come up & play Dixie
for me. After Mitchel's company killed those men they turned
Mrs. Thompson out of doors & burnt her house. The Col. left
our house with two companys & waggons, to plunder & destroy
the widow Mitchel's. When they got there & asked her if the
Captain was her son she told them "Yes, Billie Mitchel is my
son & I am proud of him. He is doing nothing but his duty & I
hope he'll continue, & sir as long as I have a crust of bread
that crust will be shared with him & his company." The Yankees turned· & left her & did not touch one thing. Her son is
such a brave fellow. Capt. Meriman told me "if her sons lack
bravery it wasnt their mothers fault."

The next set that camped on us was the 90th Ill. Irish Legion. They treated us a great deal better than the black republicans did—the Irish were all democrats. One of the officers'
wives, Mrs. Steward, staid here. She was a very nice lady. By
the way, she was almost a Secesh; she was begging me to play
for her, & I told her I played nothing but Rebel songs. She said
they were the very kind she wanted me to sing to her—so I
sang "My Maryland," "Bonnie Blue flag," "Mississippi Camp
Song," "Cheer Boys Cheer," "Life on the Tented Field," &

"Dixie." She said "Oh! they are beautiful, I dont blame you for loving them." She made me write them off for her.

The next day Capt. Flynn came up; he asked me if I knew what he came for. I told him no; he then said it was to beg a great favor of me & he hoped I would be so kind as to grant it, that he wanted me to sing "My Maryland" for him. At first I thanked him & told him I did not play for Federal officers but Pa said I must, that Capt. Flynn had kept us from starving & had been so kind to us so I consented. He was so much pleased with it that he got me to write the words off for him. I put a little Confederate flag at the top of it & wrote under it "no northern hand shall rule this land." He sent it on North to his wife.

I wish you could have seen the parting between Capt. Flynn & myself, the Major & him & a good many officers came up to tell me goodbye & the Major was saying he was going to reduce the south to starvation & then send us north. I said to him I had rather starve to death in the South than be a beggar in the North, Major. Capt. Flynn jumped up, caught me by the hand & said "Miss Scales, you are a whole-souled Rebel & I admire you so much for it. I do wish I could stay here & protect you while our army is retreating. I'd fight for you, God knows I would." That sounds strange for a Yankee, dont it?

The next we had were the "Grierson Thieves"[1] & the next the 7th Kan. Jay hawkers. I can't write of these; it makes my blood boil to think of the outrages they committed. They tore the ear rings out of the ladies ears, pulled their rings & brest pins off, took them by the hair; threw them down & knocked them about. One of them sent me word that they shot ladies as well as men, & if I did not stop talking to them so & displaying my Confederate flag, he'd blow my brains out. I sent him word by the lady that I did not expect anything better from Yankees, but he must remember two could play at that game. Capt. Bannett was telling me before they all left about Stonewall Jackson telling his men about the passage in the Bible where the South should drive the North in the sea.[2] I told him I hoped I would be at the jumping off place & see the last blue coat go under.

[1] The 6th Illinois Cavalry was commanded by Colonel Benjamin H. Grierson.

[2] See Daniel, XI.

Lou, I tell you what we've been through fiery trials, and if we did not exactly cuss, there is a great many of us *that thought* cuss mighty strong.

Oh! how I did shout when Vandorn came into Holly Springs. He made them "skeedaddle" shows you born. I was so glad I had the pleasure of seeing Mr. Yankee run; just the day before some of them asked me where our men were that they could not find any of them. . . . I would write more about it but Mr. Caldwell is waiting to start. He is going to mail it at Sardis. The girls are wearing such pretty garabaldies up here. . . .

Goodbye my dear Loulie, Your

Aff. friend

DELIA

## 11. BETTY HERNDON MAURY—"WE ARE TO BE TURNED OUT OF DOORS"

*We have now some of the concluding entries in Betty's diary. That of February 18, 1863, is the last. The pitifulness of her situation becomes apparent. Her great father, accompanied by her young brother Mathy, was in England on behalf of the Confederate government. Her mother and sisters were scattered in various parts of Virginia. Dick was with the army in Virginia. John was with the army in the West and would lose his life at Vicksburg.*

*Her husband, Will, had not succeeded in getting an appointment. They lived in the back parlor at her Cousin Hite's.*

*After Betty was forced to leave Richmond she wandered about trying to find a place of safety within the Confederate lines. She managed finally to reach Charlottesville where her baby was born. There she stayed until Appomattox.*

*When the war was over she and her husband and children returned to Washington, where Will became prominent at the bar and Betty was known as a woman of "forceful character and intellect." She died on January 8, 1903.*

*It was after her death that her daughter Alice, now Mrs. James Parmalee, found her mother's wartime diary, until then unknown in the family. Written in a clear, legible hand, it filled two large composition books. Mrs. Parmalee gave it to the Library of Congress—one of the most colorful of all extant Civil War diaries.*

Richmond, Virginia
January 30th, 1863

If I live until next May, I expect to have another little baby. Cousin Hite has been very kind in expressing her willingness to have me here then and to do what she can for me. I told her how grateful I felt and how highly I appreciated her kindness. Our board here is two hundred dollars a month!! but that is less than we would have to pay at any boarding house in town. I do not know where the money is to come from to meet all our additional expenses in the Spring. But the Lord will provide I feel sure. Will gets a little employment here sometimes through his friend Mr. Ould,[1] but nothing permanent or constant.

Jan. 31st. 1863

Mrs. Jarnete, of Caroline [County] has been on a visit to Washington (Ran the blockade of the Rappahannock at night) and through the influence of some Yankee friends was allowed to return with a quantity of baggage!

She brought a trunk from Mother, containing things for cousin Sally, cousin Martha and myself. She sent Nannie Belle a Christmas gift of the most beautiful crying doll I ever saw. It was dressed in white with red ribbon trimmings and red shoes and a red riding hood on.

Judge Hallyburton has allowed Will two thousand dollars for his services as Receiver while he was in Fredericksburg. It is a great comfort to feel we have that much ahead and owe no man anything.

We see through the Yankee papers that Papa and Matsy have reached England in safety. I miss Papa so much. I miss his guiding influence and advice in the family even though we were not always with him.

Feb. 1st 1863

The "Princess Royal," an English vessel, was captured a few days ago while attempting to run the blockade into Charleston. The papers say the Captain escaped with valuable despatches

[1] Robert Ould had charge of the exchange of prisoners.

from Commodore Matthew Fontaine Maury. I hope he had letters for us. We fear that Papa sent us a box of goods by the same opportunity. We all gave him commissions to execute in England. . . .

Feb. 12–1863

We have received letters from Papa from London of dates to the 20th of December. He did send us a large case of goods by the Princess Royal. It cost between three and four hundred dollars in gold, and is worth nearly *four times* as much in our money. If we had lost as much two years ago, I would have thought it a great calamity, but now we see and feel so much real trouble that we cannot let the loss of a few dollars trouble us much, especially when we hear that all of our dear ones are safe and well. . . .

Feb. 17–1863

Will received a written notice from Mr. McGruder yesterday to leave at the end of the month. It is a great surprise and mortification to us. We have had no falling out, no difficulty with him or cousin Hite or anyone in the house. Everything has been smooth and pleasant up to this time. I had an express understanding with her that we were to remain until after May. It was at her suggestion that I engaged a nurse and with her consent that I brought the furniture here from Fredericksburg, and now when Richmond is crowded to excess and it is impossible to get confortable even decent lodgings at any price —we are to be turned out of doors.

No one will be willing to take us when told that I expect to be confined in a month or two.

Feb. 18, 1863

I have written Aunt Betsy Woolfolk telling her of our troubles —of how homeless and forlorn I feel and asking her to let me come there as a boarder. Of course Will will have to stay in town.

## 12. MISSOURI STOKES—MY BROTHER IS AN EXCHANGE PRISONER

*A young teacher of Decatur, Georgia, Missouri Stokes was the half sister of Mary A. H. Gay. Her only brother Thomie had moved to Texas before the war. He enlisted with the 10th Texas Infantry and was killed at the bloody Battle of Franklin, Tennessee, November 30, 1864.*

Decatur, Georgia

March, 1863. On the 11th of January, 1863, Arkansas Post, the fort where Thomie was stationed, fell into the hands of Yankees. General Churchill's[1] whole command, numbering about four thousand, were captured, a few being killed and wounded. We knew that Thomie, if alive, must be a prisoner, but could hear no tidings from him. Our suspense continued until the latter part of March, when Ma received a letter from our loved one, written at Camp Chase (military prison), Ohio, Feburary 10th. This letter she forwarded to me, and I received it March 21st, with heart-felt emotions of gratitude to Him who had preserved his life. A few weeks afterwards another letter came, saying he expected to be exchanged in a few days, and then for several weeks we heard no more. . . .

May 16, 1863. He seemd much changed, although only four years and a half had elapsed since we parted. He looked older, thinner and more careworn, and gray hairs are sprinkled among his dark brown curls. His health had been poor in the army, and then, when he left Camp Chase, he, as well as the other prisoners, was stripped by the Yankees of nearly all his warm clothing. He left the prison in April, and was exchanged at City Point. How strange the dealings of Providence. Truly was he led by a way he knew not. He went out to Texas by the way of the West, and returned home from the East. God be

[1]Brigadier-General Thomas C. Churchill surrendered Fort Hindman at Arkansas Post and its garrison of 4,791 men, after a four hours' bombardment by ironclads, to Major-General John A. McClernand's army of 32,000.

thanked for preserving his life, when so many of his comrades have died. He is a miracle of mercy. After their capture, they were put on boats from which Yankee small-pox patients had been taken. Some died of small-pox, but Thomie has had varioloid and so escaped. He was crowded on a boat with twenty-two hundred, and scarcely had standing room. Many died on the passage up the river, one poor fellow with his head in Thomie's lap. May he never go through similar scenes again!

Monday, June 15th. Thomie left. I rode with him a little beyond the schoolhouse, then took my books and basket, and with one kiss, and, on my part, a tearful good-bye, we parted. As I walked slowly back, I felt so lonely. He had been with me just long enough for me to realize a brother's kind protection, and now he's torn away, and I'm again alone. I turned and looked. He was driving slowly along—he turned a corner and was hidden from my view. Shall I see him no more? Or shall we meet again? God only knows. After a fit of weeping, and one earnest prayer for him, I turned my steps to my little school.

## 13. AUGUSTA JANE EVANS—"MY NEW NOVEL IS DEDICATED TO THE ARMY OF THE CONFEDERACY"

*Augusta, the eldest of eight children, was born on May 8, 1835, in Columbus, Georgia; lived for four years in San Antonio, Texas; moved to Mobile, Alabama, in 1849. She wrote* Inez: A tale of the Alamo *in 1855 and* Beulah *in 1859, both popular novels. A love affair with her New York editor ended with the outbreak of war when she volunteered for work in the army hospital near home. In recognition of her service there General Beauregard gave her his personal pen. After First Manassas she felt inspired to write a novel which might bring glory to the Confederacy and lift the South's morale.* Macaria; or, Altars of Sacrifice, *bound in wallpaper, was published in Richmond in 1863. Augusta sent a copy of it by a blockade-runner to her old New York publisher who brought out an edition there.* Macaria *was read with enthusiasm by Southern soldiers and civilians. Its value as propaganda was recognized by Northern leaders, who called it "contraband and dangerous," and banned it among Yankee troops.*

*St. Elmo, published in 1866, was the great best seller of its day. It was shaped to meet exactly the mood of the South. Hotels, steamboats, plantations and towns were named after it.*

*In 1868 Miss Evans married Colonel L. M. Wilson of Mobile. Various novels flowed from her pen. She died at her home "Ashland" at seventy-four.*

*The letter that follows was answered by General Beauregard on March 24. "Reports of the Battles of Bull Run and Manassas," he wrote, were being forwarded. The novelist revised the thirtieth chapter of* Macaria *to accord.*

*President Davis took offense at some things Beauregard said in these reports. Thereafter his hostility was felt by the general to be watchful and adroit, neglectful of no opportunity.*[1]

*General Beauregard was ill after the Battle of Shiloh, and when the Western army retired from Corinth to Tupelo, General Bragg took over the command.*

*In April 1861 Pierre Gustave Toutant Beauregard had secured the bloodless surrender of Fort Sumter. Two years later he was back in Charleston charged with the defense of all South Carolina, Georgia and Florida. He made new installations and arrangements for the defense of the city which withstood an assault by Admiral DuPont on April 7 and later and more formidable attacks. "In neither army," says Robert S. Henry in* The Story of the Confederacy *"was there a military engineer more competent, nor one with a better eye to the uses of the artillery arm."*

Mobile Alabama March 17th 1863

General Beauregard

Fearful as I am of intruding upon your valuable time, especially at this juncture when you must be so constantly occupied, and hoping that the reasons I shall assign, will plead my pardon, you must permit me to express my earnest gratitude for your exceedingly kind and gratifying letter, and also for the confidence you repose in me, as manifested by the gift of a copy of your "Review," which it seems you deem inexpedient to publish at this crisis. As I read the analysis and com-

[1]See Beauregard's article in *Battles and Leaders of the Civil War,* I, 225.

plete refutation of the ill natured, venomous, ungenerous and jealous remarks, elicited by the presentation of that petition, which embodied the hopes and wishes of the entire Confederacy, and reflected upon the systematic injustice that had been heaped upon you, by the President, the blood tingled in my veins, and I could not forbear recalling the words of Tennyson:

> "Ah God! for a man with heart, head, hand,
> Like some of the simple great ones gone
> Forever, and ever by!
> One still strong man in a blatant land,
> Whatever they call him, what care I?
> Aristocrat, democrat, autocrat,—one
> Who can rule, and dare not lie."[1]

The day is not distant I trust, when all the facts connected with the infamous persecution of yourself, and General Price,[2] may be laid before an indignant and outraged people.

Apropos! of the Western Scipio, I recently had the pleasure of becoming acquainted with him, as he passed through Mobile en route for Vicksburg, and as I looked into his noble gentle face, beaming with generosity and enthusiasm while he spoke of *You* Sir, in terms of unmeasured admiration and exalted esteem; I felt the lines of the great Ode to Wellington, creeping across my lips:

> "Oh good gray head which all men knew;
> Ah face from which their omens all men drew!
> Oh iron nerve, to true occasion true!"

In alluding to your removal from Department No. 2, which he said he should never cease to deplore, and regarded as the most flagrant Administrative faux pas, of the war, he added with his genial smile, and humorous twinkle of the eye, "in fine, General Beauregard has certainly been treated with more *rank injustice* than any other man in the Confederacy, except *one* far less important individual." . . .

---

[1] From *Maud*.
[2] General Sterling Price had been subordinated to General Van Dorn in the West by order of President Davis.

Allow me if you please to detail my reason for inflicting a letter upon you at this time, when any interruption must be annoying. You may perhaps remember that I mentioned to you, that I had a MS. novel containing a chapter relative to the Battle of Manassas, where one of my characters was killed. I was very anxious to read it to you but could find no appropriate opportunity. At the time that I spoke of it to you, I intended not to publish it until the close of the war, but recently circumstances have determined me to bring it out, as soon as I can finish copying the MS upon which I am now employed. The chapter to which I allude is the XXXth and before I copy it I am extremely desirous to know that I am entirely accurate in all my statements relative to the Battle. I am afraid to trust to my memory of the conversation I had with you concerning it, and to avoid the possibility of error, I beg permission most respectfully to propound the following inquiries. Am I correct in saying—

1. That you and Gen'l Johnston were not acquainted with the fact that McDowell had left Washington with the main Fed. army to attack you at Manassas Junction, until a young Lady of Washington (I give no name), disguised as a market woman, and engaged in selling milk to the Fed. soldiers, succeeded in making her way through their lines to *Fairfax Court House* and telegraphed you of the contemplated attack.[1]

2. That you immediately telegraphed to Gen'l Johnston, then at Winchester, and in consequence of this information he hastened to Manassas?[2]

3. At what hour did you learn that your order for an advance on Centreville by your right wing, had failed to reach its destination?[3]

4. Did you not *lead* in *person* the second great charge which recovered the *plateau* and took the Batteries that crowned?[4] Could I satisfy myself of the correctness of my

[1]See footnote, page 62 *supra*.
[2]Beauregard sent the word of McDowell's movement at once to President Davis, who passed it on to General Joseph E. Johnston.
[3]It appears that this was about 8:30 A.M., Sunday, July 21, 1861.
[4]Beauregard says (*Battles and Leaders of the Civil War*, I, 213): "For the recovery of the plateau I ordered a charge of the entire line of battle, including the reserves, which at this crisis I myself led into action."

view or impression regarding, these points, *elsewhere* than by applying to you, believe me Sir, I would not annoy you, for I shrink from the thought of becoming troublesome to you, or imposing, upon your generosity. I regret exceedingly that I could not have submitted this chapter of my new novel to you, before sending it to press. It is dedicated to the *Army of the Confederacy.*

In view of the impending attack upon Charleston, your name is constantly on our lips, in our hearts, and believe me, *in our prayers.* Yet apprehension does not mingle with my interest in all the tidings that come from your Department; I rest in perfect assurance, that with the blessing of our God, victory will, as everywhere else, nestle upon your banner. Have you heard recently from Mrs. Beauregard?[1] Earnestly, most earnestly do I hope, that ere this, her health has been perfectly restored, and that the day, is not very distant, when in peace and prosperity, you may return laden with the love, and followed by the prayers of a redeemed and grateful people, to your rescued home, and the bosom of your beloved family. That God will shield you, from all the dangers that threaten, and preserve you to the country, which so demands your services, and rests its hopes upon you, is the *heartfelt* wish of,—

Yours most respectfully and gratefully

AUGUSTA J. EVANS

P.S. My Sisters desire me to tender you, their love and gratitude for your kind and gratifying remembrance. A.J.E.

## 14. EMMA SANSOM—"GENERAL FORREST ASKED FOR A LOCK OF MY HAIR"

*On a small farm by Black Creek in northern Alabama Emma Sansom, sixteen years old, was living with her widowed mother and a sister. Her only brother was with the 19th Alabama Infantry. Of a sudden she was caught up in the startling tides of war. General Nathan Bedford Forrest was hot on the track of Colonel Abel D. Streight, of Indiana, who with 2,000*

---

[1] In 1860 the general had married Caroline, daughter of André Deslonde, a sugar planter of St. James's Parish, Louisiana. She died in the spring of 1864.

*picked horsemen was aiming to cut General Bragg's railroad
supply line between Atlanta and Chattanooga. Forrest's force
was only about a third as large. By leading him to the lost ford
Emma helped materially in the pursuit which led to the capture of Streight and his whole force near Rome on May 3.*

*Her bold, dangerous ride with "Old Bed" was not unreward-
ed. That night he wrote: "My highest regards to Miss Emma
Sansom for her gallant conduct while my posse was skirmish-
ing with the Federals across Black Creek near Gadsden Alabama." And thirty-six years later the legislature of Alabama
voted her, as a token of "admiration and gratitude," the gift of
640 acres of land.*

*On October 29, 1864, Emma married C. B. Johnson, of the
10th Alabama. They went to Texas after the war, where her
husband died in 1887, leaving her with seven children. She
died August 9, 1900, and her grave is at Little Mound, Upshur
County, Texas.*

We were at home on the morning of May 2, 1863, when
about eight or nine o'clock, a company of men wearing blue
uniforms and riding mules and horses galloped past the house
and went on towards the bridge. Pretty soon a great crowd of
them came along, and some of them stopped at the gate and
asked us to bring them some water. Sister and I each took a
bucket of water, and gave it to them at the gate. One of them
asked me where my father was. I told him he was dead. He
asked me if I had any brothers. I told him I had *six*. He asked
where they were, and I said they were in the Confederate
Army. "Do they think the South will whip?" "They do."
"What do you think about it?" "I think God is on our side and
we will win." "You do? Well, if you had seen us whip Colonel
Roddey[1] the other day and run him across the Tennessee River, you would have thought God was on the side of the best
artillery."

By this time some of them began to dismount, and we went
into the house. They came in and began to search for firearms
and men's saddles. They did not find anything but a side-sad-
dle, and one of them cut the skirts off that. Just then some one
from the road said, in a loud tone: "You men bring a chunk
of fire with you, and get out of that house." The men got the

[1]Philip D. Roddey, the Confederate cavalry leader.

fire in the kitchen and started out, and an officer put a guard around the house, saying: "This guard is for your protection." They all soon hurried down to the bridge, and in a few minutes we saw the smoke rising and knew they were burning the bridge. As our fence extended up to the railing of the bridge, mother said: "Come with me and we will pull our rails away, so they will not be destroyed." As we got to the top of the hill we saw the rails were already piled on the bridge and were on fire, and the Yankees were in line on the other side guarding it.

We turned back towards the house, and had not gone but a few steps before we saw a Yankee coming at full speed, and behind were some more men on horses. I heard them shout, "Halt! and surrender!" The man stopped, threw up his hand, and handed over his gun. The officer to whom the soldier surrendered said: "Ladies, do not be alarmed, I am General Forrest; I and my men will protect you from harm." He inquired: "Where are the Yankees?"

Mother said: "They have set the bridge on fire and are standing in line on the other side, and if you go down that hill they will kill the last one of you."

By this time our men had come up, and some went out in the field, and both sides commenced shooting. We ran to the house, and I got there ahead of all. General Forrest dashed up to the gate and said to me: "Can you tell me where I can get across that creek?"

I told him there was an unsafe bridge two miles farther down the stream, but that I knew of a trail about two hundred yards above the bridge on our farm, where our cows used to cross in low water, and I believed he could get his men over there, and that if he would have my saddle put on a horse I would show him the way.

He said: "There is not time to saddle a horse; get up here behind me." As he said this he rode close to the bank on the side of the road, and I jumped up behind him.

Just as we started off mother came up about out of breath and gasped out: "Emma, what do you mean?"

General Forrest said: "She is going to show me a ford where I can get my men over in time to catch those Yankees before they get to Rome. Don't be uneasy; I will bring her back safe."

We rode out into a field through which ran a branch or

small ravine and along which there was a thick undergrowth that protected us for a while from being seen by the Yankees at the bridge or on the other side of the creek. This branch emptied into the creek just above the ford. When we got close to the creek, I said: "General Forrest, I think we had better get off the horse, as we are now where we may be seen."

We both got down and crept through the bushes and when we were right at the ford I happened to be in front. He stepped quickly between me and the Yankees saying: "I am glad to have you for a pilot, but I am not going to make breastworks of you."

The cannon and the other guns were firing fast by this time, as I pointed out to him where to go into the water and out on the other bank, and then we went back towards the house. He asked me my name, and asked me to give him a lock of my hair. The cannon-balls were screaming over us so loud that we were told to leave and hide in some place out of danger, which we did. Soon all the firing stopped, and I started back home. On the way I met General Forrest again, and he told me that he had written a note for me and left it on the bureau. He asked me again for a lock of my hair, and as we went into the house he said: "One of my bravest men has been killed, and he is laid out in the house. His name is Robert Turner. I want you to see that he is buried in some graveyard near here." He then told me good-bye and got on his horse, and he and his men rode away and left us all alone.

My sister and I sat up all night watching over the dead soldier, who had lost his life fighting for our rights, in which we were overpowered but never conquered. General Forrest and his men endeared themselves to us forever.

## 15. MARY ANNA JACKSON—"THEY SAID MY HUSBAND HAD BEEN WOUNDED"

*Mrs. Jackson had been with Stonewall four times after he left Lexington that spring morning in 1861.*

*In September '61 she journeyed from her father's home in North Carolina to visit the general at Camp Harman, his headquarters near Manassas.*

*The following winter, when he was stationed at Winchester,*

*they lived at the home of their friend, the Reverend J.R. Gra-
ham. With the approach of the spring campaign in the Valley
she went back to her father's again, and they did not meet for
thirteen months. She wrote to him every day; knit his socks;
made his pantaloons and caps with broad gilt bands—and for
this he scolded her. "Please," he wrote, "do not have so much
gold braid about them." She begged him to come for a visit,
but he did not feel he could leave his command. On November
23, 1862, their daughter was born in Charlotte, North Carolina, and was named Julia—for the general's mother Julia
Neale.*

*Next April Mrs. Jackson and the baby were with Stonewall
at Mr. Yerby's a mile from the camp at Moss Neck outside
Fredericksburg. The baby was baptized by the army chaplain
and christened "Little Miss Stonewall" by the soldiers. Minis,
the photographer, came from Richmond to take the general's
picture. Mrs. Jackson curled his hair in ringlets and he sat
stern and unsmiling, dressed in his new uniform, the gift of
Jeb Stuart. Henry Kyd Douglas in* I Rode with Stonewall *gives
a charming picture of the family:*

"I do not forget my embarrassment when at the mischievous
suggestion of one of the neighborhood ladies Mrs. Jackson
handed me little Julia to hold for a space. The General walked
in and amusement increased the surrounding merriment, but
he made the nurse come to the rescue. Little Julia grew up in
her beauty and was very fair to look upon. She married young
and died young, and two children take her place with her
mother."[1]

*After nine days Mrs. Jackson and the baby were hurried off
before the onset of the Battle of Chancellorsville. They stayed
in Richmond with their friend the Reverend Moses D. Hoge,
Presbyterian minister and Confederate chaplain. She had been
there only five days when the news came: Her husband had
been wounded in three places. On Saturday May 3, the second
day of Chancellorsville, after a march across the front of Joe
Hooker's army, he had completed his last and greatest flank
attack, assuring Lee of victory against double the Confederate*

[1]Chapel Hill: The University of North Carolina Press, 1940.

*strength; then in the darkness and confusion of the fighting he had been fired on by his own men.*

*Mrs. Jackson reached him at Mr. Chandler's at Guinea Station, where he had been brought in agony. On May 10 at quarter past three in the afternoon, dying, he said: "Let us cross over the river and rest under the shade of the trees."*

*Afterward they carried his body to lie by the side of his first wife, Eleanor Junkin Jackson, and her daughter who had lived only a week. Once more Mary Anna returned with Julia to her father's house in North Carolina.*

*Through the rest of her life honors were showered on General Jackson's widow. She shrank from publicity and accepted only those attentions which did not require her to speak or to appear in public. Her Memoirs of Stonewall Jackson was publised in 1895, a valuable contribution to our knowledge of his personal as well as his military life. She died at her home in Charlotte, March 24, 1915.*

On Sunday morning [May 3, 1863], as we arose from family worship in Dr. Hoge's parlor, Dr. Brown informed me that the news had come that General Jackson had been wounded. . . . On Tuesday my brother Joseph arrived to my great relief, to take me to my husband, but my disappointment was only increased by his report that it had taken him nearly three days to ride through the country and elude the raiding enemy. It was not until Thursday morning that the blockade was broken, and we went up on an armed train prepared to fight its way through.

A few hours of unmolested travel brought us to Guiney's Station, and we were taken at once to the residence of Mr. Chandler, which was a large country-house, and very near it, in the yard, was a small, humble abode, in which lay my precious, suffering husband.

From the time I reached him he was too ill to notice or talk much, and he lay most of the time in a semi-conscious state; but when aroused, he recognized those about him and consciousness would return. Soon after I entered his room he was impressed by the woeful anxiety and sadness betrayed in my face, and said: "My darling, you must cheer up, and not wear a long face. . . . My darling, you are very much loved."

Early on Sunday morning, the 10th of May, I was called out

of the sick-room by Dr. Morrison, who told me that the doctors, having done every thing that human skill could devise to stay the hand of death, had lost all hope, and that my precious, brave, noble husband could not live!

He now sank rapidly into unconsciousness. . . .

That night, after a few hours sleep from sheer exhaustion, I awoke, when all in my chamber was perfect stillness, and the full moon poured a flood of light through the windows, glorious enough to lift my soul heavenwards; but oh, the agony and anguish of those silent midnight hours, when the terrible reality of my loss and the desolation of widowhood forced itself upon me, and took possession of my whole being! My unconscious little one lay sweetly sleeping by my side, and my kind friend, Mrs. Hoge, was near; but I strove not to awaken them, and all alone I stemmed the torrent of grief which seemed insupportable, until prayer to Him, who alone can comfort, again brought peace and quietness to my heart.

The next morning I went once more to see the remains, which were now in the casket, and were covered with spring flowers. His dear face was wreathed with the lovely lily of the valley—the emblem of humility—his own predominating grace.

On Monday morning began the sad journey to Richmond. . . .

# BIBLIOGRAPHY

Full bibliographical description and credit are supplied for first listings. Additional selections from the same sources are referred back to the first listing.

## CHAPTER I. THE UNION IS DISSOLVED
### (December 1860-May 1861)

1. South Carolina Secedes from the Union
   Diary of Emma E. Holmes, 1861–1862. Manuscript Room, Duke University Library.
2. Florida Passes the Ordinance of Secession
   Susan Bradford Eppes, *Through Some Eventful Years.* Macon, Ga.: The J. W. Burke Company, 1926. (By permission of Susan W. Eppes and Alice B. Eppes.)
3. "We Are a Free and Independent People"
   Augusta J. Kollock to her brother, January 22, 1861. Susan M. Kollock, ed., "Letters of the Kollock and Allied Families," *The Georgia Historical Quarterly,* XXXIV, 3 (September 1950), 229–231. (By permission of The Georgia Historical Society.)
4. Montgomery Welcomes Jefferson Davis
   Eleanor Noyes Jackson to her sister, February 19, 1861. Jefferson Davis Scrapbook, Manuscript Room, Alabama State Department of Archives and History.
5. "I Could Not Command My Voice To Speak"
   Varina Howell Davis, *Jefferson Davis: A Memoir by His Wife.* New York: The Belford Company, 1890.
6. Charleston Prepares for War
   Caroline Howard Gilman to her children, March 12, 1861. "Letters of a Confederate Mother," *The Atlantic Monthly,* CXXXVII (April 1926), 505–506. (By permission of *The Atlantic Monthly.*)
7. Fort Sumter Surrenders
   Diary of Emma E. Holmes, 1861–1862. (*See* I, 1.)
8. "Our Home Grew Lonely"
   Mary Anna Jackson, *Memoirs of Stonewall Jackson, by His Widow.* . . . Louisville, Ky.: The Prentice Press, 1895.
9. "The Prospects before Us Are Sad"
   Mary Custis Lee to her daughter, April 20, 1861. Rose Mortimer Ellzey MacDonald, *Mrs. Robert E. Lee.* Boston: Ginn & Company, 1939. (By permission of J. Lewis Scoggs.)

10. "I Heard the Drums Beating in Washington"
[Judith Brockenbrough McGuire], *Diary of a Southern Refugee during the War, by a Lady of Virginia.* New York: E. J. Hale & Son, 1867.

11. I Set My House in Order
Mary Custis Lee to her husband, May 9, 1961. *Mrs. Robert E. Lee (See* I, 9.)

12. "They Are the Finest Set of Men"
Varina Howell Davis to Clement Claiborne Clay, Jr., May 10, 1861. Clay Papers, Manuscript Room, Duke University Library.

CHAPTER II. THE CONFEDERACY IS INVADED
(May 1861-February 1862)

1. Virginia Is Invaded
[Judith Brockenbrough McGuire], *Diary of a Southern Refugee. (See* I, 10.)

2. "We Left Washington"
Diary of Betty Herndon Maury. Manuscript Division, Library of Congress.

3. "A Battle Has Been Fought at Manassas"
From: A DIARY FROM DIXIE by Mary Boykin Chesnut. Copyright, 1905, D. Appleton & Company. Reprinted by permission of the publishers Appleton-Century-Crofts, Inc.

4. "My Home Was Converted into a Prison"
Rose O'Neal Greenhow, *My Imprisonment and the First Year of Abolition Rule in Washington.* London: Richard Bentley, 1863.

5. Our New Home
Varina Howell Davis, *Jefferson Davis. (See* I, 5.)

6. "Our Cause We Know Is Just"
Leora Sims to Mary Elizabeth Bellamy, November 14, 1861. Copy of letter in possession of Mrs. Mary Verner Schlaefer, Jr., Columbia, South Carolina. (By permission of Mrs. Mary Verner Schlaefer, Jr.)

7. "I Hope This State of Affairs Will Not Last Long"
Mrs. Dorian Hall to her son, January 6 and 9, 1862. William Hall Collection, Military Records Division, Alabama State Department of Archives and History.

8. Hard Times in Texas
Mary Byson to Margaret Butler, January 16, 1862. Butler Family Papers, Department of Archives, Louisiana State University.

9. Old Capitol Prison
Rose O'Neal Greenhow, *My Imprisonment. (See* II, 4.)

10. Personal Observations at Some of the Camps and Hospitals
Mary H. Johnstone to Alexander H. Stephens, February 3, 1862. Alexander H. Stephens Papers, Library of Congress.

11. "My Husband Was a Prisoner at Fort Henry"
Louisa Frederika Gilmer to her father, February 10, 1862.
Gilmer Papers, Southern Historical Collection, University of
North Carolina.

12. The Union Flag Was Raised in Nashville
Miss A. M. B., "Foraging Around Nashville," *Our Women in
the War; The Lives They Lived; The Deaths They Died.*
Charleston, S. C.: The News and Courier Book Presses, 1885.

13. The Inauguration of Jefferson Davis as Permanent President
Constance Cary Harrison, "A Virginia Girl in the First Year
of the War," *The Century Illustrated Monthly Magazine,*
XXX (August 1885), 610.

## CHAPTER III. A FRIGHTING SPRING (March-May 1862)

1. "The Daring, Reckless Captain Morgan Visits Murfreesboro"
Diary of Alice Ready. Southern Historical Collection, University of North Carolina.

2. "Write Me What Your Horse Is Named"
Loulie Gilmer to her father, March 16, 1862. Gilmer Papers,
Southern Historical Collection, University of North Carolina.

3. Winchester Is Occupied by the Enemy
Cornelia Peake McDonald, *A Diary with Reminiscences of
the War and Refugee Life in the Shenandoah Valley,
1860–1865,* ed., Hunter McDonald. Nashville, Tenn.: Cullom
& Ghertner, 1934. (By permission of Hunter McDonald.)

4. "My Boy Is Gone from Me"
Margaret Lea Houston to her mother, March 17, 1862. Temple Houston Morrow Collection, University of Texas Library.

5. The Aftermath of Shiloh
Kate Cumming. *A Journal of Hospital Life in the Confederate
Army of Tennessee from the Battle of Shiloh to the End of
the War. . . .* Louisville, Ky.: John P. Morton & Company,
1866.

6. Abraham Lincoln Was in Fredericksburg
Diary of Betty Herndon Maury. (See II, 2.)

7. Enemy Ships Pass the Forts below New Orleans
Sarah Morgan Dawson, *A Confederate Girl's Diary,* ed., War-
rington Dawson. Boston: Houghton Mifflin Company, 1913.
(By permission of Warrington Dawson.)

8. New Orleans Has Fallen
Julia Ellen (LeGrand) Waitz, *The Journal of Julia LeGrand,
New Orleans, 1862–1863,* ed., Kate Mason Rowland and Mrs.
Morris L. Croxall. Richmond, Va.: Everett Waddey Company,
1911.

9. The Enemy Comes to Baton Rouge
Sarah Morgan Dawson, *A Confederate Girl's Diary.* (See III, 7.)

CHAPTER IV. THEY CALLED THEM "GREAT DAYS"
(May-September 1862)

1. Stonewall Defeats Banks at Winchester
   Cornelia Peake McDonald, *A Diary with R.* (*See* III, 3.)
2. In Richmond during and after Seven Pines
   Constance Cary Harrison, "A Virginia Girl." (*See* II, 13.)
3. "I Want To See You So Bad"
   Lucy Lowe to her husband, June 1, 1862. William Hall Collection, Military Records Division, Alabama State Department of Archives and History.
4. "Jackson Is Doing Great Things"
   Diary of Betty Herndon Maury. (*See* II, 2.)
5. "What Cannot Be Cured Must Be Endured"
   Amie Kelly to her husband, July 6, 1862. Letter in possession of Miss Maud McLure Kelly, Montgomery, Alabama. (By permission of Miss Maud McLure Kelly.)
6. "I Am Proud To Be Your Wife"
   Elizabeth McGavock Harding to her husband, July 17 and 27, August 5 and 29, 1862. Letters in possession of Mrs. Jesse E. Wills, Nashville, Tennessee. (By permission of Mrs. Jesse E. Wills.)
7. "We Appeal to You as Our Friend"
   Lucy Smith to Jefferson Davis and Alexander H. Stephens, August 20, 1862. Alexander H. Stephens Papers, Library of Congress.
8. "Gone Was My Small Paradise!"
   Sarah Morgan Dawson, *A Confederate Girl's Diary.* (*See* III, 7.)
9. "The Children All Want To See You"
   Mary Frances Brooks to her husband, September 3, 1862. "Confederate Letters," Georgia State Archives.
10. "I Received My Commission"
    Belle Boyd, *Belle Boyd: In Camp and Prison.* London: Saunders, Otley & Company, 1865

CHAPTER V. HIGH HOPES WANING (September 1862-May 1863)

1. "What Shall I Name the Baby?"
   Cassie Selden Smith to her husband, October 10, 1862. Edmund Kirby Smith Papers, Southern Historical Collection, University of North Carolina.
2. "I Never Walk or Ride without My Pistol"
   Cordelia Lewis Scales to Lou Irby, October 29, 1862. Percy L. Rainwater, ed., "The Civil War Letters of Cordelia Scales," *Journal of Mississippi History,* I (July 1939), 170–181. (By

permission of Percy L. Rainwater and *Journal of Mississippi History.*)

3. We Hope To Reach Texas
   Mary Williams Pugh to her husband, November 9 and 18, 1862. Richard L. Pugh Papers, Department of Archives, Louisiana State University.

4. "Accept My Best Wishes for Your Happiness"
   Mary Cahal to Mrs. John Hunt Morgan, December 16, 1862. John Hunt Morgan Papers, Southern Historical Collection, University of North Carolina.

5. "New Orleans Is Full of Rumors"
   Julia Ellen (LeGrand) Waitz, *The Journal of Julia LeGrand.* (*See* III, 8.)

6. "The Negroes Are Having a Merry Time"
   Diary of Sarah L. Wadley, August 1859-April 1863. Southern Historical Collection, University of North Carolina.

7. "God Blessed Us with Victory at Fredericksburg"
   Diary of Betty Herndon Maury. (*See* II, 2.)

8. "Come to Me, My Darling"
   Martha Ready Morgan to her husband, January 6, 1863. John Hunt Morgan Papers, Southern Historical Collection, University of North Carolina.

9. "There Is Not a Bonnet for Sale in Richmond"
   Agnes to Sara Rice Pryor, January 7, 1863. Mrs. Roger A. (Sara Rice) Pryor, *Reminiscences of Peace and War.* New York: The Macmillan Company, 1904. (By permission of The Macmillan Company.)

10. "I Wore My Pistol All the Time!"
    Cordelia Lewis Scales to Lou Irby, January 27, 1863. "The Civil War Letters." (*See* V, 2.)

11. "We Are To Be Turned Out of Doors"
    Diary of Betty Herndon Maury. (*See* II, 2.)

12. My Brother Is an Exchange Prisoner
    Journal of Missouri Stokes. Mary Ann Harris Gay, *Life in Dixie during the War.* Atlanta, Ga.: Charles P. Byrd, 1897.

13. "My New Novel Is Dedicated to the Army of the Confederacy"
    Augusta Jane Evans to General Pierre G. T. Beauregard, March 17, 1863. Beauregard Papers, Manuscript Room, Duke University Library.

14. "General Forrest Asked for a Lock of My Hair"
    Emma Sansom. John Allan Wyeth, *Life of General Nathan Bedford Forrest.* New York: Harper & Brothers, 1899. (By permission of Harper & Brothers.)

15. "They Said My Husband Had Been Wounded"
    Mary Anna Jackson, Memoirs of Stonewall Jackson. (*See* I, 8.)